INSTRUCTOR'S MANUAL

to accompany

BUILDING THE INFORMATION-AGE ORGANIZATION
STRUCTURE, CONTROL, AND INFORMATION TECHNOLOGIES

James I. Cash, Jr.
Robert G. Eccles
Nitin Nohria
Richard L. Nolan

Prepared by

Janis L. Gogan
Graduate School of Business Administration
Harvard University

IRWIN

Chicago • Bogota • Boston • Buenos Aires • Caracas
London • Madrid • Mexico City • Sydney • Toronto

Printed in the United States of America.

ISBN 0–256–12459–0

2 3 4 5 6 7 8 9 0 WCB 1 0 9 8 7 6 5

Building the Information-Age Organization
Teaching Manual

Table of Contents

Teaching Note Authors

For each case in the book, listed alphabetically on the next page, a teaching note was prepared. Most of the notes appearing in this manual are *lightly edited* versions of notes written by Harvard Business School faculty members. Revisions were made so that all notes would conform to a common style and format, to reduce the length of the note, to add a brief discussion of a concept or framework covered in the book, or to de-emphasize discussion of a topic not covered in the book. Any such changes are the sole responsibility of the *Teaching Manual* editor. For the original version, contact the original author(s).

Harvard Business School cases, and hence their accompanying teaching notes, are sometimes revised to strengthen the rhetoric, emphasize a point, or reflect new developments in the case situation. This Teaching Manual contains edited versions of teaching notes as of May, 1994.

If you wish to determine whether a case or teaching note has subsequently been revised, contact Harvard Business School Publishing at 617-495-6117, or contact the original teaching note authors, who are noted on the next page.

Case	Number	Note Author(s)
Air Products and Chemicals, Inc.: Project ICON (A)	192-097	Donna B. Stoddard
Allen-Bradley's ICCG: Repositioning for the '90s	491-066	Nitin Nohria
Appex Corp	491-082	Nitin Nohria
Capital Holding Corporation - Reengineering the Direct Response Group	192-001	Donna B. Stoddard
Compaq Computer Corporation	491-011	Robert G. Eccles and Janis L. Gogan
Connor Formed Metal Products	193-003	Janis L. Gogan*
Control at the Sands Hotel & Casino	184-048	Kenneth Merchant and William J. Bruns, Jr.
Crompton Greaves Ltd.	491-074	Nitin Nohria
Hill, Holiday, Connors, Cosmoupolos, Inc.	491-016	Nitin Nohria
Hong Kong Tradelink: News from the Second City	191-026	
Singapore Leadership: Tale of One City	191-025	Lynda M. Applegate and
Singapore Tradenet (A): Tale of One City	191-009	Benn Konsynski
Singapore Tradenet (B): the Tale Continues	193-136	
Incident at Waco Manufacturing	189 142	Janis L. Gogan and John J. Sviokla
Internal Revenue Service: Automated Collection System	490-042.	Nitin Nohria
Jacobs Souchard	489-106	Janis L. Gogan
KPMG Peat Marwick: the Shadow Partner	492-002	Janis L. Gogan and Richard L. Nolan
Lithonia Lighting	492-003	Nitin Nohria
Mrs. Fields Cookies	189-056	James I. Cash, Jr. and Janis L. Gogan
Otis Elevator: Managing the Service Force	191-213	Keri O. Pearlson
Phillips 66 Co.: Executive Information System	189-006	Lynda M. Applegate
Safeway Manufacturing Divison: the Manufacturing Control System (A)	193-134	Donna B. Stoddard
Symantec, Rev. 2/91	491-010	Nitin Nohria

* An alternative teaching note for this case, by Lynda M. Applegate, is available from Harvard Business School Publishing.

Teaching Manual Overview

Introduction

Building the Information-Age Organization: Structure, Control and Information Technologies is the output of an ongoing effort to integrate the evolving domains of information technologies, control systems, organizational forms, and human resources practices. As stated in the book's preface,

> *Concepts that held up well for much of the century - strategy, structure, span of control, organizational boundaries - are shifting on their foundations. Many of these changes are enabled by information technologies, which managers use to fundamentally alter organizational purpose, shape, and practices.*

The Harvard Business School course based on this book offered students an integrated approach to the uses of structure, controls and information technologies in support of the organization's mission. The specific solution utilized at HBS reflected our faculty interests and complemented the other courses required in the first-year MBA curriculum. However, the specific sequence of cases and activities which we used would not necessarily be appropriate at another institution or at another point in time. For that reason we are not providing a sample syllabus. Instead, we offer a simple set of guidelines for effectively using these materials, in three prototypical situations, described below.

Fully Integrated Introductory Course

Ideally, the entire set of materials would be used in the sequence provided in the book. Each case would have its own full-class discussion (with the exception of the Singapore case series in Chapter 7, which can be covered in a single session). That translates into 25 sessions. In addition, to provide students with the necessary concepts and frameworks for understanding the cases, for each chapter the instructor would prepare a full-session lecture to weave together the common threads in the cases covered in that chapter. If an additional session is given over to a mid-term exam and another to a wrap-up lecture, that brings the figure to 36 class sessions of 80-90 minutes each. In this scenario, Chapters 2 and 3 are utilized completely. It is assumed that students do not yet have a grounding in either organization structure (Chapter 2) or control systems (Chapter 3). The cases in those two chapters do not focus on the architecture or use of information technologies.

By including 6 to 8 sessions on fundamentals of organizational structure and control systems, this version of the course provides material equivalent to at least 1 1/2 courses, and can be structured to be equivalent to two full courses. This requires close collaboration among the faculty who traditionally teach organization studies, managerial control, and MISS. As MBA programs experiment with new integrative courses, this one could be considered to cover 50% to 100% of an MBA student's introductory MIS material, 25 to

50% of introductory managerial control material, and 25% to 50% of introductory organization theory.

Partially Integrated Introductory Course

Another alternative is for MIS faculty to substitute much of the material used here for the traditional required introductory MIS course for students who are not MIS majors. In this approach, it is assumed that students have prior familiarity with the basic concepts covered in Chapters 2 (organization structure) and 3 (control systems). The cases in those chapters would be available to students for remedial or review purposes only, and no more than one session would be devoted to reviewing those concepts. Instead, the course would focus on a) the evolution of information technology architecture, applications, and impacts and b) new organizational forms, control mechanisms and issues enabled by or arising from the use of new information technologies. By assigning readings as supplementary materials used in conjunction with cases, and by using fewer full-session lectures, it is possible to structure a single full course which still conforms to the basic logical flow of the book's chapter structure.

Advanced or Capstone IS Course

The material in this book also lends itself very well to a capstone course for MIS majors. In this scenario, Chapters 2 (structure), 3 (control) and 4 (IT architecture) would be treated as review materials, and students would dig more deeply into the material covered in chapters 5 through 9, perhaps supplemented by additional contemporary readings and a substantial student project.

Summary

To summarize, the book offers instructors an unusually rich set of materials that treat information technology as an enabler of potent changes in organization structure and control systems. The cases in the book can be used to provide students with a broad overview of the interrelationships among technology, people, controls and structures in introductory courses. They can also be effectively used in a capstone or elective course for MIS majors.

This Teaching Manual

This teaching manual is organized as follows. The chapter following this one, "Teaching by the Case Method" briefly discusses how cases are used at Harvard and other educational institutions, some considerations in their use, and sources of further information about the case method of teaching. Case teaching notes are then listed alphabetically by case. We chose this organization because we realize that many instructors will not follow the book's chapter outline, and hence it is somewhat easier to locate each teaching note when they are sorted alphabetically. For each note, the *Suggested 80-Minute Teaching Plan* appears on its own page.

Teaching by the Case Method

Introduction

An increasing number of MBA programs are making full or partial uses of the "case method" of instruction. This note briefly reviews the Harvard Business School approach to using cases in the classroom.

At Harvard, case method is the predominant pedagogical method and philosophy used in our MBA and executive programs. However, we do supplement case method with various individual and group exercises and simulations, use of speakers from industry, and even an occasional traditional lecture. This note will briefly review how the case method of instruction is used at Harvard, followed by a brief discussion of the use of cases in MBA programs where the case method does not predominate.

Case Method at Harvard Business School

At the Harvard Business School, the case method of instruction is used extensively in virtually every course taught in the MBA program. This choice rests on several beliefs:

1. Future managers need to be exposed to a wide variety of organization types, industries, cultural settings, and situations.

2. When students place themselves (figuratively) in the shoes of actual decision-makers, they are more likely to internalize important managerial concepts.

3. Management students need to develop critical thinking skills, in addition to being taught specific techniques and concepts.

4. There is no "management cookbook" and there is no "one right answer" to a managerial situation. When mangers face opportunities, constraints, or problems, they can bring to bear a variety of techniques to inform their choices, and they can make a variety of coherent choices.

All four beliefs are fundamental to the case method of instruction. Cases illustrate a wide variety of actual companies in a wide variety of settings, illustrating a wide variety of situations (point #1). Because they are based on real situations faced by real managers, cases engage students' attention (point # 2). Cases can illustrate specific techniques while also forcing students to sift through the information available to a decision-maker, making choices as to what is relevant and what is not (point # 3). Finally, although students and instructors can identify clearly "wrong" or inappropriate solutions to case situations, they also face up to the realization that there is rarely just one "right" answer.

This latter point is arguably the most important aspect of the case method. We fundamentally believe that management is a highly dynamic endeavor. Managers need to be skilled at both thoughtful anticipation and flexible response. Case method helps future managers appreciate that managerial decision-making is rather like buying a gift for a loved one. There are plenty of inappropriate or mediocre selections to be made, and quite a variety of appropriate selections, ranging from "useful" to "outstanding," and from "predictable" to "path-breaking." We believe that the cumulative impact of preparing and discussing a large number of cases across every course in the MBA curriculum is a highly effective way to develop the critical thinking skills needed for thoughtful anticipation and flexible responses.

Case method takes advantage of the power of collaborative learning. At HBS, we do not believe that the instructors hold all the answers. Our students typically have two or three years' experience in a variety of jobs and industries. Each student brings to case discussions his/her experiences, which greatly enrich the discussions. Effective teachers tap into students' experiences to increase everyone's insights and learning. In the process, students learn to express themselves clearly, to listen thoughtfully, and to approach their own and others' ideas with healthy skepticism.

At Harvard, the first year class is divided into sections of 90 students each; students take all their classes as a section. A typical day consists of three classes, which usually translates into three cases to prepare each night. Most students meet with a study group late in the evening or early in the morning, after they have individually prepared their readings and cases. In this scenario, the instructors who teach students early in the first year set the expectation level concerning participation in discussions, "cold-calls" to open cases discussions, and other matters. Instructors of courses later in the sequence, such as this one, do not need to build the rationale for use of cases or for active, thoughtful participation, but they do need to work with an already-formed section culture.

The teaching notes presented in this manual were originally written by Harvard faculty with this unique setting in mind. Instructors at other academic programs should bear this in mind as they consider how to use cases in environments other than the Harvard Business School. The next section offers a few a few thoughts for consideration on this issue.

Use of Cases in Schools Where Case Method Does not Predominate

Many schools use cases, but in ways that differ from the HBS approach. The key differentiating factors seem to be:

>   Do all instructors use cases?
>   In what ways are cases used?
>   What proportion of the curriculum involves cases?
>   Do first-year students take all their courses with the same cohort of students?

If all instructors use cases to some extent, then you may not need to build a "case for cases." On the other hand, at many schools instructors use cases in varying ways. Some instructors use the Harvard case method, while others use a case as an interesting launching point for a traditional lecture. Others use the case as a starting point for an open-ended discussion which differs from our case method, and some assign cases as readings or study group exercises, but do not conduct a case discussion in the classroom. Some instructors devote most of their class sessions to cases, while others may introduce only one or two cases, which are revisited periodically throughout the semester. It is important to take stock of how your predecessors in a curriculum have used cases, since this will greatly influence students expectations at the start of your course.

Where students go through the first-year curriculum in common cohorts, the instructor can more easily build upon the foundation established by his/her predecessors, who influenced the students' norms concerning preparation quality and the nature and extent of class participation. In settings where students will not have a common shared experience in their previous courses (this is often true with part-time evening programs), the instructor will have to spend more time setting a clear expectation level concerning the use of cases in his/her course.

For a far richer discussion of case teaching than can be provided here, we urge you to pick up *Education for Judgment: The Artistry of Discussion Leadership*, edited by C. Roland Christensen, David A. Garvin and Ann Sweet (Harvard Business School Press, 1991).

Air Products and Chemicals: Project ICON

Synopsis

This case describes a proposal that Pete Mather and John Shepherd are evaluating to use computers and telecommunications equipment to consolidate a multinational company's US and UK IBM data centers. The class discussion will center on IT architecture and the risks and challenges associated with the choices that general managers make with respect to IT hardware, software, services, and structures; that is, its IT architecture.

The case provides an outstanding context for describing both a typical mainframe computing environment and for introducing students to emerging opportunities and trends with respect to computers and telecommunications. This case is (understandably) full of computer, telecommunications, and company acronyms and language. The instructor needs to encourage students to cut through this vernacular and focus on the general management issues of managing IS in a multi-national company.

Teaching Objectives

The Air Products and Chemicals case presents a multi-national firm looking to consolidate its mainframe applications in a single US data center by taking advantage of improved processing and networking capabilities. The specific teaching objectives are:

> Provide a snapshot of a global information systems (GIS) architecture in a contemporary multinational corporation; and

> Provide a context for applying McFarlan's risk framework (**Exhibit TN-1**).

Optional Additional Readings

Liana, Andres, "Applying High-Speed Channel Facilities," *Telecommunications*, July 1990, p.56. This article describes 'channel extension' technology.

Two additional cases included in this manual:

> Air Products and Chemical, Inc.: Project ICON (B) and (C)

describe the ICON implementation and other issues which arose during implementation.

Suggested Study Questions

1. Compare the baseline IT architecture in place at the time of the case, with the proposed IT architecture of project ICON.

2. What do Shepherd and Mather propose to accomplish with project ICON?

3. How would you characterize the risks associated with project ICON? From Shepherd's perspective, what issues need to be managed? As Mather, what concerns do you have?

Opportunities for Student Analysis and Discussion

Action Recommendation: Proceed with ICON?

The class can be opened by asking students to assume the role of John Shepherd, MIS director of Air Products-Europe (APE). The instructor might then ask, "Based on the information presented in the case, who in December 1990 would be willing to go forward with ICON?" Two students can be asked to present their analyses, one student who wants to go forward and one who would not. Each can describe the rationale for their respective positions.

Situation Analysis: How is IT Used within APCI?

After these presentations the class can be asked to characterize the business and competitive environment that APCI and APE managers faced in 1990. APCI is in four businesses: industrial gases, chemicals, environmental and energy, and equipment and testing. In 1990, competition in these businesses was fierce. The corporation was under unrelenting pressure to reduce costs while maintaining or improving the level of customer service that it provided.

"How is IT used within APCI?" IT had traditionally been an important resource which supported many aspects of APCI and APE's businesses. A list of typical applications will emerge. Based on the data contained on pages 180-181 of the book, we know that computers support traditional business functions (accounting, manufacturing process control etc.). Also, APCI has had an extensive telecommunications infrastructure in place for some time. Further, the case states there is a desire to do "global engineering," thereby suggesting that the company now uses IT to support engineering applications and would like to do more in that area. One of the most critical user applications which would be affected by ICON was an online customer service application.

The discussion can proceed by asking, "In light of the importance of IT within APE, why would Shepherd and Mather consider a project like ICON? What alternatives did they have to ICON? The bottom line as to why ICON was considered was that APE needed to lower its costs while providing a higher level of service to its customers. More specifically, Shepherd needed to (1) reduce or control his budget and (2) provide support to the Bassingstoke users.

APE IT and telecommunications specialists began to investigate channel extension technology as a way to provide a high level of service to those users who were moving to the Bassingstoke facility. The users who were moving to Bassingstoke, some of whom were in the customer service area, had traditionally received sub-second response time because their terminals had traditionally been directly attached to the mainframe computer. The users expected Shepherd's organization to provide them with a comparable level of service after the move.

A more traditional solution which was considered to provide IT support to Bassingstoke was to install a host computer in Bassingstoke. However the cost of establishing and maintaining such a data center lessened the appeal of that solution once the channel extension alternative was introduced.

During this discussion I would ask someone to explain the difference between case Exhibits 6 and 7. A student who has had experience with large-scale computers should be able to provide an explanation. In case Exhibit 6, mainframe computers are shown in both Allentown and Hersham. Exhibit 7 shows that the input/output devices in Hersham would be connected to the channel extension devices, giving users the illusion of being channel-attached to a mainframe computer.

Risks of Project Icon

The instructor can ask, "What are the risks associated with ICON?" The responses to this question are likely to be as follows:

> The channel extension technology may not work. According to the case, no one has ever used this channel extension technology to across the Atlantic ocean.

> Air Products Europe could experience outages (have no computing capabilities) if a telecommunications line were to go out or if the fiber cable was damaged.

> Response time may degrade.

> APCI and APE have little experience with this technology and it would be difficult to hire people who have experience with this technology.

> This seems to be a large project. There appear to be a lot of technical details that need to be ironed out for this project to be successful, and not a lot of time because of the impending move.

> Users are likely to be justifiably skeptical of such a project in light of their need to have uninterrupted service.

The risk framework developed by McFarlan (**Exhibit TN-1**) can be used to organize the discussion of the risk of this project. This is a large project of high structure. Technology risk is moderate, since APE and its parent have extensive telecommunications experience. However, the channel extension technology had never been applied in a transatlantic situation. Most students will classify this project as medium to high risk. The short window within which this project had to be completed significantly increased the risk of this project.

Another factor which increased the risk of this project to Mather and Shepherd was that there was no user ownership of the project, i.e. no one with whom to share the glory if it worked or pain if there were problems. In fact, European users were skeptical as to whether this scheme could work and not disrupt the high quality service that they had come to expect.

At this point the instructor can inform students that Mather and Shepherd announced their decision to go forward with ICON on January 2, 1991, APE's "Black Monday." Students can be asked to describe what needs to be accomplished to implement ICON by the targeted June 1991 date.

After a 10 minute discussion of implementation issues, the instructor might remind students that on January 17, 1991 the Allied bombing raids on Iraqi targets had begun. The students should be asked to assume they were Shepherd and as Shepherd, what would they would do, with the Persian Gulf War in progress, and the accompanying threats against US air travelers?

The session can be wrapped up by showing the aggressive implementation plan proposed in the (B) case and share with them the details concerning implementation highlighted in the (C) case.

Suggested 80-Minute Teaching Plan

1.　　What should Shepherd and Mather do?　(15-20 minutes)
　　　projected net savings: $1 million in 1992; $2 million by 1994
　　　70% capacity improvement
　　　improved reliability, response times for continental users
　　　improved batch processing turnaround

2.　　APCI's Use of IT　(15 minutes)
　　　traditional functions: accounting, manufacturing
　　　extensive telecommunications infrastructure
　　　online customer service applications
　　　future: global engineering

3.　　Why consider a project like ICON? (10 minutes)
　　　support Bassingstoke users with sub-second response times
　　　mainframes both in US and Europe near capacity
　　　Airlink satellite lease about to expire
　　　Alternatives:
　　　　　　outsource
　　　　　　discourage new IT applications
　　　　　　upgrade APE data center
　　　　　　small host at Bassingstoke

4.　　Risks of ICON (15 minutes)
　　　short time window: by June 1991.
　　　Already a full plate ("needed ICON like a hole in the head")
　　　channel extension: never applied trans-Atlantically
　　　small vendors; rental car agency had problems; but good line redundancy (2 cables)
　　　no ownership by users (although proposed by Bassingstoke manager Albert Lee)
　　　"American" solution. Seven jobs would be eliminated.

5.　　B Case and implications of the Gulf War (10 minutes)
　　　January 2, 1991: go forward with ICON.
　　　January 17, 1991: Gulf War starts

6.　　C Case (10 minutes)
　　　June 24: cut-over
　　　No network failures; total redundancy
　　　Faster machine --> better response times

Key Summary Lessons

Consideration of whether to introduce new IT tools (in this case, new computing hardware, significantly enhanced networking capabilities, and new software) involves consideration of the impact on an organization's IT architecture, as well as consideration of organizational and human resources issues.

The risks of information technology initiatives can be assessed using McFarlan's Project Risk Framework, which suggests ways to reduce the risks imposed by projects that are large, unstructured, and involving new technologies.

Effective IT implementation includes both extensive advanced planning and the ability to adapt to unforeseen circumstances (such as the Gulf War)

McFarlan's IT Project Risks Framework: Assessing Systems Efforts

Size: How big is this project?
Projected person/years, lines of code, function points
Is it de-composable into smaller pieces?

Structure: Is this project well-defined?
Are the outputs and data requirements clear?
Is a clear processing algorithm possible?
To what extent can structure be imposed on this project?

Experience with the technology:
Are the necessary IT tools, processes, or structures new to us?
New hardware? software?
New systems development methods?
New vendors?
Can we hire the necessary expertise? or must we learn by doing?

Organizational Readiness: are we ready to handle this?
Previous experience with projects/technologies of this kind?
Strong IS leadership?
Motivated, trainable people?
Senior management backing?

* Source: James I. Cash, Jr., F. Warren McFarlan, James L. McKenney and Lynda M. Applegate, *Corporate Information Systems Management, Text and Cases* (Third Edition). Boston, MA: Irwin, 1992.

Air Products and Chemicals, Inc.: Project ICON (B)

Just before Christmas, 1990, Peter Mather and John Shepherd decided to proceed with ICON and presented the ICON proposal to the APE and APCI management committees. The response? A cautious okay and an admonition that if Shepherd and Mather chose to undertake it, the project had better work.

Gary Pettifer, manager of technical support, remembered January 2, 1991, the day that Shepherd announced the project to the APE MIS group, as "Black Monday". He noted, "I had built a great group of IBM systems programmers who worked well together. It was difficult for me to face them and admit that some of them would have to go."

One employee, who had been with APE for five years, described his reaction as "total shock." He added:

> The operators were very disconcerted. We felt like the rug had been pulled from under our feet. In November 1990 we completed an evaluation of a number of vendors' products which would have allowed us to automate production scheduling and other areas of the IBM operation. We wondered, then, why management put those projects on hold. With the January 2 announcement of ICON, all became crystal-clear.

Equipment testing and simulation of transatlantic loads and vendor selection was scheduled for the first calendar quarter of 1991. The approved implementation plan (**Exhibit 1**) would allow Shepherd and Mather to kill ICON at the end of the first calendar quarter 1991 if the channel extension equipment failed to meet or exceed service level criteria.

At 11:30 pm, January 16, 1991, came the first reports of allied bombing raids on Iraqi targets in Kuwait and Iraq. In the days that followed, terrorist threats caused the volume of international air traffic to plummet, and reminded all APE and APCI workers of the perils of international air travel in such turbulent times. At such a time, what could Shepherd and Mather ask of their employees in the name of Project ICON?

Research Associate Robert W. Lightfoot prepared this case under the supervision of Professor Donna B. Stoddard as the basis for class discussion rather than to illustrate either effective or ineffective handling of an administrative situation.

Exhibit 1   APCI, ICON Project Implementation Schedule

ICON Implementation Schedule

Technology Evaluation and Simulation of Transatlantic Loads - **Vendor Selection**	**February/March**
Preferred Vendor Equipment Tests - **Single Transatlantic Link (Hersham/Allentown)** - **Response Time, Reliability, Performance** - **Data, Voice, Video, Interactive, Print, Remotes** - **Basingstoke Fallback**	**April/May**
Preferred Vendor Equipment Tests - **Dual Transatlantic Links & Basingstoke** - **Full Load - Pre-Production** - **Contingency, Backup, Automatic Rerouting**	**May/June**
Continental Circuit Upgrade (64 kbps lines to Paris)	**May/June**
Live Cutover	**24 June**
Basingstoke Move	**20 July**
Continental Circuits Installation	**July to October**

Source: Company records.

Air Products and Chemicals, Inc.: Project ICON (C)

European IBM processing was successfully transferred to APCI's Corporate Data Center on June 24, 1991. From the first day of operation, there were no network failures, and response times were better than Hersham users had experienced prior to ICON.

Cutover: The 500-step Plan

Bill Townsend, APCI's manager of computing services operations, crafted a 500-step plan for implementing the cutover. Though meticulous in detail, his plan enabled the cutover to proceed without trouble. He said:

> We drafted a detailed plan with more than 500 individual steps. Everything had a back-up. Tapes had to be transferred to the US, so we had shipped duplicate copies on different planes that departed from different airports in the UK and landed in different airports in the US. We prepared for customs procedures by getting all prior clearance done beforehand.
>
> The key to the process was communication. We used voice mail reports to inform everyone involved in the project where we were in the plan during the cutover. In the plan, there were detailed instructions of how to contact everyone involved. We even extended the cafeteria's hours to provide for the many shifts of people working around the clock over the three-day cutover.

100 Days of Understanding

Though ICON was immediately successful on a technical level, Prutzman—ICON's implementation team leader—pointed out that success of the project did not end on June 24, 1991:

> The US had more automated production scheduling than the UK, so the temptation was there to start changing the way European applications were run. But there were many nuances of how the system was put together and how the

Research Associate Robert W. Lightfoot prepared this case under the supervision of Professor Donna B. Stoddard as the basis for class discussion rather than to illustrate either effective or ineffective handling of an administrative situation.

business was run. So after the cutover, we adopted a policy of "100 Days of Understanding," instead of "100 Days of Changing." After the cutover, we focused on learning how European operations worked.

APCI did not provide 24-hour technical support, but it did put technical support analysts on-call during off-hours and provide them with mobile cellular phones so they could be reached at home or on their way to work. (US employees were often on their way to work during the UK's peak hours.) Noted Prutzman, "We've become much more sensitive to extending our prime shift to cover Europe. That's been a liability for the support staff because they are on-call more, but this hasn't proven to be a big deal."

Organizational Impact

Project ICON strengthened the personal relationships between APE and APCI employees, and many thought these relationships would improve cooperation between the two organizations in the future. The placement of one APE employee in APCI contributed to APE employee trust in APCI.

Internal positions proved more difficult to find than had originally been expected, though APE did place four of the seven displaced workers internally. Of the remaining three, one left the company shortly after ICON was announced to become a missionary in Australia, and one found a sales job (that he preferred to his old job) with one of the channel extension technology vendors. Toward the end of the project, APCI and APE identified a job for the last displaced employee in the Corporate Data Center, though securing a five-year work visa for him was difficult.

Almost universally, employees in the UK and the US responded that the greatest effect of the project was a feeling of "empowerment." Prutzman noted:

What we got out of it was a sense of pride in our ability to make things happen. People worked harder than they had ever worked, and they felt a real part of the organization. Because of the scope of the project and the intense time pressure, management delegated a lot of decision making. Management also freed up resources for international travel—something that wasn't traditionally done at APCI for many employees.

Townsend added that ICON had positive implications for future management practices: "Project ICON really worked, and we know why. We knew the target. We made it clear to everyone. We got the right people and told them what we needed from them. And we kept their path clear."

Allen-Bradley's ICCG: Repositioning for the '90s

Synopsis

The case describes a broad set of organizational changes undertaken by a division of Allen-Bradley (A-B) in anticipation of changing environmental conditions. The key environmental change driving organizational transformation is an increasing emphasis on computer integrated solutions in the market for industrial automation. Allen-Bradley's strengths have historically been in the controls area, especially in programmable logic controllers (PLC). To better compete in the integrated solutions market, the ICCG division has restructured itself in order to break down traditional boundaries among its various divisions. IT is hoped that the new structure will allow A-B to develop integrated products while staying focused on core competencies and presenting a single point of contact to customers. The division has adopted cross-functional teams as basic building blocks of the new organization, in an attempt to respond in a more timely yet integrated manner to customer demands. The firm has also changed its information architecture and control systems to support the new strategy and structure. The changes being undertaken at Allen-Bradley offer a good example of what Drucker calls "the coming of the new organization."

Teaching Objectives

This case focuses on how organization structure, control systems, and information systems must be managed in combination in order to enhance an organization's effectiveness. The case supports three broad teaching objectives:

> To examine a case of organizational transformation in which significant changes have been made in the organization's structure, information systems, and control systems.
>
> To discuss how such a sweeping transformation should be implemented. Is change best accomplished by top-down direction or bottom-up initiative? How should changes be sequenced? What are the conditions that facilitate effective organizational transformation?
>
> To discuss the emergence of the "new organization" that is heralded by so many contemporary observers.

Optional Additional Readings

Brian Dumaine, "Who Needs a Boss?" *Fortune*, May 7, 1990, pp. 52-60.

Brian Dumaine, "The Bureaucracy Busters," *Fortune*, June 17, 1991: 36-50.

Peter Senge, "The Metanoic Firm," *New Management*, Summer 1986, pp. 6-13.

Suggested Study Questions

1. What are the main characteristics of the organizational transformation at Allen-Bradley's ICCG? Do they make ICCG a more effective organization?

2. How important are these changes for the firm's competitive success in the 1980s?

3. What challenges does ICCG face in the future? What should Rody Salas do?

4 Are the changes at ICCG an example of the emergence of a new organizational paradigm?

Opportunities for Student Analysis and Discussion

Context of ICCG's "Second Repositioning"

Understanding the drivers of change at Allen-Bradley (A-B) is important for students to be able to critically assess the transformation underway. The class discussion can be started by asking: What is driving A-B's "second repositioning?

A-B's "first repositioning" took place when they switched from electromechanical to programmable logic controllers (PLCs) in the late '70s. This shift was made in anticipation of changes in the controls marketplace that were subsequently borne out, and hence A-B was able to build a leadership position.

In the mid-1980s, Tracy O'Rourke, who envisioned the first repositioning initiated a "second repositioning" in anticipation of new changes in the controls marketplace. O'Rourke felt that in order to retain leadership in the late '80s and the '90s, A-B would have no choice but to:

become a "global supplier of computer-integrated solutions" in the computer-integrated-manufacturing (CIM) area.

compete not on the basis of cost but on the basis of innovation (e.g., Pyramid Integrator) and customer service.

His rationale was that US firms would never compete successfully on price alone in the face foreign competition based on low labor costs. They needed some other source of comparative advantage. In light of that reasoning, the bet that A-B is making—and evidence suggests that they are right—is that their customers will increasingly look for integrated "solutions" for their CIM needs. This, A-B's executives believe, will force all vendors to become more "systems" oriented—selling stand-alone "boxes" or even PLCs as ICCG used to do will no longer be viable. It will also require vendors like A-B to focus more on "customer service" and to build deeper relationships with their customers.

One of the most interesting competitive challenges in the market for CIM solutions is the customer's choice of "prime contractor." The prime contractor's role is necessary because no firm can independently offer all components that go into a fully integrated solution. Any integrated solution requires assembling many vendors, including suppliers of :

> controls (like A-B);
> computers (like DEC),
> software (like Computervision and Autodesk), and
> systems integrators (like Arthur Andersen)
> (see case Exhibit 4).

The integration of products from multiple firms not only presents formidable technical challenges of subsystem compatibility, but also political challenges of balancing competition and cooperation among the players. For example, a major brewing company wanted a CIM solution for a new plant they were trying to build. They invited several different vendors to the table and charged them with coming up with an entire solution and a single point of contact for future service. The brewing company wanted a single vendor whom they could call in the case of a service request, regardless of whether the DEC Vax system or the Allen-Bradley PLC needed service. Allen-Bradley won this bid, and acted both as the prime contractor and prime source of service. In other situations, Allen-Bradley competes with the same players that it cooperated with to provide the solution for the brewing company. In yet other situations, Allen-Bradley been a subcontractor, not the prime contractor. While such complicated projects were not the norm at the time of the case, they are becoming increasingly common.

The challenge these environmental conditions present for Allen-Bradley is to be clear about its own strategic intent and distinctive competence, so that its identity does not get lost in this jumble. Defining its own identity clearly and then making sure it remains at the leading edge in that domain becomes an imperative. It also forces the firm to focus more clearly on customer needs. The firm also needs to switch from a single product focus to an integrated solution focus which will require greater internal coordination among its existing product divisions. Finally, it requires the firm to open itself to creating coalitions with other firms in an opportunistic and yet consistent manner.

Problems with ICCG's existing organization

The limitations of ICCG's old organization in effectively meeting the requirements of the second repositioning envisaged by O'Rourke can be discussed from the standpoint of the old structure, the old information architecture, and the old control system.

Old Organization Structure: A discussion of the drawbacks of ICCG's existing structure should surface the following points:

1. Internal divisions that were each technology focused and autonomous — and in some cases even competitive, leading to incompatible products and confused customers.

2. Unfocused marketing departments that were redundant across the divisions.

3. Sales were done through distributors and there was little direct interaction with the final customer.

4. ICCG had lots of relationships with other firms, but no clear vision for partnering.

5. Most decision rights were concentrated within each of the internal divisions.

6. Although there was no dearth of innovative initiatives, they were random and not institutionalized.

Old IT Architecture: A discussion of the existing IT architecture should raise the following concerns:

1. Internal disconnects across departments like engineering, manufacturing and administration.

2. Lots of information redundancy and information overload.

3. Lack of a common information architecture. Islands of information systems.

4. Lack of good customer information.

Old Control: Discussion of the old control system should highlight the following problems:

1. The P&L responsibility of each division created problems of goal congruence and coordinated effort.

2. The proliferation of engineering projects without any purpose or priority led to frequent slippages on schedules and low productivity and satisfaction for the engineers.

3. The exclusive focus on financial measures led to a neglect of the growing importance of customer satisfaction.

4. The focus on the technical superiority of products led to a neglect of inefficiencies and flaws in business processes.

The "New" ICCG

Having discussed the limitations of the old ICCG organization, one can ask students to assess the new ICCG organization. This discussion can also be organized under the categories of organization structure, information architecture, and control systems.

New Organization Structure: Both internal and external structural boundaries have been redrawn in the new ICCG. A circular structure has been introduced. Its purpose is to abolish the previous divisional fiefdoms and provide a clear focus and identity for the company. The new structure reflects what ICCG sees as its "core competence" — the programmable controller business. Accordingly, it is placed at the center of the circular structure. ICCG management believes that they must always be at the leading edge of this core competence. Any other firm with a similar core is a competitor, with whom ICCG should be especially wary of entering into collaborative deals. The next ring is the communication and information systems area, which builds interfaces so that ICCG controllers can be used as components of an integrated CIM solution. Here, ICCG is willing to develop close partnerships with firms like Digital, who provide additional hardware that is required for an integrated CIM solution. The next outer ring is defined by the application systems area which deals with software and systems integration vendors. Third-party relations abound in this ring, as it is farthest from ICCG's core competence. Outside this ring are customers, the marketing and sales organizations, the management and administration organization, and two manufacturing operations.

The circular structure has more rhetorical and communication value than it has a direct influence on the division of labor, the coordination of activities, and the distribution of decision rights. The cynical view would be that the only change is that the old divisions have been redrawn as circles instead of boxes on the organization chart. The one identifiable difference is that marketing has been centralized. While this cynical view has an element of truth, the symbolic importance of the new representation of the firm's structure should not be underestimated. Symbolic acts are rhetorical devices that managers can use to force the organization to reconsider existing organizational relationships. The new representation helps Salas to communicate a new focus for the organization.

In addition to symbolically redefining the boundaries of organizational structure, Salas has also attempted to change the structure more fundamentally through the "team-based organization" shown in case Exhibit 5. The basic building blocks of the new structure are cross-functional teams, which can be put together for a variety of purposes. We see in the case examples of teams assembled to develop products (the T60 team), develop a new information architecture (the Kent-Mesko-Kreuger team), address customer service issues (the Ghostbusters team), and so forth. While some teams are more permanent than others, teams have become the dominant mode of doing work at the new ICCG. Forming and disbanding teams is overseen by business teams who can either establish a team or approve one proposed by any organizational member. Business teams play a significant coordination and resource allocation role. Teams are overseen by four executive councils, each charged with providing overall leadership and vision for a crucial aspect of ICCG's mission.

The purpose of this team-based structure is to push responsibility and decision making down and to empower people to act as they see fit to meet well defined organizational goals. While the ends are clearly defined, few constraints are imposed on the means for achieving those ends.

If this structure works, the benefits will include:

> more innovative, expeditious implementation because all parties whose efforts must be coordinated will be involved from the outset,

> a focus on the crucial aspects of the business because of the oversight of councils and the business teams, and

> a broader sense of opportunity in the firm.

The skeptic might quite reasonably ask if this new structure is just old wine in new bottles that over time — once the enthusiasm of being on the most number of teams dies down — will become a new and probably even more bureaucratic mess than the one it was intended to replace. This debate can be very lively, especially since the virtues of teams have been so widely touted in the contemporary management literature. If teams are "good," then should they be adopted with the giddy enthusiasm that we see at the new ICCG? This question causes at least some students in the class to pause and reexamine the presumed benefits of teams that have often been accepted uncritically.

New Information Architecture: The main change is an attempt to create a common information architecture on the principle of a single closed loop. Al Hails captures the design principle that underlying the single closed loop architecture aptly: "The idea is to get the right information to the right place at the right time, using common data. The flip side is to collect the information at all the distributed points of activity and put them together in a database that can be accessed by anyone on the other side." The new information architecture has two notable characteristics. First, it maintains a universal underlying database that forces a common vocabulary upon all the divisions. Second, it allows users to choose their own hardware and application programs as long as the inputs can be received from and the outputs can be stored in a common company-wide data repository.

The new information architecture has had a direct impact on coordination across departments and on the time taken to execute various business processes. It also gives management much tighter control over the business. An important side benefit of this internal change in the way ICCG manages information flows is that the lessons they have learned have enhanced their ability to understand and sell CIM solutions.

This information architecture is still lacking external data on sales, competition, and customer satisfaction. Managers at ICCG have recognized this problem and are trying to address it.

New Control: A much broader set of performance measures are at the heart of the new control system. As case Exhibit 2 shows, there is much greater emphasis on measuring operational efficiencies, quality, customer satisfaction and service, and human resources. These measures have been chosen so that they can be easily understood, measured, and tracked. They are constantly revised, which ensures that they are perceived as being continually fair and relevant. There are also a number of interesting changes in the process by which performance is monitored and reviewed. Particularly notable is the separation of the review of financial performance from other non-financial measures. These two meetings take place separately, and more time is spent on reviewing non-financial metrics, thus ensuring that these are not perceived as being secondary to financial measures. Also notable is the emphasis on translating the periodic review of performance measures into concrete actions by identifying the "top five" factors limiting better performance and determining the actions (with dates and assigned responsibilities) to be taken to address these factors.

The general manager milestone review serves as a way for top management to remain on top of critical projects, since these are now the main vehicle for getting things done in the firm.

Finally, the executive councils provide overall direction and establish priorities that guide resource allocation. In this regard, a simple but fascinating new control system is a periodic review of "priorities." I was quite stunned to learn that in the last such review, by cutting two thirds of the projects, the firm was able to improve the number of new product introductions over the next year by 33%. This points to the enormous effect the priorities system has had on resource allocation within this firm.

The discussion of control systems can be enriched by discussing how "tight" or "loose" it is, how "robust" it is to gaming, what "functions" it serves, and what underlying assumptions of human behavior it makes?

Implementing change

After assessing the changes that have been made in the organization of ICCG, it is useful to spend some time discussing the manner in which these changes were implemented. There are several important lessons that can be drawn from this discussion:

Importance of a clear guiding vision like that provided by Tracy O'Rourke.

The need to translate the vision into simple, easily understand messages or slogans such as Rody Salas's five "guideposts."

The willingness to learn from spontaneous efforts undertaken at lower levels of the organization, such as the Kent-Mesko initiative (this is a key finding of Mike Beer's research on change).

Importance of "organizational prototyping," such as ICCG's efforts to learn teaming from the Pyramid Integrator and T60 projects.

Sequencing. Starting with large scale structural change would probably have been a mistake. It was best to wait until everybody acknowledged that it was necessary and could thus be implemented with greater buy-in.

Importance of perseverance and commitment on the part of top managers.

The interconnectedness of information, organizational, and control systems problems. Inevitably changes in one domain require changes in the other.

Future challenges

The biggest challenge facing Salas as the case ends is to get the new structure and control system to work. There is still a lot of uncertainty about just how the team approach will play out. Previous definitions of authority are recognized as being no longer valid, but new definitions have yet to emerge. This is a time of opportunity and risk. Some employees are thrilled, others paralyzed, yet others quite upset. I heard several employees express hope that things would soon settle down, but Salas wants to create a self-designing organization that is always in flux. He hopes that employees will learn to live with much greater uncertainty and ambiguity. The relative roles of project teams, business teams, and executive councils is still being shaped. A big concern: what if, instead of breaking up the bureaucracy and creating focus, the changes lead to even more bureaucracy and even more unfocused projects?

The HRM system, as might be expected, has been the slowest to adapt to the changes. The new structure will profoundly impact career paths, skills required of employees, and performance measurement and rewards. Periodic evaluations by a single boss and rewards based on purely individual accomplishments seem to be inconsistent with the new ICCG. The new organization requires more team-based performance assessment and rewards, and the HRM department is experimenting with ways to change in that direction.

Finally, for ICCG to be successful, Salas must coordinate his efforts with the parent Allen-Bradley organization in Milwaukee. The Milwaukee organization has complementary products and still controls the sales function. Don David, who picked Rody Salas to succeed him as head of ICCG, is now president of Allen-Bradley, so we can expect the parent to be receptive to ICCG initiatives. However, there may be some resentment in Milwaukee about the ascendance of the upstart Cleveland division.

Suggested 80-Minute Teaching Plan

1. Introductory remarks (5 minutes)

2. What are the forces driving ICCG's "second repositioning"? (5 minutes)

3. What were the limitations of the old organization, with respect to its ability to effectively meet the challenge of this second repositioning? What were some limitations of the way the firm was structured? with its information architecture? with its control systems? (15 minutes)

4. What changes has ICCG made? Will these changes make ICCG more effective? (20 minutes)

5. What do you think of how Salas implemented these changes? (10 minutes)

6. What are the future challenges confronting Rody Salas? How should he address them? (10 minutes)

7. Is ICCG an example of "the coming of the new organization?" How prevalent do you think this new model will be in the 1990s? (10 minutes)

8. Wrap-up and concluding remarks (5 minutes)

Key Summary Lessons:

Is ICCG an example of the coming of the new organization?

With its emphasis on core competencies, custom solutions, customer satisfaction, time-based competition, team-based organization, strategic partnering, common company-wide information architecture, and broad performance measures, ICCG is an exemplar of the new organization. Discussion of the coming new organizational model often has a great deal of energy. Some students take the stance that the new organization is a necessary response to demands of the contemporary business environment, while skeptics view the new organization as a fad that will soon be replaced with another. To push this discussion, one can bring in a historical perspective and describe the conditions that led to the emergence of the multi-divisional organization. Then ask if a similar sea-change is currently underway.

Appex Corporation

Synopsis

This case describes the challenges faced by Shikhar Ghosh, when he took charge of this faltering start-up in the cellular communications industry. The case examines a series of structural changes that enabled Ghosh to turn the company around and grow it faster than all projections. Having inherited an ad-hoc entrepreneurial structure that was being stretched to its limit, Ghosh led the company through six different structures in thirty months.

In Fall, 1988, he first implemented some innovative egalitarian structural designs—most notable of which was a circular representation. This failed to bring order and control to Appex. In February 1989, he implemented a second change: a traditional hierarchical, functional structure. This improved the reliable execution of functions, but suffered from problems of poor integration across functions. To address these problems, around May 1989, Ghosh overlaid a product team structure on the functional design. In November 1989, he added a twist to this hybrid structure by creating business teams with responsibility for families of products. This fourth structural change quickly outgrew its usefulness as it increased the total amount of "bureaucracy" and diluted accountability. In August 1990, Ghosh implemented a fifth design: a divisional structure. This was to bring greater accountability and responsiveness.

The case describes some problems with this divisional structure, and changes being contemplated. Another major change that is not discussed at length in the case is the October 1990 acquisition of Appex by EDS. By the end of the case Appex not only has to address the problems with its own divisional structure, it also has to adjust to being one of many divisions of a larger corporation.

Teaching Objectives

This case introduces concepts of organization structure. It presents most of the archetypal structural forms and shows how each affects organizational behavior and performance. The case clearly demonstrates that no one "best" design solves all organizational problems. Instead, it shows the importance of dynamically aligning structure with changing circumstances. It highlights the close linkage between structure, control systems, performance measurement, career paths, and information architecture. The main pedagogical objectives are:

> make students aware of the critical role of organization structure in shaping the behavior of its members and their individual and collective performance.

> acquaint students with the main organizational forms and their strengths and weaknesses.

explore the circumstances under which structural change is a useful management tool and how frequently one can change structure to address emergent problems.

Suggested Optional Readings

Larry Greiner, "Evolution and Revolution as Organizations Grow," *Harvard Business Review*, 1972.

Jay W. Lorsch, "Note on Organization Design," Harvard Business School Case Publishing # 9-476-094

Suggested Study Questions

1. What were the challenges that Shikhar Ghosh faced when he joined Appex?

2. Evaluate the importance of each structural change. What problems did each new structure address? What problems, in turn, did it create?

3. What would you have done in Shikhar's place? Was every structural change necessary? How would you address the challenges confronting Appex at the end of the case?

Opportunities for Student Analysis

The major opportunities for student analysis are the strengths and weaknesses of each design and the circumstances to which each is suited (see Chapter 2, Exhibit 8.)

Consider the situation Appex when Ghosh was appointed COO in May 1988. A good trigger for discussion would be: Do you agree with Ghosh's assessment that Appex needed control and structure? This should lead to a discussion of the strengths and weaknesses of a start-up entrepreneurial structure. It should also induce discussion of key success factors for Appex. The main strength of the entrepreneurial structure is that it facilitated fast, innovative responses. This was how Appex established itself in the cellular communications industry; as evidenced by its ability to successfully defeat the ACT alliance led by GTE. The company was founded and run by self-driven, technically competent entrepreneurs who worked hard together, and did whatever was required to ensure the company's survival. There was no formal structure or control system. In its early years, Appex probably did not need it.

28

With growth, this highly informal organization began to encounter its limits. One big problem was reliability, a key success factor in the cellular business. If Appex failed to verify "roamers," their clients (cellular phone companies) were unable to allow their customers to complete calls. For Appex's clients, this could lead to loss of revenue and customer defections. Moreover, these clients depended on Appex to manage their accounts; here, too reliability was of the essence. Missed installation dates, product and system failures, inconsistent service, were of major concern, particularly since the cellular phone business was growing rapidly and increasingly required greater reliability. Moreover, since each cellular phone company was a large account, the penalty of defections was very high. A second concern, especially to the venture capitalists who had invested in Appex, was the lack of planning and adherence to projected targets. This was one of Shikhar's main mandates when he was made COO, so his own future was also at stake.

These critical failures were in large part due to the poorly defined division of labor, responsibility, authority, and accountability in Appex's early structure. As Ghosh points out, there is a fine line between being entrepreneurial and chaotic. Appex was crossing this line as demand for its products and services increased to the point where everyone could not do everything on an ad-hoc basis. It is hard to disagree with Shikhar's assessment that Appex had reached a juncture where structure and control were needed.

Next students can address what can be learned from the failure of Shikhar's innovative circular organization structure. The main lesson here is that the structure of a firm serves as a road-map that helps organization members define their and others' positions. Thus, the organization chart helps define employees' identity within the firm and how they relate to each other. Shikhar's organization chart was like a map without any markings indicating directions or roads. It provided little guide for action and did little to address the limitations of the previous entrepreneurial structure. The division of labor remained ambiguous. Responsibility and accountability were poorly defined. Note also that Appex was recruiting new employees who did not see themselves as entrepreneurs and were used to a more traditional organization chart Shikhar's innovative ideas created even more confusion than existed previously.

Even though most students are critical of this structural intervention, it is worth asking if Shikhar would have been able to implement a hierarchical structure without having gone through this intermediate stage. Would that change have been too drastic for earlier employees? Might they have felt too tied down? Could Appex afford to lost them? One might also discuss Shikhar's view that it is easier to go from a traditional structure to a more innovative one, but very hard to got from no structure to an ambiguous one.

One can then direct student's' attention to the functional structure. A good discussion question might be: Was the functional structure a good way for Appex to solve its problems? This can lead to discussion of the benefits of a functional structure, particularly the clear division of labor it creates for essential activities. By clearly defining who had responsibility for the main functions—sales and marketing, operations, software development and services, engineering and technology, and finance, human resources and administration, the functional structure enabled Appex to focus on completing its tasks. This helped bring under control several problems. Reliability improved. With greater accountability, targets could be set with greater confidence, and the functional structure helped people define their identity and career paths.

Why did Shikhar have to change this structure? Analysis should reveal some dysfunctions of bureaucratic functional structures: the importance attached to titles, the proliferation of jobs as each function builds its own empire (for a classic example, see case Exhibit 4 which shows how complex the marketing function can get for even a small organization), and the emergence of organizational politics. The functional structure at Appex wonderfully illustrates the classic concepts of differentiation and integration advanced by Lawrence and Lorsch. The case clearly shows how functions get differentiated and develop their own distinct identities, leading to problems of integration across them. For example, consider the problems between engineering and operations. Nor does the functional structure promote the development of good general management skills. It also puts a lot of pressure on the CEO, who is the only person able to resolve conflicts between functions. Moreover, as stated in Paul Gudonis's memo (see case Exhibit 5), the functional structure dilutes accountability for financial performance and can diminished employees' motivation to produce innovative products and services. Strategic planning for issues that cut across the firm (system architecture, capacity planning, network integrity) can also be neglected.

Analysis of the functional form can set up discussion of hybrid solutions. One could ask: Did the Product and Business team structures address the limitations of the functional structure?

The greatest benefit of the **Product Team Structure** was that it brought a strategic focus to the development and performance of each product and service, since this was now the responsibility of a product manager. It reduced the integrative role that Shikhar had to play, since product managers had to secure the necessary effort from the functions. It also placed greater emphasis on product development and strategic planning. Inevitably, though, it generated its own problems. It created ambiguity and conflict over decision rights. Who had the right to propose, who had the right to approve, who had the right to decide how to implement the plan, and who had the right to review performance became muddied. Resource allocation was also a big issue, as product managers competed to get the most out of the various functions for their own products. Organizational life became increasingly political, and partisan issues were too often escalated to top management.

The **Business Teams Structure** gave strategic and resource allocation responsibilities to families of products. This hybrid was closer to a divisional structure, while retaining the underlying functional form. It may have been too much of a "kludge," as it added administrative work and obfuscated decision rights and accountability. In Shikhar's words, "there was more tail than tooth." It did give some of managers more general management responsibilities and helped Shikhar identify future divisional general managers.

This analysis should help students recognize that hybrid designs are rarely permanent solutions, even though they can be useful interim solutions.

Analysis of the **Divisional Structure** can follow the discussion of hybrid designs. This discussion should include the benefits of a divisional structure, particularly its emphasis on greater accountability for financial performance and responsibility for planning and budgeting. This structure frees up the CEO from involvement in day-to-day operational details, but increases his responsibility for making resource allocation decisions across divisions. As the case shows, divisions can also develop partisan interests just as fierce as those among functions. This can lead to an unwillingness to share resources and a loss of scale economies (e.g., each division needing its own database manager); to detrimental competition among divisions (each vying for a larger share of product development money or gaming to improve their relative numbers); and to issues "falling through the cracks" because they do not fall neatly in a particular division.

Students can be asked, What are the structural implications of the EDS acquisition of Appex? While the case does not speak to this question, one can see that being part of EDS should greatly improve Appex's access to resources. EDS may take away some of Appex's autonomy, and require that Appex modify various systems and procedures to be consistent with EDS's systems (e.g., will purchasing procedures change?). Furthermore, Appex will likely command only a small fraction of the attention of EDS management. This may cause delays in critical decisions that require EDS approval.

In my interviews, Shikhar felt that EDS had given Appex a free hand in most matters, although they set tough financial targets. Appex did have to deal with some new bureaucratic procedures, such as for purchasing (EDS wanted Appex to benefit from the volume discounts). EDS required that employees take a test for substance abuse. Appex managers also began to realize that their firm was but a small speck in the attention horizon of EDS management. Shikhar told of how one manager called the VP of Purchasing at EDS to inquire about delivery of a $500,000 computer. He did not realize that this VP at EDS was probably four levels above the person responsible for managing the Appex order. At Appex, the manager had always called a VP when he wanted to check on something like that. Despite such incidents, there were no voluntary or involuntary separations of key people, and, Shikhar was pleased to be part of EDS..

Having analyzed the main structural forms implemented by Shikhar Ghosh at Appex, students can be asked what would they do to respond to the problems with the divisional structure? One option was to centralize those key activities that truly cut across divisions, such as data-processing and new product development. Another would be to create company-wide programs such as Total Quality Management or a Customer Satisfaction program that would be overseen by a cross-functional, cross-divisional team. Managers could be rotated across divisions so that they did not develop strong partisan loyalties and instead helped serve as linking pins across divisions. A more radical solution might be to break the divisions up into a number of smaller divisions (perhaps organized on the basis of key customers) while retaining some centralized functions. This would reduce the power of existing divisions and encourage a sharper customer focus. In 1992, Shikhar was contemplating such a move.

Finally, students can be asked what they think of Shikhar's philosophy toward structure. Would they, with the benefit of 20/20 hindsight, have done anything differently? Would they anticipate making a major structural change in the coming six months? In answering this question, students must take into account the rapid growth of the company. They should also see that Appex could probably not have implemented a divisional structure right after the functional structure. A critical contingency was the cast of characters as Appex grew. Individuals who were great at managing a function were not necessarily capable of managing a division. As Shikhar noted, it takes time to grow or recruit management talent. Bringing in people from the outside to manage existing "stars" can be difficult and emotional. Structures have to be designed with egos in mind.

There is also the issue of incremental versus radical change. It is often easier to take small steps that are headed in a particular direction than to try and make one large-scale change. At Appex, the circular structure was a small step between the start-up and functional structures, and the product and business team structures were two steps between the functional and divisional structure. Shikhar viewed these interim forms as experiments to see if more drastic structural changes were warranted and if structural change would actually yield the results he expected. These incremental moves were also a good way for him to learn, since he had previously been a consultant and had little direct management experience.

This case suggests that structure should not be thought as static or inertial but as a continuously changing response to problems. Any structure deals with some problems at the expense of others. Any particular form focuses attention on some things and not on others. Thus in choosing a structure managers make trade-offs among various contingencies. Managers must be willing to change the structure when different contingencies become more important.

Structural change (as Shikhar notes) evokes an immediate and sharp behavioral response. But structural change can be disruptive and cause a great deal of stress in the organization. An interesting question to explore is: Under what circumstances and with what frequency should structural changes be made in organizations? This discussion usually generates very different student responses and can be a productive way to surface student assumptions about structure. To sharpen this discussion, one can ask students whether they would use the same criteria to determine when to change an organization's incentive system as they would use to change its structure?

Suggested 80-Minute Class Plan

1. Do you agree with Shikhar's assessment when he joined Appex that it needed "structure and control?" "What were Appex's key success factors? How well was it meeting them?" (10 minutes.)

2. Why did the **circular structure** fail to achieve its desired outcome? What does this tell us about the role that structure plays in an organization? (10 minutes.)

3. What were the strengths and weaknesses of the **functional structure**? How well did the product and business teams address the problems with the functional structure? (10 minutes.)

4. What do you think about the change to a **divisional structure**? What are its relative advantages and disadvantages compared to the earlier structures? How would you address the problems with the divisional structure? (10 minutes.)

5. What implications might the acquisition by EDS have for the structure of Appex? (5 minutes.)

6. What do you think of Shikhar's views of organization structure? Would you have done what he did over the last 30 months at Appex? Would you anticipate making another major structural change in six months? (15 minutes.)

7. Under what circumstances are structural changes a useful management intervention? When might such changes be undesirable? (10 minutes.)

8. Wrap-up and summary: Discussion of the main elements of organization structure. Review of the strengths and weaknesses of each major form. Importance of a dynamic alignment between structure and organizational context. (10 minutes.)

Key Summary Lessons

Importance of structure as a general management tool.

Basic dimensions of organization structure.

Comparison of different forms of organization structure.

Advantages and disadvantages of different organization structures.

Aligning an organization's structure and environment.

Using structure as a flexible tool to focus attention and solve problems.

Capital Holding Corporation: Reengineering the Direct Response Group

Synopsis

This case describes a strategic change initiative which was underway within Capital Holding Corporation's Direct Response Group (DRG) in 1991. DRG's senior management viewed reengineering as a process which would allow them to significantly change how DRG, a direct marketing insurance company, identified and sold products to their customers. In the late 1980s, Norm Phelps, president, joined DRG; Pam Godwin was hired shortly thereafter as vice president of strategic planning. Godwin led the DRG executive team through a strategic planning process which resulted in identification of "a new business model," which highlighted the executives' vision of how DRG would identify and service customers in light of their new strategy. Reengineering was initiated to enable them to realize that vision.

At the time of the case, several reengineering projects were underway. The tone of the case is quite up-beat; management felt they were on the right track in light of what they wanted to accomplish. Yet, the case ends with questions of concern to DRG senior management: "Can we make the dramatic changes that will be necessary to fund our growth into the 21st century? Do we have the right vision? What else do we need to do to ensure the success of our business?"

Teaching Objectives

This case can be taught alone or as a part of a case series on business process reengineering, in which it would follow the Safeway case (No. 193-134). The teaching objectives:

Introduce the concept of reengineering, and its benefits and challenges.

Examine and evaluate one organization's approach to reengineering.

Discuss the role of information technology in reengineering.

35

Suggested Optional Readings:

Davenport, Thomas, *Process Innovation*, Boston, MA: Harvard Business School Press, 1993.

Hammer, Michael, "Reengineering Work: Don't Automate, Obliterate," *Harvard Business Review*, July-August 1990, 104-112.

Hammer, Michael and James Champy, *Reengineering the Corporation*, New York: Harper Collins Books, 1993.

Stewart, T., "Reengineering," *Fortune*, August, 1993.

Suggested Study Questions

1. What is reengineering? How does reengineering differ from other organizational change initiatives?

2. Describe the reengineering approach undertaken by DRG management. What obstacles should DRG managers anticipate as they move forward with reengineering?

3. What recommendations would you make to DRG management as they try to institutionalize some of the initiatives that were started under the reengineering umbrella?

Opportunities for Student Analysis

What is reengineering?

It is worthwhile to start with a generic discussion of reengineering. The class can be opened by asking: "What is reengineering? How is reengineering different from other organizational change programs?"

Reengineering has been defined as "the *fundamental* rethinking and *radical* redesign of business *processes* to achieve *dramatic* improvements in critical, contemporary measures of performance, such as cost, quality, service, and speed."[1] Furthermore, information technology is an "essential enabler" of reengineering: "Information technology acts as an enabler that allows organizations to do work in radically different ways."[2] Many ambitious information systems implementations involve applying IT to existing processes; these would not constitute reengineering. Nor would an ambitious attempt to re-organize processes without employing information technology. Such efforts might be examples of very effective business process redesign, but they would not be reengineering (according to Hammer and Champy's definition).

Reengineering may also differ from other IT-enabled change programs in the *scope* and *magnitude* of the change involved:

> *scope of the change*: reengineering typically cuts across traditional departmental or functional boundaries.

> *magnitude of the change*: effective use of IT can enable dramatic performance improvements from reengineering efforts.

Reengineering also differs from other organizational change programs in that a <u>process</u> perspective is assumed. A process refers to a collection of activities that, taken together, create value for a customer. "A process perspective implies a strong emphasis on *how* work is done within an organization, in contrast to a traditional <u>product</u> focus emphasis on *what*."[3] Students should be challenged to describe what it means to take a process perspective. To stimulate discussion on this topic, the instructor could ask, "Envision a typical business. What are some generic processes that exist within business enterprises?" Students can be expected to respond with product development, order fulfillment and after sales service. Advanced or insightful students might add that some "internal" processes - such as human resources and information resources management - are cross functional in nature and need to be closely managed. The instructor could then ask whether we should expect all organizations within an industry to have the same core processes. The answer is to that question is yes and no. The "core" or critical processes should vary in light of the strategies of various organizations within an industry.

Situation analysis

Following the generic discussion of reengineering the dialogue will naturally shift to a discussion of DRG's reengineering initiative. The following questions can help effect a transition to that topic:

> What are the key success factors for DRG?
> What prompted DRG to undertake "reengineering"?
> What do they hope to accomplish with their reengineering initiative?
> What core processes have DRG's senior management identified?

DRG is an insurance company which uses direct response methods. The case explains that TV, newspaper inserts, and direct mail are the primary methods used to reach potential customers. Telephone contact and mail are used to provide customer service. DRG has no agents who can meet face-to-face with customers.

During the late 1980s performance measures began to suggest that DRG's traditional mass marketing approach was not working. DRG management concluded that a more targeted approach was needed. To be successful, they needed to become closer to their customers. In fact they sought to provide a level of service that characterizes agent-based insurance companies using direct response methods.

A new vision and a new business model were defined. The vision highlighted their commitment to each customer. The new business model communicated how they would identify and sell to prospects and customers.

Reengineering was initiated to realize their new vision and implement the new strategy. According to the case, "Reengineering was viewed as an umbrella for a series of projects, pilots, prototypes, and tests where successes could be quickly built upon and failures could be learned from and quickly discarded." To regain market share, senior management believed that the business and its core processes needed to be re-conceptualized. As a result of reengineering, management expected both to offer new, innovative products and to support customers in new, innovative ways.

Once the New Business Model was in place, key business processes were identified and prototypes developed to test out new ways of carrying out key business processes. The case describes how DRG had begun to experiment with new ways of dealing with customers (CMT) and identifying new market segments (MMT). The CMT concept is an outgrowth of work with personal service representatives in the late 1980s, in which senior citizen customers who purchased Medicare supplements were assigned to a team who handled the senior's interactions with the company. That program was considered successful. CMT was an attempt to expand the PSR model and apply it on a broader scale.

Many organizations begin reengineering initiatives by identifying the organization's core processes and proceeding to work on those processes that are "broken" or need to be sped up. DRG's new business model can be viewed as a **very** high level process map. Management seemed to believe that their marketing approach was an area upon which they needed to focus attention. Case Exhibit 8 summarizes reengineering projects associated with their back office functions that were underway at the end of 1991.

Management of the reengineering initiatives

Prescriptions for managing change are typically based on *evolutionary* change theories, which argue for gradual or incremental change, or *revolutionary* change theories, which propose radical, discontinuous change.[4] For any change project, managers who wish to motivate employees to participate in a change must make decisions such as:

1. who will participate in the project,
2. who will lead it,
3. how and when project details will be communicated to organization members,
4. how to justify or communicate the need for the reengineering effort,
5. determine the nature of milestones, and
6. identify needed changes in the current root structure of the organization.

38

Prescriptions for decisions in these areas vary, depending on whether one wants to foster incremental/evolutionary change or radical/revolutionary change.

Exhibits TN-1 and **TN-2** summarize the approach taken by DRG management for each change tactic and the risks of each change tactic in light of their goal to enable radical change. The framework provides the structure for discussing how the DRG reengineering initiatives were managed.

Employee involvement: DRG management used current employees - some of their best and brightest - to work on the new business model and to brainstorm how existing processes could be enhanced. Consultants and existing managers facilitated the process design meetings.

Leadership: A new senior management team initiated the reengineering efforts. Outside consultants worked with this team to develop a new strategy and helped them to get the reengineering projects started. Often reengineering consultants seek to lead and control efforts. DRG management wanted to become independent of their consultants, who were phased out after the redesign phase was completed.

Communication: DRG management sought to widely communicate what reengineering projects were underway and the expected impact of those projects. Phelps and Godwin met with employees at all levels to explain the new business model and how reengineering initiatives would affect employees. A videotape simulating new work processes was shown in small interactive round table discussions. The reengineering teams prepared numerous articles for the parent company's newspaper and for the organization's own newsletter, and set up an kiosk in a lobby to inform employees and customers of the reengineering initiative. A course that covered the basics of the new processes was added to the organization's training curriculum. Still, a middle manager involved in the reengineering initiative commented:

> *One can never communicate enough, particularly to the middle management level. There is no one right form or medium; all possible forms and media must be used. Still, communication to the rest of the organization is one of the toughest challenges of the change process.*

DRG management believed there had been an unanticipated benefit from broad communication of the new business process design. An officer of the company noted:

> *Communicating and engaging people in the blue print of the design seems to help even if the blueprint isn't exactly what you will implement. It seems to help people to start preparing themselves for change. You will also find that some of the design gets implemented without attempting to be implemented.*

A potential risk of wide communication during early stages of a reengineering initiative is that often management does not know what the outcome of the initiative will be. On the other hand, too little communication can make employees fear the worst and believe that management is trying to hide things from them.

Need for Reengineering: Management at DRG tried to communicate that reengineering was necessary because of a crisis. DRG employees were told that financial results were poor and that if the organization was to be successful in the long-run, things would have to change. DRG was in the midst of downsizing to cut costs when the reengineering program was announced.

Milestones: An overall time frame was developed for the company-wide reengineering initiative; yet during the early stages of an individual project, flexible milestones were set. Once an approach had been tested and results suggested a project would yield positive results, firm milestones were set. For those projects initiated to test "new" approaches, milestones were more flexible.

Firm milestones arguably keep a project team focused. Where milestones are set too early, however, experimentation may suffer as the group tries to complete an initiative within the defined time frame. On the other hand, without firm milestones, participants may not grasp the need to produce results and may get caught up in experimentation.

Changes to structure and culture: The first major step in DRG's reengineering initiative was a cultural audit. This audit allowed management to "take the temperature" of employees and to learn, from the employees' perspective, what norms of behavior existed and were rewarded.

The students should be challenged to discuss why a senior management team would undertake a cultural audit, what they would want to uncover in the process, and what actions they would take in light of the findings? In the case of DRG, management recognized that "hidden" aspects of the existing culture might hinder the organization from achieving its new goals. Revolutionary change theorists agree with their view; to achieve radical or revolutionary change, the culture of an organization must be changed. In order to change the culture, one must understand it. Frequently management's assessment of an organization's culture will be very different from employees' perceptions.

Several of the cultural audit findings were surprising to DRG senior management. For example, they were surprised and concerned that employees felt that the customer was incidental, especially since the customer was at the core of their new strategy.

The role of IT

IT was the "engine," but not the driver, for reengineering at DRG. The IT organization was working hard to develop Windows-based IT prototypes to support the work of the CMTs and other organizational prototypes that were underway.

In early 1992, the DRG data center was consolidated with the Capital Holding Agency Group's data center in Louisville, KY. DRG utilized IBM's DB2 relational database technology and had installed a Sybase 486-based server to enable data management in the LAN-based environment being installed to support the Window-based personal computing environment.

In many ways, IT was perceived as an inhibitor to reengineering because the new working environments, e.g. the CMT, could not be tested or scaled-up without significant IT development. Thus the IT organization faced a difficult challenge.

Future

Will they be able to institutionalize the lessons learned from and approaches taken to reengineering? What concerns do you have as they move forward? What can DRG management do to mitigate those concerns?

As of the time of the case, only one tenth of the employees in Godwin's area had been involved in the reengineering initiative. It will be a challenge to get others on board since the reengineering initiative represents a major change initiative for the organization.

Management should be concerned about scaling up - many IT systems were put together quickly to support the prototypes. One might question how much effort it will take to support a large number of people with information-based tools. From an HRM perspective, employees need training and support as DRG becomes more customer focused.

Comparison with Safeway case

If the Safeway case has also been taught, then **Exhibit TN-3** can be developed on the board, as students attempt to develop some robust reengineering principles.

Suggested 80-minute class plan

1. What is reengineering?
   How does reengineering differ from other organizational change programs? (10 minutes)

2. Let's understand the context for DRG's business. What business are they in?
   What do they need to do well to be successful?
   What prompted DRG to undertake "reengineering"?
   In light of our definition of reengineering, would you characterize what they are doing as BPR or is it something more or less? (20 minutes)

3. Evaluate the approach to reengineering taken by DRG management.
   How would you characterize the change tactics they have employed for reengineering?
   How appropriate are these change tactics in light of what they seek to accomplish?
   How would you compare DRG's approach to change management to that used by Safeway? (25 minutes)

4. What has been the role of information technology in DRG's reengineering initiative? (15 minutes)

5. Will they be able to institutionalize the lessons learned from and approaches taken to reengineering? What concerns do you have as they move forward?
   What can DRG management do to mitigate those concerns? (10 minutes)

Key Summary Lessons

1. Reengineering should support strategic initiatives defined by senior management. Significant gains may sometimes be achieved when reengineering is accompanied by changes to structures, systems, and human resources practices.

2. It is important to choose change management tactics in light of the scope of the change that is planned.

3. IT is a key enabler of reengineering.

Exhibit TN-1   Change Tactics

Change Tactics		
Management of the change process		
Employee involvement		
Communication		
Communicated need for BPR		
Milestones		
Changes to structure and culture		

Exhibit TN-2   Change Tactics Utilized at Capital Holding DRG

Change Tactics	Capital Holding DRG		
Management of the change process	* new senior management team * BPR emerges as way to implement new strategy * outside consultants used		
Employee involvement	* teams of employees design and prototype new work approaches		
Communication	* management widely communicate about reengineering projects within the organization		
Communicated need for BPR	* crisis: loss of market share, eroding margins		
Milestones	* flexible		
Changes to structure and culture	* cultural audit identifies need to change culture, organizational structure		

Exhibit TN-3   Change Tactics Utilized at Capital Holding DRG and Safeway Manufacturing Division

Change Tactics	Capital Holding DRG	Safeway Manufacturing Division
Management of the change process	* new senior management team * BPR emerges as way to implement new strategy * outside consultants used	* new manager brought in to manage BPR * outside consultants develop initial case for action * consultants also used for application development
Employee involvement	* teams of employees design and prototype new work approaches	* high performing plant supervisors and manager selected, relocated to headquarters to design new approach to work
Communication	* management widely communicate about reengineering projects within the organization	* reengineering team somewhat isolated during design phase * broadly communicate plans as design firms up
Communicated need for BPR	* crisis: loss of market share, eroding margins	* self-improvement
Milestones	* flexible	* firm initially; subsequently flexible
Changes to structure and culture	* cultural audit identifies need to change culture, organizational structure	* changes deemed necessary, but not explicitly addressed at start of project

Compaq Computer Corporation

Synopsis

The Compaq Computer Corporation case illustrates a company in a rapidly-moving industry using *continuous planning and budgeting*, in contrast to traditional approaches.

At the time of the case, Compaq is a very successful company which set many growth-rate records. Its success in the personal computer industry is especially striking in light of the many companies which tried and failed, and in light of the fact that it did not compete against IBM on price. Instead, Compaq offered IBM compatibility with superior functionality and premium prices.

Key to Compaq's success has been its ability to match technology to market needs. To be too soon is to be on the bleeding edge; to be too late is to miss a window of opportunity in which sales and market share are obtained. In the personal computer industry, product innovation and introduction is a timing problem. To be successful, the company must move quickly, yet avoid moving too quickly. In this situation, traditional long-range *strategic planning* is virtually useless. Instead, the focus must be on *product planning,* where timing decisions about matching technological and market capabilities are made. It is no surprise that CEO Rod Canion and his other senior managers spend a lot of time on this activity.

Achieving this timing requires the easy and rapid flow of information from and to the market, and within the company. Anything which inhibits or distorts the flow of information makes timing difficult. The company's culture and its approach to financial control and planning facilitate the flow of information and getting the right resources in the right place at the right time to take advantage of opportunities which can quickly appear and disappear.

Teaching Objectives

This case can be used for three main objectives:

1. to explore the relationship between company culture and its approach to financial control and planning.

2. to contrast Compaq's approach to financial control with that found in other companies.

3. to contrast Compaq's approach to financial planning with the typical budgeting process found in most companies.

Suggested Optional Reading:

Webber, Alan M. Consensus, continuity and common sense: an interview with Compaq's Rod Canion. *Harvard Business Review* 68(4): 114-123, July-August, 1990.

Suggested Study Questions:

1. Analyze Compaq's approach to financial planning and control.

2. Would you anticipate that Compaq will have to make any changes in its approach to financial planning and control as it grows and diversifies?

3. How applicable is Compaq's approach to financial planning and control for other companies? Under what circumstances?

Opportunities for Student Analysis

Culture   *"Bad news is good, as long as it is reported."*

The description of the company's culture in the case is fairly comprehensive and self-explanatory (and consistent with Rod Canion's description in the July-August 1990 HBR article). The rule of inclusion, teamwork, "working the issue," and consensus building all encourage the flow of undistorted information between people within and across functions. Norms about not shooting the messenger and actively exploring all sides of an issue reinforce this information flow. This culture is based on a model of human behavior and motivation that views people as basically honest, hard-working, competent and wanting to do the right thing.

Some students are skeptical of whether Compaq's culture is really as it is described in the case. I myself was initially skeptical. Geoff Love (the case writer) and I pushed hard on this by interviewing people with varying degrees of tenure, up and down the organization. It really seems to be a supportive culture. In executive programs I pointedly ask people if they believe a place can be so "nice." You can go with this discussion for a while and then ask, Is there anything wrong with this culture, whether or not it is real? After all, the elements of Compaq's culture are what most companies are trying to attain.

Although it is somewhat of a detour, you can discuss whether a culture like this has to be shaped in the beginning (this seems to have been the case at Compaq, with Texas Instruments being the model for many things to avoid). Or, can it be created from a different existing culture? Students can be asked to contrast the culture of the companies they have worked in with that of Compaq. Where they are different, what do students think would be involved in changing the culture?

Financial Control

In some ways, Compaq's approach to financial control looks fairly typical. If anything, there appears to be an awful lot of it. Much emphasis is placed on financial measures and analyses of many different cost centers. These measures and analyses are facilitated by information systems which give CFO Daryl White and others the ability to perform ad hoc analysis at a moment's notice. "What-if" analysis is important in a rapidly changing business in order to understand variations from expectations and the consequences of adjustments made in response to changes.

The controllers spread throughout the organization are a "grapevine" to White about what is going on in the company. Sophisticated financial systems were created at the beginning. In fact, a short article about this in *Newsweek* led me to approach Compaq. I saw this firm's approach as a contrast to Datapaq, where sophisticated financial controls early in the company's history were soon discarded because they were felt to be oppressive.

At Compaq, although there are lots of numbers and control systems, how they are perceived and used is different than at many organizations. The difference is based upon a model of human behavior that assumes that peopled are honest, competent, hard-working, and wanting to the right thing, rather than dishonest, stupid, lazy, and out to undermine the company's best interests. According to managers quoted in the case, information systems are used less to "control" managers (in the sense of keeping them in line) than in helping them achieve their objectives. Canion does not use financial measures as a club. It appears that he does not spend a lot of time delving into details. In White's view, managers have a sense of "ownership" of the numbers provided by finance. He adds, this is not the case in most companies. Students can be asked if White's assessment is valid.

Financial Planning

The most subtle aspect of the case is Compaq's approach to financial planning, which is described in detail. One could get all of the steps of what-happens-when on the board, but this is not the most interesting thing to discuss. It is worth noting how much effort is made to get input from relevant individuals, and how the company's culture facilitates this.

The central difference between a typical budgeting process and financial planning at Compaq lies in an assumption about how predictable the future is. Implicit in most budgeting processes is the belief that the future is predictable enough to use a budget as a baseline for resource allocation and performance measurement. The budget is a type of contract which commits resources under the expectation that if resource commitments are not changed, expected results should be achieved. For this reason, budgets are established and fixed for 12-month periods. Life is taken in annual bites, with monthly and quarterly checkpoints along the way for examining the variances of actual from budgeted numbers.

In the PC business, 12 months is long-term planning. Many events certainly cannot be predicted. The attitude at Compaq is: the further one projects into the future, the more likely one is to be wrong. For this reason, Compaq uses a rolling 12-month financial projection. Although the purpose is to make resource commitments, these are not considered permanent. As conditions change, the best return on resources will require reallocations across functions and projects. Thus, to produce positive variances - a laudable thing in most companies - is considered a disaster at Compaq. Money not spent in one function has a huge opportunity cost if it is not spent in another function (such as to increase manufacturing capacity, distribution capability, or marketing impact). If money isn't spent where it can get its biggest benefit, opportunities will be missed, perhaps forever.

This is not to say that financial performance isn't taken seriously. As a public company, Compaq must be concerned about reported earnings and stock price. Compaq has developed a financial model that depicts what the business should look like in terms of P&L and balance sheet ratios and their implications for stock price. Projections which vary from the model are closely examined, as are actuals, and decisions are made whether or not to achieve forecasted targets. Management is sensitive to inherent short- versus long-term trade-offs. However, the company's culture encourages people to "do what makes sense," rather than slavishly adhering to financial projections and results. I also encourages people to take actions which are in the best interests of the company as a whole.

In contrast to many other companies (and, in my opinion, the dominant current practice) managers at Compaq place financial measures in a broader strategic perspective. They recognize measures' inherent uncertainty and the timing trade-offs which have to be made. This observation illustrates that it is inappropriate to view "tight" control as necessarily "good," or "loose" financial control as necessarily "bad." Rather, one can compare companies where managers let numbers run the company versus companies where numbers are used to let the managers run the company by interjecting a substantial amount of their own judgment and encouraging flexibility.

People crunch lots of numbers at Compaq, all the time; perhaps even more often than in most companies, since their "budget" is redone every month. The difference is how these numbers are used. They are not the basis of binding commitments which are inviolate. Rather, they measure what is happening, assess what resources commitments should be made in light of events, and project what results can be expected.

Exhibit TN-1 summarizes Compaq's approach to planning versus traditional approaches.

Motivation and Compensation

At many companies, managers debate how aggressive their budget targets need to be in order to motivate people without discouraging them. At Compaq, this is a moot issue. Financial results, other measures, and subjective judgments determine Compaq managers' compensation. However, there is no formula that ties bonuses to actual results compared to budget. Instead of focusing on financial results, performance evaluation focuses on managers' contribution to the team and the integrity of the process. Both assessments of past performance and expectations about future potential go into determining a person's compensation (I know of only one other place that factors the future into current bonuses: Salomon Brothers). Compaq again has a different perspective than that found in most companies. Instead of focusing on results and letting managers use whatever process they want to produce them, Compaq focuses on the process, believing that if it is adhered to, then results will follow. Compaq is reluctant to manage to objectives, under the belief that this can limit expectations.

Money is not considered the primary motivator, at least past a certain point. Nonetheless, Compaq compensates its people well in terms of salary, bonus, and stock options. The company's success has made a number of people wealthy. It is always easier to say that money isn't everything when you already have a lot of it.

What Lies Ahead?

Even if you are willing to believe my interpretation of the case, the question remains, How long can it last? The end of the case points to some indicators that current management practices may have to change. The following changes would all put strains on the company's culture:

Larger size

Slower or even negative growth (especially accompanied by layoffs),

Product diversification (which strains the functional structure; recall that the brief experiment with a multidivisional structure failed);

New distribution channels (Compaq had always used dealers, but can they sell the more sophisticated, higher-priced client-server machine?)

Greater overseas manufacturing and sales activities (the company is already very international)

If Compaq's culture changes, would its approach to financial control and planning have to change as well? If the culture does not change, will larger size and product and geographical diversification result in a heavier emphasis on managing by the numbers?

The general issue is: how fragile or robust is the overall management approach being used at Compaq? How tightly or loosely are its elements coupled to each other? One view is that the company is young and has yet to undergo a major crisis, particularly one based on failure. In this view, Compaq will lose its youthful optimism and glow, and start to look more like other companies. Another view is that the company is well-positioned to deal with change and adversity. Going through it will only reinforce its character and make it stronger. Only time will tell.

Postscript

Following the case, Compaq suffered a loss of market share as aggressive new PC clone-makers undercut Compaq prices. In second quarter 1991, Compaq reported a short drop in sales and profits, and on September 30, 1991 they reported their first ever loss of $70 million. This resulted in a 12% staff reduction, the firing of Rod Canion, and the hiring of Eckhard Pfeiffer. The company was restructured for separate focus and distribution mechanisms for low-end, business, and systems products. By second quarter 1992, following drastic price cuts, Compaq recorded a 43% increase in net income. 1993 and 1994 results were excellent as a new line of desktop and notebook computers were introduced, including the pen-based 486 Concerto notebook.

Exhibit TN-2 consists of sample article abstracts from an ABI-Inform search on Compaq in early 1994.

Suggested 80-Minute Class Plan

1.   How would you describe Compaq's culture? (10 minutes)

2.   Evaluate Compaq's financial controls. What do they look like?
      What do they feel like to Compaq managers? (15 minutes)

3.   How do Compaq managers do planning?
      What are the assumptions underlying the company's approach to financial planning?
      (20 minutes).

4.   What challenges do you see ahead for Compaq? (10-15 minutes)

5.   Wrap-up
      Hand out article abstracts describing recent Compaq goings-on (**Exhibit TN-2**).
      Contrast Compaq's approach to strategic planning versus traditional approaches.

Key Summary Lessons

1. In high-velocity industries, traditional approaches to strategic planning
   are completely inadequate.

2. In such industries, continuous planning and budgeting are necessary.

3. Rapid, timely, accurate information flows, from both external and
   internal sources, are essential to support continuous planning and
   budgeting; hence, close attention to the firm's IT architecture is a
   prerequisite capability.

Traditional Planning	Compaq Planning
The future is predictable	The future is uncertain
A budget is a commitment	A budget is a starting point
A positive variance is good; results were better than expected	A positive variance is bad; resources were not available elsewhere
The budget is the target basis for bonuses	Bonuses are based on following "process"

Stalking the best PCs   Wood, Lamont Electronic Business Buyer Nov 1993 v19n11 page(s) 115-120
The state of the personal computer market makes purchasing decisions difficult. . . . Business Buyer
magazine concluded that leading companies like IBM, Tandy, Digital Equipment, Compaq, and Texas
Instruments are providing the best new products for the money. With sales of notebook computers expected
to rise by 20% in 1993 and reach 3.1 million units by 1996, that product category heads the list in a buyers
guide that also covers subnotebooks, low-end PCs, and high-end PCs.

Compaq boxes focus on ease of use   Klett, Stephen P Jr Computerworld 27(44): 15, Nov 1, 1993
In an attempt to cover every segment of the market from major corporations to small business users to first-
time home buyers, Compaq Computer Corp. will introduce 46 desktop machines emphasizing ease-of-use
features from the graphical user interface to the packaging.

Compaq announces healthy third quarter   Polilli, Steve InfoWorld Oct 25, 1993 v15n43 page(s) 30
Compaq Computer Corp. has virtually eliminated its product backlogs, an act that helped the company post
exceptionally strong 3rd-quarter results in 1993. Compaq reported sales of $1.75 billion, up 64% over
the same quarter in 1992. Profits more than doubled to $107 million.

Compaq wants pen mightier than mouse   Melanson, Daniel Info Canada 18(10): 8,10, Oct 1993
With the introduction of Concerto, a full-featured, 486-based notebook using a pen as its pointing device,
Compaq may establish a new pinnacle for notebook computers...

**As top PC makers regain edge, cloners lose, price war...   Fitzgerald, Michael Computerworld Oct
25, 1993 v27n43 page(s) 1,16**
Analysts project that the top 10 PC makers will boost their share by 7% to 11% in 1993 at the expense of
smaller vendors. The resulting consolidation could mean a return to orderly price decreases based on
component pricing, rather than the price wars that have characterized much of the 1990s.

**EDI expands its role into management   Carbone, James Electronic Business Buyer 19(9): 89-92, Sep
1993**
Initially developed and applied to speed the ordering of goods by transmitting orders electronically, electronic
data interchange (EDI) is being adapted by companies to transmit build schedules, designs, forecasts, and
payments. Using EDI, Compaq Computer transmits forecasts to suppliers for the next 9 months and then
updates those forecasts weekly.

Heavy hitters: Barbara Krumland   Smith, Dawn Marketing Computers 13(10): 34, Oct 1993
Compaq Computer Corp. is cautiously reveling after a successful turnaround that included a dramatic
overhaul of its product lines, pricing, and distribution methods. In March 1993, Barbara Krumland, vice
president, rolled out Compaq DirectPlus, the company's first direct sales division. The division is expected
to account for 5% of its business in the fourth quarter of 1993. Careful pricing and customer targeting have
eased tensions between the dealer channel and DirectPlus.

**The expert's opinion Palvia, Shailendra Journal of Global Information Systems 1(2):43-44, Spring
1993**
Harold Chong, chief information officer and director of information management at the Asia Pacific division
of Compaq Computers, discussed the importance of IT, the lifeline of the company. Compaq manufactures
and markets IT products, and, therefore, IT systems and hardware are very important. Compaq's facility in
Singapore far outshines both the US and European facilities in terms of productivity and cost. Compaq looks
for worldwide systems solutions. From the international standpoint, Compaq has a wide IT communication
network linking all of its offices worldwide. Electronic data interchange (EDI) has been the driving force
that has facilitated the company's international expansion.

Compaq results counter PC trend   Fitzgerald, Michael Computerworld 27(30): 105, Jul 26, 1993
During the first half of 1993, Compaq Computer Corp.'s sales doubled from the year-earlier period, while net profit almost tripled. Compaq officials attribute those results to the company's continued focus on cost-cutting and aggressive product introductions.

Master of the universe   Craggs, Keith International Management Jul/Aug 1993 v48n6 page(s) 25-26
Eckhard Pfeiffer is the German CEO of Houston-based Compaq Computer. Turnover in 1992, Pfeiffer's first full year at the helm, leaped ahead 25.3% to $4.1 billion, yielding net profits 62.9% up a $213.2 million. Recruited in 1983 as Compaq's first European employee, he built up its European operations from an office in Munich into a network of 13 wholly owned subsidiaries that account for 46% of group turnover. In 1991, Pfeiffer was named president and chief executive. Pfeiffer moved quickly, repositioning Compaq with a raft of new products launched in June 1992 that reignited its performance.

Compaq flexes its pecs   Burrows, Peter Business Week Aug 2, 1993 n3330(Indu page(s) 24-25
In the personal computer market, Compaq Computer Corp. is the only standout performer. On July 21, 1993, Compaq reported that its sales increased 97%, versus 1992's 2nd quarter, to $1.63 billion, while earnings more than tripled to $102 million. Compaq has managed to lower prices while raising margins by squeezing excess from its once-bloated infrastructure. It doubled production over 1992 and now is running its 3 plants around the world 7 days a week, 24 hours a day. Given its higher purchasing volume, Compaq also expects to save more than $400 million in materials costs in 1993, on top of $200 million in 1992. Chief Executive Eckhard Pfeiffer's main goal now is to boost market share from the current 6.5%, displacing market leader IBM by the first quarter 1996. Pfeiffer plans to continue the company's push into direct mail and mass-market retailers, bolster research and development, and introduce new products.

A Tale of Two Lost Heads . . .   Heller, Robert Management Today Sep 1992   page(s) 35-38
The ultimate cause of the oustings of Robert Horton of British Petroleum and Rod Canion of Compaq lay in loss of confidence in the corporate government by the governed. Both chief executive officers had golden track records and implemented swinging reforms in their respective companies but were tried and found wanting by their peers. ...In management, ancient or modern, actions speak louder than words. ...

Ex-Compaq Chief Rod Canion Starts Over   Brown, Priscilla C. Business Marketing Sep 1992 v77n9 page(s) 101
In October 1991, Joseph R. Canion was ousted as president and chief executive officer of Compaq Computer Corp., the IBM-compatible PC maker he co-founded in 1982. That move by Compaq's board took place one day after the company announced its first-ever quarterly losses and layoffs. Canion is now chairman of a new company, Insource Management Group (Houston, Texas), which plans to distinguish itself by offering a service called "business integration." Canion says that the first step in providing that service to clients is to assess where they are and how they operate their business on a day-to-day basis. On the basis of that assessment, Insource will help clients apply technology that is cost-effective, productive, and in the safe mainstream areas of technology. The company will also help clients manage their technological resources efficiently and learn how to observe new technologies evolve.

DEC Loses, Compaq Comes Back   Eastwood, Alison Computing Canada Aug 17, 1992 v18n17: 1,10
Compaq Computer Corp., which in October 1991 sustained a first-time quarterly loss of $70 million, followed by the firing of its chief executive officer Rod Canion, recently reported a 43% increase in net income for the 2nd quarter of fiscal 1992. Meanwhile, Digital Equipment Corp. (DEC), which will gain a new chief executive officer, Robert Palmer, on October 1, 1992, revealed a $2.8-billion net loss for fiscal 1992. Of that total, $1.5 billion went toward restructuring charges for employee separations. DEC also blamed the economy and competitive pricing for its losses. Drastic reduction of its prices appears to have benefited Compaq, which claims that it will continue to reduce costs in order to maintain price competitiveness. DEC has reduced its employee count by 23,000 since the end of fiscal 1989; this includes 3,700 people in the US who left via an early retirement program. The company is relying on its 64-bit RISC chip, Alpha, to see it through to the next century.

Compaq Set to Announce Low-Price Product Strategy   Anonymous Info Canada Jun 1992 17(6): 1,4
After the board-of-directors-led ouster of Compaq Computer Corp. founder Rod Canion in the fall of 1991, industry observers agreed that the company probably would shift direction under newly installed CEO Eckhard Pfeiffer. Pfeiffer, who had built the company's European Division into the continent's 2nd-largest personal computer (PC) manufacturer - representing about $2 billion per year in sales and accounting for 54% of the company's overall revenue - was widely seen as a no-nonsense manager who would refocus the foundering computer maker in a profitable direction. Compaq, in a sweeping change of direction, is expected to unveil its own line of clone-killer machines, as well as a renewed effort focused on improved channel distribution and enhanced support, including 2nd-day on-site service. Compaq is also expected to expand its distribution channels in order to get the competitive new products to the customers it hopes to reach.

Regrouping of Compaq   Barker, Paul   Computing Canada Jun 22, 1992 v18n13 page(s) 1,4
After the sudden firing of Compaq Computer Corp. co-founder and chief executive Rod Canion, Eckhard Pfeiffer was named as his replacement. Pfeiffer immediately began redefining and restructuring the company. The process began with an advertising campaign proclaiming a new Compaq. Unlike the old Compaq of high price structures and high revenues, a low-cost strategy has been implemented with the release of the Compaq ProLinea desktop line which is designed to compete against such companies as AST Corp., Dell Computer Corp., and Advanced Logic Research Corp. Other developments include the release of the Contura 3/20 and 3/25 low-priced notebooks, the Compaq LTE Lite/25C color notebook, the Deskpro/i line of desktops, and Insight server management hardware and software tools. Compaq is also upgrading its service and support programs. The projected target from all of these efforts is a revenue increase of 8% to 10% by the end of 1992.

Compaq Net Income Takes 71 Per Cent Fall Eastwood, Alison Computing Canada Feb 17, 1992 18(4): 1,4
Compaq Computer Corp. ended fiscal 1991 with a 71% drop in net income. Eckhard Pfeiffer, president and chief executive officer, blames the results on intense price competition.   In September, Compaq introduced and cut prices on a line of modular personal computers. The company also sustained a loss of $70 million for the quarter ended September 30. A 12% staff reduction in November was followed by the replacement of Rod Canion, co-founder and president of Compaq, by Pfeiffer, whose strategy for reversing the downturn in profits included cutting prices and expaning distribution channels. Compaq Canada Inc. president Don Woodley hopes that Compaq's lower-priced products will help the company enter new market segments such as individual users and employee purchase programs.

Compaq - "It Simply Better Work"   Coursey, David   InfoWorld Dec 9, 1991 v13n49 page(s) 45-50
Where other vendors have adapted to a changing industry, Compaq Computer Corp. has - until the last 2 months - stuck with its business plan of producing high-end machines at a premium price. With the departure of president Rod Canion, Compaq acknowledged that its plan was designed for a different industry than the one that exists today. Industry analysts who attended a recent Compaq briefing say that they saw a new, humbler company emerging from the restructuring being implemented by new president Eckhard Pfeiffer. With the division of Compaq into separate business units for personal computers (PC) and systems will come significant changes in product focus, support, and marketing. Compaq will have 3 product lines - low-end, business, and systems - each sold and supported through their own, sometimes overlapping, channels.

Compaq's New Boss Doesn't Even Have Time to Wince   Ivey, Mark Business Week Nov 11, 1991 n3239(Indu page(s) 41
Compaq Computer's board of directors has appointed a new chief executive officer, Eckhard Pfeiffer, who built the company's fledgling European unit into a $1.8 billion operation. Pfeiffer replaces company founder Rod Canion, whose departure came after weeks of high-level wrangling aimed at pulling the company out of a 6-month decline in revenues, profits, and market share. After Canion had failed to provide a sharp enough recovery strategy, board chairman Benjamin M. Rosen and Pfeiffer devised a plan to reorganize the company into 2 units: plain-vanilla personal computers and more sophisticated computer systems. Perhaps the most important change Pfeiffer must make is to accelerate the pace of new-product introductions.

Connor Formed Metal Products, Inc.

Synopsis

This case describes a custom metal spring and stamping manufacturer. President Bob Sloss (a member of the family which controlled the company since 1947) attempts to re-position Connor by changing the company's structure, human resources practices, control systems and information technology applications. The changes, taking place from 1984 to 1990, are driven both by his recognition that this once slow-paced, steady business is facing significant new competition from offshore manufacturers with lower costs and better quality, and from a personal desire for a more democratic corporate culture and an empowered workforce.

After reviewing an apparently successful IT-driven change in the LA division, Sloss considers how to promote a PC-based order tracking system in the other three divisions, which vary in size, production processes, customers, IT literacy, and other dimensions.

Teaching Objectives

The Connor case is an excellent vehicle for illustrating the dynamic interplay of strategy, controls, structure, people, and technology. Early in Bob Sloss' tenure, changes in the company's structure and human resources practices - including an employee stock ownership plan (ESOP), although well received, were apparently insufficient for restoring profitability and growth in an industry undergoing significant change. Sloss considers a personal computer-based system for order tracking and inter-plant communication. Although the system is simple and inexpensive, using "plain vanilla" hardware and off-the-shelf, partially customized software, its powerful design supports improved operational controls and cross-functional communication. The case can be used to discuss several Chapter 6 concepts:

> *IT Eras:* progression through the DP, micro and network eras.

> *Automate/Informate:* what are the implications for system design and use?

> What role does IT play in supporting *empowered workers*?

The case can also be introduce concepts of IT-enabled organizational transformation. Positioned in Chapter 6 *(IT in Organizations)* following several examples of companies coping with significant change (Cypress Semiconductor, Allen-Bradley, Phillips 66), the Connor case can highlight issues of timing. Sloss first changed structure and human resources practices, then considered strategic changes and new investments in information technology. Was this an optimal sequence of changes, or should strategic changes and an examination of the IT architecture have preceded structural and human resources changes? When this topic is to be emphasized, the case can be taught either in the sequence provided in the book, or along with the Chapter 8 materials *(IT and Business Transformation)*.

Suggested Study Questions

1. Evaluate the actions taken by Bob Sloss since he assumed control of Connor Formed Metal Products.

2. What role did IT play in the changes Sloss made?

3. The technology developed at the LA division will be transferred to the San Jose, Portland and Dallas divisions. What advice would you give Sloss on the implementation?

4. What advice would you give Sloss on future directions for the use of IT at Connor?

Opportunities for Student Analysis and Discussion

Evaluation of Bob Sloss' Presidency

The discussion can begin by asking a student to evaluate the steps Sloss has taken since he assumed the presidency of Connor in 1984. One or two students or teams could be asked in advance to prepare a summary and assessment to present to the class. These students can be asked to consider two time periods in Connor's recent history:

before 1984   (George Halkides)
1984 - 1990   (Bob Sloss hired spring 1984)

Each is summarized below in terms of the People, Information and Technology framework. It may be useful to give students a handout for subsequent reference during the wrap-up **(Exhibit TN-1)**.

Connor Formed Metal Products, Before 1984:

Strategy and Performance: George Halkides ran the company with a traditional command-and-control approach. One student commented that Connor then was "a low-tech, labor-intensive supplier to local customers with low expectations." Throughout the industry, which was comprised of hundreds of small (20-30 employee) job shops, poor quality and service were the norm. Founded in 1947, Connor grew at a slow, sometimes stagnant, marginally profitable (3% to 5%) rate through the seventies and early eighties (see case Exhibit 2).

People: The case does not provide information about skill levels and backgrounds of employees, but does state that the company did not have engineers during this era.

Information Technology: Computers first used to automate back-office transaction-intensive processes such as payroll, accounts receivable and accounts payable. Goal: efficiency. IBM System 34 minicomputers, accounting software.

Culture:
Incentives and Rewards: Employees were paid "standard wages."

Values: culture of "working in small groups."

Organization:
Informal Networks: not described for this era.

Formal Reporting Relationships: traditional centralized hierarchy:

San Francisco headquarters
Los Angeles   San Jose
Phoenix   Portland

Business Processes: job shop; each new order required a new estimate, new setup, etc. Time-consuming manual processes included cost estimates, shop orders ("10 carbons deep"), labor-time, sales reports (handwritten trip reports; customer letters filed in loose-leaf binders).

Decision Rights: managers and supervisors decide; workers do.

Control:
Data: poor data management; little access to information needed to make informed decisions.

Planning: the case does not describe the planning process.

Performance Measurement and Evaluation: broad, rough, bottom-line financial measures

Connor Formed Metal Products, 1984-1990

Strategy and Performance: Sloss, president in spring 1984, changes the company name, retains its regional strategy, adds more complex products, and re-positions: differentiate through '100% reliable" quality and service. Products: 20% coiled springs (commodity); 80% more complex wire forms, assemblies, metal stampings. Participates in the Baldrige Award process, and invest in manufacturing technologies and quality techniques. Despite a sales increase, the company suffers a loss in 1989 (case Exhibit 2). Offshore competition is becoming a significant factor, and the company may be at risk of a takeover.

People: Begin to hire top-notch engineers. Shop floor employees, expected to monitor and take responsibility for the quality of their own work, are trained in quality techniques.

Information Technology: IT is mostly used to automate back-office accounting. $300,000 to upgrade to IBM System 36, with mixed success. No dedicated MIS function. Interest in personal computers grows in the late eighties. Michael Quarrey is hired in August 1989 to develop an order tracking system for LA. He chooses a relational DBMS, Clipper.

Culture:
Incentives and Rewards: Competitive wages. discretionary and regular bonuses. Employee Stock Option Plan (ESOP) established in 1986. Quarrey's goal: "empower employees with information... information and ESOP's should be married together."

Values: retain culture of "working in small groups;" add cross-functional teams. "Employees should act like owners." "The more employees know, the better the company will be." Value embedded in the software: "the purpose is not to manage people, but the other way around." No individual employee productivity reports.

Organization:
Informal Networks: management-by-walking-around; team building; Sloss encourages all kinds of cross-functional meetings and task forces, as well as rotating leadership responsibilities, which helps convey that every person's opinion counts.

Formal Reporting Relationships : Decentralizes: all four divisions report directly to San Francisco; each has "autonomous" P&L accountability.

Business Processes: job-shop; manual processes included cost estimates, shop orders ("10 carbons deep"), sales reports (handwritten trip reports; customer letters filed in loose-leaf binders). Processes defined by the forms employees fill out.

Decision Rights: (case Exhibit 3) LA workers expected to do "shop holds" whenever they believe circumstances warrant. Employees monitor their own product quality, using SPC.

Control:

Data: Expectation that information should be shared widely; but data management is weak. Cannot answer questions like which products/customers are profitable, etc.

Planning: case does not describe the planning process.

Performance Measurement and Evaluation: emphasizes team effort. Metrics are improving; include quality, sales-in, backlog, payroll, credits issued to customers, customer satisfaction, etc. Not clear whether they have identified 2 or 3 key metrics as yet.

Issues

Assessment of the actions taken by Sloss through the People, Information and Technology framework reveals issues for each dimension, as summarized below. It is useful to reserve a large blackboard for recording students' comments in the categories below.

Strategy: Students may criticize Connor's strategy as "fuzzy," in that it seems that Sloss has not decided if his firm should be in the commodity spring business or the value-added, complex metal products business. Others might question Sloss' belief in a regional organizational structure. Sloss believes that manufacturing needs to be located geographically close to customers in order to best serve their needs. This may be true for engineering-intensive products (at least until full multimedia networking capabilities are ubiquitous) . However, it is difficult to understand why that would be a necessary constraint for producing commodity-like products at high volumes, where price is likely to be the key differentiating feature. Similarly, why would plant location necessarily be a critical constraint in dealing with large OEM's, many of whom are themselves dispersed among multiple locations? This discussion is worth pursuing for a few minutes, because the instructor can use this as an opportunity to discuss the value of questioning assumptions and engaging in what Argyris calls "double-loop learning." One student characterized Connor's strategy as "do what we have always done, but better" - another way of saying they do fine single-loop learning, not enough double-loop learning. This theme can be revisited at multiple points in the case discussion, which will be noted below.

People: One of Sloss' priorities has been to upgrade the work force. He personally recruits engineers from the best schools, for example. But it is not clear from the case whether Sloss accurately perceives the full range of changes that should be made in order to make best use of an empowered work force. One student commented: "adding engineers to the company, like salt to food, will not turn Connor into an engineering-oriented company." This perceptive comment might be generalized to the following: "Adding or altering any single element will not transform Connor into a strong competitor."

Mention is made of team-building and quality training, but the case does not provide sufficient detail for the reader to determine whether Connor is making an adequate commitment to upgrading employees' skills so they can effectively use the information and systems that are to be made available to them. It is most definitely not enough to merely tell employees that they are "empowered;" employees at all levels need to shed old roles and take on new roles in order to realize that goal. Nor is it enough to provide employees with financial incentives such as the ESOP and bonus schemes. It is not clear whether Connor shop-floor workers have been equipped as yet with sufficient skills and knowledge to work effectively within the new structure. For example, how does the production employee know whether or not it is appropriate to issue a shop hold? Have they received training that will adequately guide their judgments in that regard, and will they receive on-the-job feedback to verify that a particular hold was appropriate or not? Nor is any mention made of the role of the shop-floor supervisor, which should change dramatically in an empowered organization (from line-of-sight control to a coaching and gate-keeping role). Here there is yet another opportunity to use the concept of double-loop learning. When structures, systems, and basic tools are being called into question, shouldn't peoples' roles also be re-examined?

Information Technology: The discussion of changes in the use of IT at Connor raises several concerns. The first is regarding the IBM System 34/36/38 minicomputers. The case states that these machines and the software running on them were "too generic," "unwieldy," "counter-intuitive," "unacceptably complex," and "a dog." Given the many successful System 36/38 installations in use in businesses worldwide, these comments may not convey the full dimensions of the situation. Neither the San Francisco headquarters nor any of the four divisions had an MIS professional on staff, a decision which is understandable given the size of the company, but which also explains much of the users' reactions. Yet the option of hiring an MIS specialist - perhaps someone who would rotate among the divisions or train master users in each location - does not seem to have been considered. Indeed, when Michael Quarrey was hired Sloss stated, "The idea of a little company like ours hiring a computer programmer was mind boggling."

A second IT-related issue concerns Quarrey. He seems to be a talented programmer with a knack for system design, and an ESOP specialist. The issue with Quarrey, and indeed the issue with many talented personal computer users who have not had formal systems training is: does he know what he doesn't know? Data management at Connor is potentially an area where Quarrey is unaware of an entire set of methodologies for verifying data accuracy and ensuring its integrity and security. There may be similar issues regarding networking or IT architecture issues. One solution would be to bring in an information systems consultant to audit the current IT architecture, identify weak points, and suggest options for strengthening the foundation before further development work or networking are done.

A third IT-related issue concerns Sloss' hands-off approach to IT. He is not networked to LA, and he has a propensity to delegate details. One student remarked that Sloss was too much of a "spectator" in a game where he needs to be an active "player." If he wants to achieve IT-enabled organizational transformation, he himself needs hands-on experience with the systems Quarrey is building, so he can be a strong and informed champion to convince the 20-year veterans who cut their managerial teeth in the old DP era, when most managers kept their hands off computer keyboards.

A fourth, and crucial IT issue concerns design of the new order-tracking system, which appears to be an example of "automating history." See *Business Processes*, below.

Finally, there is the issue of implementation timing and site selection. Students may criticize the choice of Los Angeles as the first site for the new order-tracking system. LA has the worst performance in the company, and Spanos, its manager, is a 20-year veteran who has shown little enthusiasm for re-thinking "how we do things around here." The case indicates that the choice of LA worked out (although perceptive students may question how much of the dramatic performance improvements can be attributed to the software, which had been in place only a few months), but it is still reasonable to question whether, in general one would want to choose a site with poor computer literacy and poor management commitment for an IT project as important as this.

Culture: Quite a lot of attention has gone into modifying <u>incentives and rewards</u> at Connor. However, the apparently weak performance metrics (see performance measurement and evaluation, below) would suggest that there may be considerable room for improvement, in terms of matching strategically useful measurements with rewards.

As for <u>values,</u> there are some discrepancies between the "walk" and the "talk" at Connor. Sloss says he wants to empower employees; however, this value is not always consistently carried out. Connor does not yet have the flat structure of an empowered organization, there is little indication that supervisors and managers are changing their roles, and employees may not yet have the skills and knowledge to really be empowered.

<u>Informal Networks:</u> Networked information technologies could provide for new means of informal information exchange, but this capability does not seem to be exploited yet at Connor. Sloss encourages many useful mechanisms for information exchange, in the form of a variety of meetings and meeting reports, "management by walking around," "lunch with the boss," and the company newsletter. However, the potential for widespread IT-facilitated organizational learning is not yet being exploited. The order tracking system automates structured information exchange, but electronic mail and bulletin boards could facilitate informal networks, especially across sites.

Organization: As for <u>formal reporting relationships,</u> Sloss believes the company has undergone a major re-structuring. However, within each division, a traditional hierarchy is retained; each division has its own administration, quality control, engineering, sales, manufacturing functions. Some students will observe that the fundamental structure, complete with functional "stovepipes" and a hierarchical chain of command within each division, has not changed significantly in the decentralized organization. The primary role changes have occurred at the level of plant management; these individuals may have more authority and autonomy than previously, but other decision rights and reporting relationships have remained pretty much intact, as case Exhibit 3 indicates.

A second important structural issue is that of timing. Networked information technologies, combined with sound data management practices, can enable a company to be organized in a dramatically flatter form, without loss of control and operational efficiency, and possibly with an increase in organizational responsiveness and creativity. Connor's structure was changed *before* the IT architecture was in place, and this structural change apparently had little initial effect on Connor's mediocre performance. Some students will also argue that the structure was altered before management had a clear understanding of where to position the company strategically. Just as an architect normally expects to elicit the client's functional requirements before designing a building, the organizational architect normally expects to gain a basic understanding of profit drivers and organizational competencies before re-designing its structure. Students can be encouraged to debate where management can and should start in organizational change efforts. The "trite but true" answer: do everything at once. The feasible answer: do what you can, when you can.

Most <u>business processes</u> have been automated, rather than redesigned - what Michael Hammer would call "paving over the cow paths." The order tracking software seems to have been designed around existing paper-based forms and manual processes. This has the advantage of a resulting system which feels familiar to users; it has the obvious disadvantage of failing to take the opportunity to design an entirely new, potentially far more efficient or effective process design. In many respects, Connor has gotten merely incremental improvements from automation, and this may be because they automated existing practices before really understanding either the processes or the profit drivers. For example, above we questioned the assumptions about a regional focus. Networked IT can give customers a perceived local presence even while manufacturing and order fulfillment take place elsewhere. This is another example of an apparent need for double-loop learning (challenging and questioning assumptions) at Connor.

In terms of <u>decision rights</u>, shop-floor employees have a new area of decision-making responsibility: shop holds. But it is unclear whether they clearly understand when a shop hold is appropriate, and the implications (for throughput performance, particularly) of each hold.

Control: Michael Quarrey wants to "empower employees with information," a laudable goal which pre-supposes that management has made available to employees accurate, timely <u>data</u>. Again, a timing issue is involved: how can Quarrey empower employees with information if his boss has not yet identified the relevant information, and the ends toward which information-based controls will be directed? One student put it this way: "Why would you concentrate on brining more and better information to the shop floor when you don't yet know what type of business you should be chasing?" There is also little indication in the case as to whether Quarrey is schooled in data base management principles, or aware of the need to make someone responsible for ensuring data integrity, access, security, common definitions across functions and divisions, etc. Just because he is building the order tracking system using user-friendly data base management system software in no way guarantees that data management issues have been adequately addressed. Students may need to be reminded of the discussion of data management issues in Chapter 4 (which they probably read a few weeks' earlier in the term). For the instructor's convenience, I have reproduced that discussion as **Exhibit TN-2.**

There is little information in the case about planning; perhaps because Sloss is not doing enough of it.

Bob Sloss doesn't seem too concerned about performance measurement and evaluation; he prefers to delegate "details," even though he complains that he doesn't know why the firm lost money in 1989. His routine indicators - sales-in and payroll - are not going to help him monitor the extent to which the firm is moving in the right direction. Ongoing participation in the Baldrige Award process could lead to improved metrics - if Sloss reinforces the concept of measuring and rewarding behaviors that support strategic objectives. Michael Quarrey has built a reasonable IT foundation for gathering data for good metrics, once it is clear what metrics would be most useful.

Roll-Out

It is not necessary to raise every issue presented above before asking students whether Quarrey's information system should be rolled out to Dallas, Portland and San Jose. This discussion should reveal additional concerns. Two broad themes should also emerge from the discussion of roll-out choices:

* the benefit of common systems versus the benefit of division autonomy;

* the benefit of immediate roll-out versus the benefit of deferring roll-out in favor of comprehensive organizational redesign.

These are discussed next.

Common systems versus site autonomy: The instructor can ask students if the system that Michael Quarrey has implemented in LA should be rolled out to Dallas, San Jose and Portland. Students may approach this question by offering comments on the apparent turnaround in LA as a result of the system. It can be useful to let this discussion go on for several minutes - long enough for at least one student to question how much of the turnaround can be attributed to the system. A healthy skepticism is in order here, since a system implemented in May of 1990 could hardly be the sole determinant of improvements measured at the end of the same year. Still, there are indications that the system is having a positive effect, and the instructor can direct students' attention to case Exhibit 10 in order to emphasize the changes in the order entry and tracking processes.

What about the roll-out? Students will probably point out that each division is different in size, customers, leadership, and IT literacy. These differences are summarized in **Exhibit**

TN-3. It is not difficult to get students to note these differences, but the instructor may have to push students to see the potential benefits of common systems and data definitions (such as ease of user support, possible purchasing/site licensing savings, comparable data and performance metrics) across the four sites.

Immediate roll-out versus comprehensive organizational redesign: Some students may suggest that roll-out to other sites is a premature step at this time. They may note that Sloss needs a more clear understanding of the strategic, structural, and operational choices available to him. The introduction of a new system can be an opportunity to redesign inefficient processes and structures, in light of new strategic initiatives. This is an ideal point at which to drive the double-loop learning lesson home. The instructor might ask students, "Now that Sloss has some indication of what can be accomplished with new systems and a new organizational structure, is it time to roll the system out, or is it time to re-evaluate his earlier choices about strategy, structure, and employee involvement? Has Sloss gone far enough?" This can generate a vigorous discussion. Some students will express an aversion to the idea of "further study," while others will express frustration at the idea of "automating history."

These comments lead directly into the last discussion question, "what advice would you give Sloss and Quarrey on the continued evolution of Connor's organizational structure, control systems, people and technologies?" The key theme to drive home here is that Sloss will need to *simultaneously* consider all of these items, each of which is a key piece of the puzzle, whose solution is organizational effectiveness.

Wrap-Up

The instructor can conclude the session by reporting that Sloss and Quarrey next chose to roll out the system to the Dallas office, but in a manner that gave Dallas managers considerable latitude to customize to their needs. People from Dallas visited LA to learn about the system in use there, and people from LA visited Dallas. Dallas made some changes in the software to suit their needs, and subsequently LA adopted some of these changes - a nice example of organizational learning.

The instructor can then summarize with the key points offered next.

Key Summary Lessons

A coherent information technology architecture and sound data management are a required foundation for a flatter, empowered organization.

Providing "empowered" employees access to relevant data is a necessary, but not sufficient condition for success. New skills must be developed, in order for employees to effectively use the data and tools to which they have access, and employees need to take on new roles and shed old supervisory relationships and norms.

When existing practices are automated before business processes and profit drivers are fully understood, incremental improvements are likely. Significant IT-enabled process improvements require close examination of business processes, combined with double-loop learning.

IT-enabled business transformation requires dynamically piecing together many different elements. No single change - in strategy, organizational structure, IT applications, human resources policies, or other measures - is sufficient to renew an organization. Rather, many elements must be changed simultaneously and in a coordinated fashion in order to achieve significantly improved performance.

Suggested 80-Minute Class Plan

1. Evaluate the steps Sloss has taken since he assumed control of Connor in 1985. (20 minutes)
    Board plan: Before 1984
                    1984-1992

2. Should Michael Quarry's information system be rolled out to the other plants (Dallas, San Jose, Portland?) If yes, how? (20 minutes)

3. What advice would you give Sloss and Quarry on the continued evolution of Connor's organizational structure, control systems, people, and technologies? (15-20 minutes)

4. What happened: implemented in Dallas. Customized to their needs. (5-10 minutes)

5. Wrap-Up (10 minutes)

Exhibit TN-1   **Comparison of Connor Formed Metal Products in two Eras**

Connor Before 1984	Connor, 1984-1990
small	small
slow growth	moderate growth
traditional	innovative (ESOP, etc.)
hierarchical: centralized decision-making and control	flatter; divisions have P&L authority; some decision rights delegated to lower levels
managers, supervisors decide; workers do	"empowered" workers decide and do; employees are part-owners
line-of-sight supervision	"empowered" workers monitor own production
"secretive" culture; little information-sharing	"open," team-based culture; extensive information sharing
labor-intensive production	investment in factory automation
paper-intensive, manual processes	some processes automated
poor quality	participation in Baldrige Award; training in SPC and other quality techniques
unresponsive service	service-based differentiation
coarse metrics: bottom-line emphasis	more varied, relevant metrics
poor data management	somewhat improved data management
no MIS function	Michael Quarrey hired

Exhibit TN-2   Data Storage discussion: Cash, et al. , pages 167-169.

Data Storage includes verifying the *accuracy,* ensuring the *viability*, determining who will have *access*, and protecting the *security* of data resources. Inaccurate data cannot be transformed into meaningful information. Someone must decide on an accuracy standard (e.g., how many digits of precision for numeric data?) and a process for verifying data accuracy (who is responsible for verification? how can the software prevent or resolve data "collisions" in real-time, multi-user systems?) and timeliness (how often will the database be updated? how will users verify the update version they are viewing?). Data *viability* refers to the value of the data. Although data storage costs have declined dramatically, retrieval can be costly when users must navigate through unnecessarily large data bases. Hence, data storage processes must include measures for periodically and systematically purging data that is outdated, inaccurate, or no longer useful.

Data management software and techniques have evolved to handle these and other data storage issues. There are two important principles of data management. First, data are *separable* from applications. Early-generation systems did not employ this principle; applications programs defined the data they would operate upon. A single data item could exist in multiple locations, leading to redundancies and inaccuracies. This greatly inhibited data sharing and caused other problems. For example, in many firms the first-generation payroll systems defined "employee number" as a 4-digit field. That worked fine as long as the firm had no more than 9,999 employees. When employee number 10,000 was hired, the 4-digit field had to be adjusted in every application in which it was used - a costly and common exercise for many companies.

The second principle is that data definitions are *durable*. *If well-specified at the outset*, data definitions are stable over time, even though the values may change. Hence, once an organization has undergone a rigorous process of defining its data definitions and relationships, and established a data administration function, ongoing modifications are reasonably straightforward. Data managed according to these principles are readily accessible for transformation into meaningful, timely information. Unfortunately, many organizations did not take that first step and now apply Band-Aid solutions to serious data management problems.

Many organizations have data stored in *hierarchical* database management systems, which are analogous to traditional file cabinet systems (first locate the file cabinet, then the drawer, the folder, the document, the data item). Hierarchical databases work well for pre-defined searches that conform to the file structure (such as, "find all books written by this author"). However, data retrieval is slow or impossible when the query involves complex logic or a search that does not start at the top of the hierarchy (such as, "find all books written before 1980 and containing the word "computers" in the title and published by Irwin.") A more recent approach, *relational* database management, stores data in a more flexible form. Using techniques based in relational algebra, data in separate files can be easily extracted and combined, as long as they share common fields, or "relational keys." But retrieval can be slower than in a hierarchical database. Hypertext systems enable even greater flexibility in managing data, since any hypertext data element can be related to any other data element. However, systematic methodologies for developing and maintaining hypertext have not yet emerged. Lately, *object-oriented* databases have also emerged. This approach adds efficiency and flexibility by treating images, film clips, groups of data or programs, etc. as objects which can be accessed and manipulated as single units. Software designers are also working on techniques that produce the rapid retrieval possible in hierarchical databases while preserving the flexibility of relational, hypertext, and object-oriented databases.

Data access and security issues are becoming more critical in firms with matrix, hybrid or network organizational structures, and/or firms confronting high uncertainty and rapid change. In hierarchical organizations, data access could be specified according to reporting relationships and other readily-identifiable criteria. In stable environments, disputes over data access could be resolved in an orderly fashion. This is now a time-consuming luxury that many organizations can no longer afford. Access to the right data at the right time by the right people may mean the difference between winning or losing a bid, identifying and fixing a small problem before it becomes a big one, and jumping on a profitable opportunity ahead of the competition.

Dallas: purchased by Sloss in 1984.
Leadership: Bill Wilt, turnaround specialist (previously in Phoenix)
                       "managing the numbers" (p. 5): plant-wide incentives
                       bonus based on efficiency, on-time delivery, safety

Performance: not profitable yet.

LA:
Leadership: Gary Spanos: since 1986; "spirited leader", 20-year veteran, "anti-
                       technology"(previously managed Portland, San Jose)

IT Literacy: limited; use System 36 for "basic administrative," upgraded to 38
                       PC system implemented 5/90

Size: largest: 100 employees

Products: high-volume, low margin products

Performance: poor; margins declining in 80's
                       1990: improvements in late jobs, run speeds, defects, credits issued

Portland
Leadership: Neil Allen = 20 year vet; receptive to new system; entrepreneurial style

IT Literacy: experienced computer users; used System 36, experimenting with PC's

Size: small; 30 employees

Products: customers = trucking and related companies

Performance: good profitability

San Jose:
Leadership: Stan Petty, young MBA

IT Literacy: no one knew how to use System 36's
                       Job Boss developed on PC's for estimating, order entry, A/R,
                       purchasing. "invested a lot in training;" "concerns about switching"

Size: 60 employees

Products: diversified in 1980's: short-run prototypes for high-tech customers

Performance: Very good profits

Controls at the Sands Hotel and Casino

Synopsis

Stephen F. Hyde, President of the Sands Hotel in Atlantic City opens and closes a conversation with a case writer by describing his company's control system. The controls at the Sands Hotel and Casino go beyond those required by the state of New Jersey, which are designed to assure that the state captures its shares of gaming revenues. Furthermore, Hyde tells the case writer that his organization is always looking for ways to improve, especially in areas where they can relate a player's activity and skill to complementary services which the Hotel may provide to encourage guests to gamble at the Sands.

A casino presents unique challenges for the design and use of control systems. Games are paid in chips and cash. Chips must be available at each gaming location so that money can be exchanged for them. For this reason an enormous amount of cash and cash equivalents are on the gaming floor at any time, and stocks need to be controlled and replenished continuously. Although the imprest system used by the Sands is similar to that used by many companies that have petty cash funds, the importance to the Sands is many times greater because of the amounts involved.

The case focuses on controls and procedures affecting all games but especially the game of Blackjack. Exhibits detail how cash is controlled from the beginning of a shift to its end and in the cash counting rooms. Reports on the results from different pits and Blackjack tables and on different games are sufficiently detailed to show the futility of trying to apply results controls in this environment.

Teaching Objectives

This case was designed with several purposes in mind:

> First, it illustrates a control system that is dominated by action and personnel controls, rather than results controls. Analysis of the Sands Hotel and Casino case leads to insights about some of the factors that limit the feasibility of results controls.

> Secondly, the case supports a discussion of so-called "tight" control. An excellent example of the application of tight action controls is seen in the table games areas of the casino.

> Finally, the case can lead into a discussion what auditors refer to as "internal control." The case describes an excellent system of controls of cash stocks (using imprest funds) and movements of cash. These controls are necessary for, but not sufficient to guarantee, good management control.

Suggested Optional Reading:

Kenneth A. Merchant, "The Control Function of Management," *Sloan Management q Review*, Summer 1982, pages 43-55.

Suggested Study Questions:

1. List the controls described in the case. What control problems is each designed to address?

2. Focus on three key roles in the casino: blackjack dealer, blackjack pit boss, vice president of casino operations. How would you characterize the "control strategy" used over each of these roles?

3. Is Stephen Hyde justified in being proud of his company's control s ystem? Why or why not? Are any of the controls at Sands applicable to firms in other industries?

Opportunities for Student Analysis

Discussion of Student Questions

I generally start the class by having students analyze each of the organizational roles and the controls over them. I start with the lowest level role described in the case -- blackjack dealer -- and build the chart shown as **Exhibit TN-1** on the blackboard. Some students are not familiar with the game of blackjack, so some discussion of how it works and what the dealer is expected to do is generally necessary. The chart shows that results controls are not important at the dealer and pit boss levels in the organization.

A minor, but interesting point: I asked casino managers if they thought that control was enhanced by the high salaries they paid line personnel. The rationale would be that well-paid employees would be less inclined to become involved in illegal activities. The casino managers' reply was a resounding "No!" They said that it was not possible to pay salaries large enough to remove the temptation provided by the large sums present on the casino floor.

Evaluation of Controls

Evaluation of controls in use should be based on consideration of what can go wrong. A list of things that can go wrong at the blackjack tables is presented in **Exhibit TN-2**. Students can be asked to build such a list and discuss whether the controls in place were sufficient to reduce the incidence of each undesirable activity to a reasonably low level. Casino managers are aware of the risk of these problems (although new schemes are constantly being invented), and they have taken steps to reduce their incidence. As a consequence, the evaluation of the controls in place should be very favorable as long as cost constraints are kept in mind.

Another interesting and important problem casinos face is "skimming." Discussion of this problem can lead into consideration of internal control in general, and specifically the ways in which cash is controlled in the casino. The two major purposes of internal controls are to safeguard assets and to ensure the reliability of financial records. In the area of cash, the casino maintains imprest cash balances to safeguard cash and chips; this means assigning individual responsibility for a certain amount of money. They also have elaborate procedures to ensure that the financial records are reliable (e.g., multiple approvals of transactions, checking of the audit trail).

A question to motivate discussion of the adequacy of internal controls is: Do these procedures prevent skimming? Skimming can occur in any of several forms:

Cash is taken from the counting room.

Cash is taken from the cashier's cage, and a forged fill slip is written.

Checks are cashed at the cashier's cage, but someone in the office rips them up before they are deposited, and alters the audit records.

The answer to the question is a tentative yes, the controls are effective against skimming, *unless* (and this is a frequent limitation to internal controls) collusion is involved.

Tight vs. Loose Control

Students can be asked whether control over the dealers is tight or loose. Invariably the answer is "tight." Labeling any control system as "tight" or "loose" leads into a discussion of what constitutes "tight" control. My definition is that tight controls provide a high degree of certainty that the person(s) being controlled will act as the organization wishes. I believe the Sands certainly does have tight control over dealers and pit bosses. However, because they do not use action controls and do not have good performance measures, they do not have tight control over the VP of Casino Operations.

75

Weaknesses of Results Controls

Results controls are not very important in the casino, and it is important to spend some time to understand why this is so. Results controls are simply not feasible for control over dealers, because results are not measured until a shift is complete, and during that period more than one dealer has worked at a table. It would be possible to measure dealer productivity by having someone keep track of deals per hour, but that is not done.

Results can be measured for individual pits and the casino as a whole, and these measures could be used for control over pit bosses and casino managers. They are not so used, because they are not considered good indicators of desirability of actions taken. The key indicator is the hold percentage (win/drop); but as is discussed in the case, this is a flawed measure. Even if the "handle" could be measured instead of drop, the win ratio would not be a reliable indicator of the desirability of the actions of the person being controlled, because of statistical variations. On any given day, week, or even month, poor results might b blamed on a "high roller on a hot streak."

This can be illustrated by asking if the results for the table on which the case has focused (#40 swing shift on 6/23/83) indicate good performance. Direct student attention to case Exhibits 11 and 12. The drop for this table was relatively low ($2,140). This cannot be taken to mean that dealers were not productive, because drop depends on the table's minimum and the number and type of players. Similarly, the high hold percentage (52.22%) does not rule out the possibility of bad actions (e.g., overpaying bets). To illustrate the down side of this point, ask if the results for table 50, swing shift (hold percentage of -30.30%) suggest that the dealer was doing something bad?

Results measures are more reliable the larger the increment of the casino being measured (e.g., an entire shift versus a single table) and the longer the periods of time involved. Just how much the measures are affected could be calculated, but the Sands had apparently not done this analysis (or at least they did not show it to the case writer).

One other problem with results measures is mentioned by Stephen Hyde in the case. Pit bosses and casino managers can resolve disputes by deciding in the casino's favor, thereby increasing the daily hold percentage. Sometimes, up to a reasonable limit, it is more profitable to decide in favor of the player, because happy customers will continue to play in the house. This is one form of short-term versus long-term trade-off.

Control is looser at the level of the casino management. The casino does not have good information as to whether the key decisions are done properly. They are working on improved reports, but such reports will still be subject to the limitations of the hold number.

Applicability to Other Industries

Are the controls observed at the Sands applicable to other industries? The casino industry is in some ways unique, but some of the principles included in the Sands control system are of use in other firms. Tight security and good controls over movements of assets are necessary where valuable, liquid assets are involved (e.g., gold in semiconductor firms, money in banks). Personnel and action controls, such as those used in the casino, will dominate wherever good results measures are not available. Managers in any organization have to go through the process described here of thinking through what is wanted and what can go wrong, and designing controls which reflect these contingencies.

Suggested 80-Minute Class Plan

This plan works well when the case is the first in a module on management control systems.

1.   Brief introductory lecture, defining management control systems. If the Merchant reading was assigned, review his control framework (see **Exhibit TN-3**), describing the control which can be obtained through personnel controls, action controls, and results controls. Stress that a single control is rarely as effective as a combination of several types of controls. (10-15 minutes)

2.   "A visit to the casino," via discussion. Start by making sure that everybody understands how the game of Blackjack is played, and the atmosphere in the casino and at the Blackjack table. Usually it is possible to get a student to volunteer to be the "expert," describing Blackjack and casinos. The discussion should highlight the speed at which the game is played and the atmosphere which prevails at a Blackjack table, during a time when players are making bets, receiving cards, and claiming winnings. (10 minutes)

3.   What are the key actions and controls that affect a Blackjack dealer? What can go wrong at a Blackjack table? (10 minutes)

4.   What are the key actions and controls for a pit boss? What can go wrong, for which the pit boss should be responsible? (10 minutes)

5.   (somewhere between the beginning of the discussion of roles and the end of the pit boss discussion): What can we learn about the control process by looking at case Exhibits 5 through 12? Why aren't results controls possible in the environment of the table games at a casino? (10-15 minutes)

6.   What are the key actions and controls for the Vice President of Casino Operations? How will we know whether the Vice President of Casino Operations is doing a good job? Why can we use results controls for this role where we could not for others? What is necessary for implementation of effective results control? (15 minutes)

7.   How could controls at the Sands Casino be improved? (5-10 minutes)

8.   Briefly summarize key summary lessons (5 minutes)

Key Summary Lessons

1.   Effective managers use a mixture of controls to assure that what needs doing gets done in the way that managers intend it to get done.

2.   Of all controls, personnel controls are the most important. Controls rarely give people skills, nor are they sufficient to assure honesty, integrity, and effort unless people are willing to allow them to do so.

3.   Action controls create boundaries that make it easier for people to do what they should do.

4.   Results controls should be used wherever possible because they allow the controls to relate directly to the organization's goals and objectives, and the roles which each member of the organization should play in trying to achieve them. Results controls direct and motivate contributing behaviors by members of the organization.

Exhibit TN-1

Analysis of Roles and Controls
(This exhibit assumes that the Merchant reading has been assigned)

Role	Key Actions	Controls	Evaluation (in light of things that can go wrong)
Blackjack dealer	Accurate, honest deals Productive, cheerful	Licensing (P) Hiring (P) Training (P) Supervision (A) Surveillance (A) Frequent rest breaks (P)	Good, tight control, some risks
Pit Boss	Good supervision. Marketing (give comps to good customers)	Licensing (P) Hiring (P)	Have to (and probably can) trust these experienced people
VP, Casino Operations	Decisions: - hiring - labor scheduling (when to open a pit) - when to change minimums - casino layout	Licensing (P) Hiring (P) MBO system (R)	Loose

R = Results Control
A = Action Control
P - Personnel Control

Exhibit TN-2

Things that Can Go Wrong at a Blackjack Table

1. Dealer overpayment, when debts are paid or change made.

2. Dealer payoff of a losing bet.

3. Player peeking at dealer's hole card or dealer signaling (showing the card).

4. Player "past posting" (adding a bet to a hand that looks promising), or "copping" (decreasing a bet on a hand that looks lost).
   Stephen Hyde on the past posting problem:

   We constantly have to be alert. We had a situation the other day on a craps table of "past posting." A guy at one end of the table created a disturbance which distracted the entire table, and a guy at the other end of the table put down a $2,000 wager on a winning roll of the dice. Nobody at the table detected it, but it was detected by the "eye." So now we're putting all of our casino people through a class in past-posting. It's a constant threat. We have a number of dealers who have only been in the business a few years and haven't seen all these tricks.

5. Dealers stealing chips. Dealers have discovered many devious ways to remove chips from the tables. Common schemes have been to cup chips in their hands or slip them into "subs," such as elaborate hairdo, false bandages, or hidden pockets in their apron.

6. Players counting cards. Skilled blackjack players can keep track of the aces and face cards that have been played and gain an advantage in their betting. In Las Vegas, casino managers can ban these people from their casinos. In New Jersey they can only order to dealers to shuffle more frequently to reduce the advantage that such tactics provide.

7. Players introducing counterfeit money or chips.

8. Pit bosses granting bad credit (Casinos protect themselves by having this decision made by personnel in the cashier's cage. Communication to the tables is done through computer terminals).

9. Players stealing chips from each other (commonly by having an accomplice create a diversion).

10. Players marking or switching cards. This is a potential problem in Las Vegas and elsewhere, but in New Jersey, customers never touch the cards.

Exhibit TN-3

Merchant Control Classification
(This exhibit assumes that the Merchant reading has been assigned)

ACTION	RESULTS	PEOPLE
Behavioral: Physical Administrative	**Accountability:** Standards Budgets	**Upgrade Capabilities:** Selection Training Assignment
Accountability: Work Rules Policies Procedures Codes of Conduct		**Improve Communications:** Clarify Expectations Provide Information for Coordination
Preaction Review: Direct Supervision Approval Limits Budget Reviews		**Encourage Peer Control:** Work Groups Shared Goals

Crompton Greaves Ltd.

Synopsis

Crompton Greaves is a large multi-divisional firm based in India. The new CEO, Kewal Krishan Nohria (KKN) confronts declining performance in an increasingly competitive market. KKN turns the firm around by building on the Crompton Greaves' historical strengths and by motivating employees to achieve aggressive growth targets. He adopts a performance-driven control system that focuses managers' attention on a wide array of measures that are consistent with the strategy of the firm. Though successful in reversing Crompton Greaves' competitive decline, KKN's approach to management raises questions as to whether it will be robust to future growth, diversification and succession by a new CEO when KKN retires.

Teaching Objectives

Control systems require making choices about what to measure, how to set targets and review performance against them, and how to reward people and make adjustments in the light of their performance. Each choice involves assumptions about "good" indicators of performance and human motivation and behavior. This case provides an opportunity to examine the different ways in which managers can address these issues.

Suggested Optional Readings

M. Edgar Barrett and LeRoy B. Fraser, III. "Conflicting Roles in Budgeting for Operations," *Harvard Business Review*, July-August 1977, pp. 137-146.

John Dearden, "Measuring Profit Center Managers," *Harvard Business Review*, Reprint 87503.

Robert G. Eccles, "The Performance Measurement Manifesto," *Harvard Business Review*, January-February 1991, pp. 131-137.

Kenneth Merchant, *Rewarding Results: Motivating Profit Center Managers*. Boston: Harvard Business School Press, 1989.

Suggested Study Questions

1. Describe and evaluate KKN's approach to control at Crompton Greaves Ltd.

2. What assumptions regarding human motivation and behavior underlie KKN's approach to control?

3. How robust is this approach to control? What are its strengths and weaknesses?

Opportunities for Student Analysis and Discussion

This case offers five major themes:

> performance measures used for control,
> approaches to setting performance targets
> processes to monitor, evaluate, and reward performance,
> underlying assumptions of human behavior, and
> robustness of the control system.

Performance measures: key points

The performance measures at Crompton Greaves:

> are simple, quantifiable, easy to understand, and closely tied to a clear, shared statement of strategic intent.

> distinguish explicitly between outcomes ("operations management") and the key processes that generate them ("improvement management").

> go beyond purely financial measures and include measures of quality, productivity, customer satisfaction, idle time, and human resources.

> are benchmarked against the best practices in the world (e.g., quality at zero defects, productivity by US. standards, employee involvement by Japanese standards) and against relevant Indian competitors.

> focus on continuous improvement and learning (e.g., the PIP program for constantly finding incremental cost savings), in all aspects of the business.

> focus on investments that improve quality or productivity and can be justified on that basis instead of financial hurdle rates. Similarly, decisions to enter into new businesses are made based on potential competitive performance (can we be in the top 3 in the target business?), not on hurdle rates.

The performance measures adopted by Crompton Greaves demonstrate a progressive and effective approach to performance measurement. If there is one weakness, it is in the area of externally based measures, but the firm is aggressively moving in that direction. There may also be too many performance measures, and students might explore what an appropriate number of measures should be. Exhibit 1, Chapter 3, reproduced below, can help communicate the message that the traditional focus on purely financial measures of performance leads to a performance measurement system that is restricted to the lower right hand corner of the grid (Internal/Results). Effective performance measurement covers all quadrants of the grid.

84

Setting performance targets

Senior managers choose who will set targets, how aggressive targets will be, and whether they will be revised in light of new information or unforeseen contingencies. At Crompton Greaves, targets are:

> set once a year by the divisional general manager, based on meetings with the CEO. Targets are public commitments (all managers present their targets in a meeting with their peers). They are not set by the CEO or corporate management, although managers are expected to meet external benchmarks.

> revised downwards by KKN, but never upwards. KKN believes that individuals over-commit, especially in front of their peers. This philosophy is in marked contrast with the traditional approach of setting "stretch" targets.

> never revised subsequently. KKN wants managers to accept full responsibility for their performance and to serve as a reflection of the manager's judgment.

Research suggests that, in order to motivate the greatest effort, targets should be neither too hard nor too easy to meet. Typically, targets are the outcome of negotiations between managers and their superiors, with managers presenting a rather easy target and superiors demanding higher targets. KKN believed that his system circumvented this traditional negotiating game. In his view, Crompton managers were already subject to pressures to stretch themselves because, in committing to targets in front of their peers, their self-esteem would push them toward aggressive targets. Also, each target was benchmarked against external best practices. KKN felt that most managers would not to commit to targets that were much lower than these benchmarks, especially since managers' performance was judged relative to these external benchmarks.

KKN often revised targets downward because he wanted them to be demanding yet achievable. In his view, success reinforced a manager's confidence and future performance (a belief which is supported by empirical research in social psychology).

KKN's unwillingness to revise targets (even in the face of contingencies that were outside a manager's control) is a more debatable choice. While this approach does foster complete accountability and responsibility on the part of Crompton's managers, it also puts pressure on managers to submit conservative targets to insure against unforeseen events.

This discussion of how targets are set is also an opportunity to discuss the underlying assumptions of human behavior that guide this control system (see below).

Budgeting Process—monitoring, evaluating, and rewarding performance

The main features of Crompton's budgeting process can be summarized as follows:

> Emphasis on making the performance assessment "open, transparent, and fair."

> A standard annual budget preparation process that is keyed off the fiscal calendar. Budgets prepared by divisional general managers in consultation with the CEO and presented to all members of the top management team.

> Quarterly review of every division's performance against budget in a meeting of all 60 top managers.

> Each division's performance also reviewed quarterly by KKN in scheduled site visits. Except for this quarterly review, division general managers have complete autonomy.

> Performance of managers one level below general managers reviewed twice a year during peer meetings.

> Assessment based on peer rankings and demonstrated performance. The assessment process includes the bottom line, improvements from a starting point and performance against competitive benchmarks. Emphasis is placed on long-term consistency in hitting targets.

Open, public review of performance among peers.

No bonus or pay-for-performance. Rewards are primarily in the form of promotions (relatively infrequent) and symbolic rewards (many) based on competition among peers.

Failures of subordinates are not punished. Rather, these are seen as a failure on the part of top management.

Two elements of this process are worth noting. The first is the public character of performance appraisal at Crompton Greaves. KKN has adopted an entirely open system in which there are no subjective elements and each individual's relative ranking on each performance measure is public knowledge. Moreover, peers rank each other's performance and that, too, is part of the public record. This system eliminates quibbling about a manager's relative performance, avoids the usual tendency of low variance in performance evaluations, and maintains peer pressure and competition among managers. Another, more subtle consequence derives from the large number of measures. Since it is hard for any one manager to excel on all dimensions, every manager always has areas for improvement. This ultimately gives KKN a great deal of leverage because he can decide how much emphasis he places on performance against any particular class of measures.

KKN's approach to rewards and sanctions is more debatable. He does not believe in any form of variable compensation linked to annual performance. He takes a long-term view, tying consistent performance in a job over a reasonably long period of time (4-5 years) to the reward of promotion. In the short run, he believes that symbolic rewards such as trophies and peers recognition are sufficient. Indeed, KKN believes that firms which reward superior performers with huge bonuses, most companies end up demotivating those who did not perform as well.

KKN's view on failure is even more controversial. He does not fire managers for poor performance, under the rationale that their failure reflects his failure to train and help them improve. However, in a sense he does punish poor performers by sidelining them in marginal jobs. The benefit of this approach is that it prevents managers from adopting a short-term orientation and from gaming the performance measurement system to achieve bonuses. However, this approach may also inhibit motivation and creates a disadvantage for Crompton Greaves in terms of hiring the best managers in a competitive labor market.

Assumptions of human motivation and behavior

It is clear that the performance measurement and control system hinges on key assumptions that KKN makes about human behavior. These assumptions should be explicitly surfaced at some point in the class discussion:

People like to perform to their fullest and will respond if challenged. "You must inspire in people the will to succeed." "People will work as hard as they can. They are driven to be the most they can be."

People like to succeed, so they should be given an opportunity to do so. This produces a self-reinforcing cycle of success. "Success teaches success. Failure does not teach success. . .The moment people start succeeding, their own self-image is enhanced and that enables them to set higher standards in the future."

Peer pressure works wonders; managers will neither commit to a miserly target nor accept sub-standard performance when targets and performance are reviewed publicly in a community of peers. "People like to test themselves in a community of peers. They don't mind failing in the presence of their boss, but do mind in the presence of their peers."

People should be given an opportunity to take ownership for their performance expectations and should be held strictly accountable for meeting their commitments. No excuse should be allowed, since it lets people off the hook and dilutes their sense of responsibility for their performance. "Managers must own responsibility, live with the burden of responsibility, and achieve according to their commitment of results."

People will accept relative failure and lower rewards without being demotivated if they view the performance evaluation system to be open, transparent, and fair.

It is interesting to contrast this set of assumptions regarding human behavior with a more utilitarian or economic view, in which individuals are seen as acting entirely in self-interest and as being willing to cheat or shirk were possible. Contrasting Crompton's system with the assumptions of agency-principal models stimulates an interesting discussion. To spark this debate one might ask students, which kind of performance measurement system would you like to work in? What kind of system would you prefer to employ in order to manage the performance of your own organization?

Robustness of the system

Finally, one can examine how robust this control system is to several different contingencies:

Cheating or gaming of the targets and measures: This is minimized by (a) setting clear external benchmarks so that it is hard for managers to set overly conservative targets; (b) setting a clear set of performance measures that are not all susceptible to accounting tricks; (c) extensive visits to plant sites to meet face-to-face with general managers as well as her direct reports; (d) encouraging peers to openly discuss performance, with a view to create a community of watchdogs; and (e) keeping managers in their jobs for a long period so that they are accountable for long-term performance.

Increasing heterogeneity of the businesses as Crompton diversifies: The system emphasizes equity and fairness, with everybody playing by the same rules -- same measures, same measurement procedure, same reward system, etc. This standardization, essential for equity and fairness, may be inappropriate for a more diversified business. The case suggests there are already some concerns in this regard. The firm's success has been limited against more nimble entrants in new businesses such as computers and televisions.

Growth: The budgeting process and the sheer volume of information required could become overbearing as the firm grows to its target of "2,000 by the year 2000." Growth will put an immense strain on face-to-face contact and the intimate familiarity that the CEO and top managers share. This could weaken the main foundation of intense peer and superior-subordinate interaction on which this control system is built.

Increasing environmental volatility: The rigid nature of annual targets prevent rapid adjustment to events in the firm's environment. While there are rolling forecasts of year-end performance Crompton sets fixed target. In contrast, firms like Compaq match rolling forecasts with rolling targets.

CEO succession: This is probably the system's greatest weakness. It is driven by a charismatic CEO who is likely to have a long tenure. It suits his style of intense employee contact and a focus on simplicity. The MIS systems have been poorly developed and do not provide an information architecture that can be tapped to monitor performance in real time. The system as it is configured will require the next CEO to adopt a similar approach to control as KKN's, which may not be in tune with the next CEO's style. This is a potentially big problem.

Students often maintain that the system is only suited to an Indian context and would not work in the United States. This is worth pushing hard on, because it helps further flesh out the assumptions one makes about human behavior. In my own view, there is almost nothing uniquely Indian about this case. The only relevant institutional constraint is that in India there is a cap on CEO compensation. There are no restrictions at lower levels, and there are certainly other companies, unlike Crompton Greaves, which have performance measurement and reward systems that are much more along the lines of pay-for-financial performance.

Suggested 80-Minute Class Plan

1. Introduction (5 minutes)

2. Describe and evaluate the different categories and measures of performance employed by KKN. Are these a "good" set of measures of the firm's performance? (15 minutes)

3. What do you think of the way targets are set in this firm? What are the strengths and weaknesses of this approach? (10 minutes)

4. Describe and evaluate the budget review process. How effective is this process in monitoring, assessing, and rewarding performance? Does this system allow the CEO to guide the firm in the desired direction? (15 minutes)

5. What assumptions regarding human motivation and behavior are being made here? Are these reasonable assumptions? Would they apply in other countries? (15 minutes)

6. How robust is this approach to control? Can it be easily "gamed?" Will it be as effective for the new businesses that Crompton Greaves is diversifying into? Will it be effective if the company grows as planned? What will happen when KKN retires? (15 minutes)

7. Wrap-up and summary (5 minutes)

Key Summary Lessons

1. Adopt a broad set of performance measures that are consistent with the firm's strategy (see Case Exhibit 1).

2. Set targets that are challenging but achievable and are benchmarked against best practices.

3. Assess and rewarding performance in a manner that maintains the motivation of all employees. This requires balancing rewards for good performance with perceptions of fairness and equity.

4. Be aware of the assumptions of human behavior that underlie any control system.

5. Control systems must be robust to key contingencies.

Hill, Holliday, Connors, Cosmopulos, Inc.
Advertising (A) & (B)[*]

Synopsis

Faced with declining revenues and increasing costs, Jack Connors, principal of Hill, Holliday, asked Felice Kincannon, managing director of the Boston office, to develop a plan of action. Kincannon, with the help of other senior Hill, Holliday executives, decided against a makeshift approach of firing a certain percentage of people from each division. Instead, she decided to reconsider the structure of the firm to increase its effectiveness.

At the time, the firm was organized on a product basis, with general advertising and the different "integrated disciplines" (including direct marketing, market research, design, and sales promotion) each offering different advertising services and organized as a separate profit center. Each profit center had its own account executives and creative staff. Some executives felt that this led to unnecessary duplication of resources. Others, however, felt this duplication was necessary since each discipline required a unique approach to clients and creative work.

To improve efficiency, Kincannon was contemplating a reorganization which would divide the firm into client groups that would exist alongside pared down versions of the current discipline-based groups, leading to a matrix-like organization structure (though it was not labeled as such). The case describes the reactions of several senior employees to the proposed reorganization. However, the proposal has not yet been implemented, so this leaves students the opportunity to modify the proposed new structure or propose alternative structures that would achieve the desired objectives.

The "B" case (included in this manual), describes how, six months later, the pressures on the firm to cut costs vanish. The firm wins a string of new accounts and now probably needs additional resources. This dramatic turnaround forces an interesting reexamination of the earlier discussion.

Teaching Objectives

This case provides an opportunity to discuss issues that arise when the structure of an organization must respond to different contingencies that present difficult trade-offs. In such a situation, a matrix structure is often selected. But as this case shows, the matrix structure is no panacea and leads to ambiguous definitions of responsibility. The case also permits a discussion of the close relationship between how an organization is structured and how responsibility centers (such as profit and cost centers) are defined. It can thus be used as a transition case between modules on organization structure and control systems.

Finally, the case also permits a rich discussion of issues to consider when implementing a change in an organization's structure. The main teaching objectives of this case are:

Introduce students to the advantages and disadvantages of a matrix organization.

Discuss the relationship between organizational structure and the definition of responsibility centers.

Give students an opportunity to propose and implement a new organizational structure in a complicated business.

Suggested Optional Readings:

Richard Vancil, "What Kind of Management Control Do You Need?" *Harvard Business Review*, (March-April 1973). Reprint No. 73213.

Stanley M. Davis and Paul R. Lawrence, *Matrix*. Reading, MA: Addison Wesley, 1977.

Suggested Study Questions

1. What challenges is Hill Holliday facing? What problems must the new organization address?

2. What are the strengths and weaknesses of the existing structure and the proposed new structure that Kincannon is evaluating?

3. What structural changes, if any, would you recommend and how would you implement your recommendations?

Opportunities for Student Analysis

Organizational diagnosis

The firm is projecting declining revenues due to a recession in its local market and a recent failure to win new business. This reveals the strong regional (New England) dependency of the firm, its weakness in other geographic markets, and the decline of its creative department.

The firm is being challenged from two flanks. If it loses its creative edge, it is likely to lose out to "mega agencies," and if it does not offer a full line of communication services on a national basis, it could lose out to smaller firms that specialize by region or by offering only a particular advertising service, such as design or direct mail.

To address its root problems, the firm has to rejuvenate its "hot" creative reputation while continuing to offer personalized, high-quality account services. In the short run, the firm faces the urgent problem of cutting costs.

The firm's managers must be careful, in selecting people to let go. The firm has a reputation of a "caring culture." This has enabled Hill, Holliday to attract the finest talent in the past. Indiscriminate layoffs could damage the firm's employment reputation. The firm is also top-heavy. During the firm's previously rapid growth, stars were promoted into top positions and paid top dollar. Letting these people go would produce the greatest cost savings. But they are the firm's best talent and could take some clients with them if they left (as happened previously in the firm's New York office).

This background discussion enables a richer discussion of the relative advantages and disadvantages of Hill Holliday's existing organization and the new structure that Kincannon is considering.

Advantages of the current organization

The discipline-based profit centers had a number of justifications.

> The integrated disciplines of market research, direct marketing, design, and sales promotions were different in a number of ways from general advertising, and people in those departments had distinct skills.

> The current structure allowed the integrated disciplines to maintain their own relationships with each client, separate from those of general advertising. This was considered necessary because there was no guarantee that general advertising account managers would effectively sell the value-added integrated disciplines.

93

The integrated disciplines and general advertising staffs often dealt with different people at the client level. Some executives felt there was little to be gained by integrating management of a particular account, when individual clients might have distinct points of contact without any internal connection.

Each integrated discipline recruited from separate labor markets. The division of the firm along disciplinary lines allowed each area to tap into its related external labor market with relative ease.

The profit center nature of the integrated disciplines allowed for measurement of and accountability for profit and loss within each discipline. Each discipline had to justify its existence financially. Management could judge what products and services were successful, giving them the latitude to add new ones with the knowledge they could be easily measured and could be disbanded if they were unsuccessful (as they had done with their public relations profit center).

Disadvantages of the current organization

The current organization was not without difficulties:

Perhaps of most concern was the replication of effort involved in having numerous separate creative departments and account management teams.

The division of disciplines also meant that Hill, Holliday could not present clients with one point of contact and responsibility.

Under the current structure there were complications in coordinating and disseminating information. It was important for everyone working with a particular client to have an idea of all the work done for that client, in order to avoid embarrassment resulting from not being aware of all the elements of the client's program or from suggesting ideas which the client had already considered.

The divided nature of the agency meant that it was more difficult to present consistent quality. There was a clear risk that work sent to a client from different creative departments would not always be thematically unified.

When a client used services offered by only one discipline inside Hill, Holliday, there was the risk that there would be insufficient cross-selling of services.

Issues raised by the proposed reorganization

Though not labeled by the executives in the firm as such, the proposed reorganization is a matrix structure. Kincannon planned to put together account groups, perhaps five in total, and make each a separate profit center. Each account group would have representatives from general advertising and every integrated discipline. They would also be fully staffed with creative directors and writers. Kincannon could then divide accounts among the newly formed groups, which would unite all services performed for each client. This would remove some double staffing in account services and creative areas and would thus cut costs. The reorganization would retain smaller integrated disciplines (still to be run as profit centers).

The proposed reorganization had the following potential advantages:

> Cost cutting was the impetus for the reorganization, and Kincannon felt that it could be achieved. By uniting all services performed for a group of clients, the new structure would remove some double staffing in the account services and creative areas and would thus cut costs.

> The reorganization creates new opportunities for some of the best account managers, who were beginning to feel a ceiling on their growth in the previous structure.

> If there are opportunities for cross-selling, this structure creates incentives for account group managers to aggressively seek them.

> The structure ensures greater consistency and quality of creative product within and across different clients.

> The structure permits the firm to market itself more convincingly as being able to provide a full-service communications strategy for its clients.

> The reorganization puts to test a hitherto unchallenged assumption that creative staff were not transferable across disciplines. It could well lead to a discovery of unrecognized internal creative talent.

However, there were certain areas of concern that were not addressed by the reorganization, many of which can be expected in any matrix structure:

> Who made what decisions would change. Questions arose as to who would decide what would should be done and who should do it, who would determine quality, how work would be charged, who would assess performance and determine rewards, and so on. Since decision rights were now unclear, they would have to be shared or negotiated across product

areas or account groups. The plan did not specify how potential conflict would be resolved. Kincannon believed that the firm was small enough and everyone knew each other well enough to work through such issues as they arose.

The new structure would make accountability less clear. For instance, it was no longer clear what the smaller integrated disciplines would be held accountable for, since the primary profit and loss statements would be drawn by the account groups.

The new organization was likely to generate considerable competition among account groups as they vied for the biggest, most interesting clients. While some competition would be healthy, it could also create unhealthy conflict and political maneuvering.

The new organization ran the risk of diluting the expertise of various disciplines, as employees were no longer nurtured and developed by others in the same discipline.

There were concerns about how career structures would be defined. In the existing structure, employees could rise up the disciplinary ranks based upon their disciplinary expertise and performance. In the new structure, it was unclear what the performance standards would be.

It was unclear who would be responsible for assessing performance. How would account group managers and heads of disciplines resolve disputed performance evaluations?

The new structure would differ from that of most other agencies. Given the high mobility in the industry, and the importance attached to titles, there were concerns about how this would affect the "marketability" of Hill, Holliday employees if they chose to look for career opportunities outside the firm.

There were concerns about how the reorganization might affect moral, since there would likely be perceptions of winners and losers in the transition.

Given that neither organization structure is a perfect solution, one can open the discussion to alternative proposals that the students might have. This discussion often leads to proposals for hybrid structures, in which a project or client group is overlaid over the existing structure. It is important to push students to specify how they would define responsibility centers and performance measures in any structure they propose.

Implementation questions

Finally, it is useful to confront students with the task of implementing the proposed reorganization plan. Some of the questions that can be used to flesh out various aspects of the implementation problems are outlined below.

In the case itself, the need for cost savings is discussed only in the introduction. This is clearly a pressing impetus for the reorganization. Should management determine how smoothly the new groups can run before firing people? Or, should excess personnel be let go even before a reorganization takes effect? How should a cutback be handled; should current department heads decide who should be let go, or should group heads bid for personnel they want and the leftovers be fired?

How should a transition to the new structure be managed? How long in advance should it be announced? Kincannon has a rare opportunity to set an entirely new tone. What are the issues involved in this large-scale change?

Should the Los Angeles office be restructured along the same lines as the Boston office? Since most of the LA's efforts are directed at one client (Infiniti), would such a change be called for?

Kincannon seems sure that client groups will successfully negotiate with each other for resources and that group heads will resolve intragroup conflicts. Are there processes for conflict resolution should a stalemate arise? How can account group heads be trained to deal with conflict management? Alternatively, should they, and others in the firm, learn through experience?

How will intragroup cohesiveness be developed and maintained? Hill, Holliday will throw together people who traditionally had little contact with each other. The groups will have to develop a spirit of internal cooperation, as people from different integrated disciplines and general advertising learn to work together. How can such a spirit be produced and nurtured?

How will the reorganization affect sales efforts? Who will be responsible for making sales calls? Will top management, i.e., above the level of the account group, be responsible for the entire new business effort? If account groups make sales calls, will a particular group earn special rights in the internal competition to serve that client? What if the salesperson is not part of the group chosen to serve the client? Will the so-called "above-the-line" services still be sold separately? If so, what group will serve those clients that do not use general advertising services? What if no group wants to service a small account that will not bring much revenue or glory?

How will information be disseminated among account groups? Before the reorganization, the core team approach forced the disciplines to communicate, at least around shared clients. If the account group system is adopted, how will successful strategies be disseminated into other account groups?

What is the potential for the account group system to be a divisive force at Hill, Holliday? Will employees identify with their account group more than with the firm? If all of a client's "hooks" to Hill, Holliday are within one account group, would it be possible for the group to leave the firm and set up shop independently, stealing clients in the process?

How will a reorganization affect the creative reputation of the firm? With creative personnel divided among the groups, how will a consistent Hill, Holliday creative product be produced? Are there enough good creative people to fully staff each group? Do creative people need to stay together to maintain a creative atmosphere, perhaps necessary to produce ground-breaking work? Do they need to stay together and be protected from administrative and conformist pressures of working in a group dominated by account management personnel?

The "B" Case

Events in the "B" case suddenly eliminate the short-term pressures to reduce costs. Indeed, the firm is now stretched for additional resources. Given this dramatic turnaround in the environment, the question is, "Should the reorganization that has already been implemented now be reexamined?" This raises the issue of how frequently one should reorganize and in response to what circumstances. This discussion should be familiar to students who have previously wrestled with this question in the context of the Appex case (typically used as an introductory case before this one) and should help to deepen their understanding of how and when structure can be used to influence an organization's performance.

Suggested 80-Minute Class Plan

1. What are the major challenges confronting Hill, Holliday in January 1991?
    What are the main external pressures? Internal pressures?
    What are the companies' residual sources of strength?
    What degrees of freedom does the firm have in implementing change? (10 minutes)

2. What are the advantages and disadvantages of the present structure? (10 minutes)

3. What do you think of the proposed reorganization?
    What are its potential advantages? What concerns might you have?
    Do you have an alternate plan? (15 minutes)

4   How would you implement your proposed plan? (20 minutes)

5. Hand out the "B" case to read. (5 minutes)

6. What would you do under these dramatically different circumstances?
    What are the   factors you would consider in arriving at a decision to further
    reorganize or do nothing? (15 minutes)

7. Wrap-up. (5 minutes)

Key Summary Lessons

While a matrix structure can be a useful way to direct attention to different
contingencies, it does not resolve all trade-offs that a manager must make,
and thus presents its own difficulties.

An organization's structure is usually closely tied to the way responsibility
centers are defined and control is exercised.

Hill, Holliday, Connors, Cosmopulos, Inc. Advertising (B)

By July 1990, conditions at Hill, Holliday had changed significantly. The following headlines from various news features tell the story.

"Reebok Laces Up With Hill Holliday"
        — *Advertising Age*, April 16, 1990.
The Reebok account had an estimated $40 million in billings.

"Hill Holliday Gets Lotus"
        — *The Wall Street Journal*, June 22, 1990.
Lotus planned to spend $15 million on advertising.

"Upjohn Co. awards Motrin IB account to Hill, Holliday, Connors, Cosmopulos"
        — *The Wall Street Journal*, May 22, 1990.
The Motrin IB account had an estimated $30 million advertising budget.

"Harvard Health Plans on Hill, Holliday"
        — *New England Advertising Week*, July 2, 1990
The Harvard Community Health Plan account was estimated at $4 million.

"Creative Star Shaine Joins Hill, Holliday"
        — *New England Advertising Week*, June 18, 1990.
Shaine joined Hill Holliday as Co-Creative Director and was expected to work in partnership with Vice-Chairman Dick Pantano. Along with two other recent hires to the creative department, Shaine was part of a new creative team at Hill, Holliday that had earned the label of "The Four Horsemen."

Even though some of the pressures for reorganization had diminished under these remarkably changed conditions, much of the proposed reorganization had occurred. Hill,

Professor Nitin Nohria prepared this case as the basis for class discussion rather than to illustrate either effective or ineffective handling of an administrative situation.

Holliday's clients had been divided among four account groups, each of which had responsibility for servicing all of the clients' needs, including general advertising, direct marketing, marketing research, design and strategic planning. However, members of the creative department had not yet been formally assigned to the account groups.

The agency was adjusting to the new structure, and account executives were cautiously optimistic that it would work—that is, that they would be able to service the clients better and to operate more efficiently. Hopefully this would translate into even more new accounts won and a much stronger bottom line. About the reorganization, one account manager said "We expected conflict under the new system, and conflict we have got. In abundance."

Hong Kong TradeLink / Singapore TradeNet

Synopsis

The Singapore/Hong Kong series - *Singapore Leadership, Singapore TradeNet (A), Singapore TradeNet (B)*, and *Hong Kong TradeLink* - enable discussion of the challenges in harnessing information technologies in support of a country's competitive position[5]. The Singapore cases present the story behind the development of an industry-wide information technology (IT)-based platform to facilitate trade documentation processing. TradeNet is critical for the competitive position of Singapore. It involves a partnership of government agencies, bureaus, statutory boards, private agencies, and private companies involved in all aspects of shipment of goods. The Hong Kong case presents a contrasting example of a similar, but less successful initiative.

Singapore Leadership (No. 191 025) examines the political leadership of Singapore, and the so-called "Singapore Miracle. It examines the influence of leadership style and culture in implementing an ambitious IT initiative. The case is written in 1990, just as Prime Minister Lee Kuan Yew prepares to step down. His immediate successor will be Goh Chok Tong, but Yew's son, B.G. Lee, is waiting in the wings. Looking to the future, the case asks: has Singapore laid a solid, sustainable foundation for an information economy?

Singapore TradeNet (A) (No. 191 009), describes Singapore's government and resources, and the country's efforts to "become a world leader in the creation and use of information technologies." It then describes in detail the creation of TradeNet and its use until spring, 1990. The case introduces the following key players:

> Yeo Seng Teck, Chairman of the Trade Development Board (TDB)
> Phillip Yeo, Chairman of EDB and NCB
> Pearleen Chan, CEO Of the newly-formed SNS
> Joe Huber, head of the IBM TradeNet development project

Singapore TradeNet (B) (No. 193 136), continues the story of TradeNet from 1990 through 1993, and briefly describes numerous other commercial networks subsequently built by SNS, including MediNet, LawNet, GraphNet, BizNet, EPCNet, RealNet, StarNet, ProfNet, ApparelNet, ColnNet, OrderLink, MailLink, $Link, InfoLink, COMET, and ManuNet. Pearleen Chan, CEO of SNS, wants her organization to be "the EDI provider for Singapore." They appear to be well established in that role as of 1993.

Hong Kong TradeLink (No. 191 026) maintains that EDI was a "dormant issue" from 1984-1987. This compilation of public-source articles describes the TradeLink project from 1987-1990. They illustrate a poorly coordinated EDI initiative, in contrast to the well-coordinated, rapid development of TradeNet and many subsequent Singapore EDI initiatives.

Teaching Objectives

The apparent success of the Singapore TradeNet effort, and problems in the Hong Kong TradeLink project, invite a review of the factors that contribute to major IT-enabled initiatives and their implementation.

Set in Singapore and Hong Kong, the cases offer students a glimpse of previously developing political economies emerging as major players in the information age. Both political entities have only limited natural and human resources, so information technologies offer a particularly compelling avenue for future growth. Hence, these cases enable discussion of political and societal issues, in addition to the technical and organizational issues.

Finally, the cases also expand the theme of IT-enabled business transformation from an organizational to an *interorganizational* perspective.

Optional Additional Readings

_____, "The Seduction of Singapore," *The Economist*, September 7, 1991, p. 33.

Kelly, B. and M. London. *The Four Little Dragons*. NY: Simon and Schuster, 1989.

Porter, M. *The Competitive Advantage of Nations*. NY: The Free Press, 1990.

Simons, L. "Brave New Singapore." *The Atlantic*, July 1991, pp. 26-31.

Suggested Study Questions

Note: As noted in the "Suggested 80-Minute Lesson Plan" below, the cases can be taught in a single 80-minute session or two 80-minute sessions. For greatest flexibility, we offer separate questions for the Hong Kong case, followed by the questions for the Singapore cases.

Hong Kong TradeLink:

1. What are the arguments in favor of the Hong Kong Government sponsoring an EDI initiative like the Hotline project? What are the arguments in favor of private industry sponsoring an EDI initiative like TradeLink?

2. What do you think of the Hong Kong Government's commitment to the $9 million joint venture with TradeLink?

3. What challenges do the TradeLink sponsors face in planning this system?

Singapore TradeNet (A), (B), and Singapore Leadership:

1. What was Lee Kuan Yew's vision for Singapore? What challenges did he face in reaching his goals?

2. Describe the trade documentation process before and after the implementation of TradeNet. Who were the major stakeholders involved in the process redesign?

3. Evaluate the process used to implement TradeNet. Was it successful? If so, what factors contributed to its success? If not, why not?

4. Compare Hong Kong's TradeLink initiative to Singapore's TradeNet.

5. What impact will TradeNet have on countries outside the Pacific Rim?

6. How close is Pearleen Chan to her goal of making SNS the "EDI leader of Singapore"?

Opportunities for Student Analysis and Discussion

Hong Kong TradeLink

Like Singapore, Hong Kong is a trading center that depends heavily on trade. As in Singapore, visionary leaders saw that EDI offered promise for improving trade; in fact, Hong Kong started an EDI project for trade *before* Singapore did. Yet today, there is no EDI system for trade in Hong Kong. **Exhibit TN-1** reviews the TradeLink story, which centers on the themes, *Who pays?* , *Who benefits?* , and *Who reconciles conflicting interests?*

As promising as Hotline looked, the Hong Kong Trade Facilitation Council had neither the means nor the charter to pay for the system. They asked the Hong Kong government to build it, but the government's position was that businesses, who would benefit from Hotline, should build it. A survey of trading companies noted that most businesses were uneasy about placing competitively sensitive trade data on a system hosted by anyone other than the government.

The government's unwillingness to take the lead on Hotline resulted in a stalemate, until several companies formed the TradeLink organization to study the issue. By the time their report came out, Singapore's TradeNet was turned on, and it was clear that a partnership between the Singapore government and private business had been an appropriate way to bring TradeNet to fruition. SPEDI was created as a result of this realization; as of 1991, their initial report was expected soon.

Lee Kuan Yew's vision for Singapore

The Singapore discussion can begin by asking students to *describe Lee Kuan Yew's vision for Singapore*. This can then lead to a general discussion of the challenges and opportunities that faced Singapore from its birth as an independent city-state to early 1990, the time period covered in *Singapore TradeNet (A)*. Lee's publicly stated vision for Singapore was that it be "recognized as a developed nation by the year 2000." To that end, he embarked on a focused program of economic, educational, and infrastructural development that, many believed, enabled the country to move remarkably close to its goal by the late 1980s. Exhibit 1 in the *Singapore Leadership* case, along with the mention in *Singapore TradeNet (A)* that they had achieved an 87% literacy rate and 74-year life expectancy, confirm this achievement.

Many students are critical of Lee Kuan Yew's methods for moving the country forward. Some students complement Lee on his brilliant, charismatic, visionary leadership; while others criticize his dogmatic, repressive control. Because such a discussion is critical to the later analysis of the TradeNet implementation, it is helpful to capture students' comments for later use. It is important that they consider the possibility of a leadership style that includes both *charismatic, motivational leadership* and *strong control* as elements critical to managing "transformational" change. It may be helpful to have students compare Lee Kuan Yew to Jack Welch, CEO of General Electric, who was leading his company through a major organizational transformation during the same period.

A study of *leadership styles* during the implementation of strategic change[6] identified four tactics - edict, persuasion, participation, and active intervention. The most frequently used, but least successful tactics were edict and persuasion. The most successful tactic was *active intervention*. Students can be asked to classify Yew's approach according to this framework.

At this point, it is helpful to have students turn to Exhibit 1 in the *Singapore TradeNet (A)* case, and consider the *importance of trade to Singapore's success*. Its location, between the Pacific and Indian oceans, makes Singapore a key strategic port for trade in Asia and beyond. The case states that Singapore has "no natural resources" beyond its location and people. Students can be asked to identify Singapore's key competitors for trade business. Hong Kong, Indonesia, and Malaysia are readily identified as key local competitors. Astute students may recognize that TradeNet could influence the competitive picture by expanding Singapore's range of influence. The implication is that Hong Kong and Southeast Asian port cities were not the only ones that could threaten Singapore's trade business by implementing a computer-based trade documentation system.

Establishing direction and developing the Singapore infrastructure

Next, students can address the process by which Singapore's trade process was redesigned to increase its competitiveness. The pre-boarded timeline of activities (**Exhibits TN-1** and **TN-2**) helps students trade the complex series of events. As they review these actions, the three-stage transformation process and key success factors within each stage can be listed on a separate board or series of flip charts (see **Exhibit TN-3**).

Lee's early efforts in defining the vision for Singapore and the infrastructure needed to implement that vision were critical first steps in ensuring TradeNet's success. During the 1970's, the country embarked on a series of initiatives to identify key opportunities for its future economic growth. IT was targeted, and a blue-ribbon Committee on National Computerization was established to identify specific recommendations. The committee's 1980 report confirmed the importance of IT to Singapore's future and the need to create a coherent plan for its development. A massive education effort was mounted, and Singapore also stimulated the use of IT within private industry and government through subsidies and tax-incentive programs. The National Computer Board (NCB) was created and charged with "building Singapore into an IT society." The Government Computerization project was one of the first programs instituted by the NCB.

These early efforts established the importance of IT to Singapore. Networks of key actors were in place to communicate and implement the vision. Capital was invested to ensure that an appropriate technical, organizational, and human infrastructure was in place. By 1986, when TradeNet design and development began, Singapore already had a decade of infrastructure development and education in place. Government agencies were automated, more than 4000 IT professionals were available in the labor force, and the organizational structure to manage a critical system implementation was in place. The instructor may wish to *compare Singapore's actions to those needed within organizations that embark on IT-enabled business transformation*.

Clarifying the focus for change and establishing a transition organization

Whereas early efforts were directed toward IT in general, events in the mid-1980s helped focus efforts on trade. A recession in 1985 caused concern about the country's future, and a high-level committee identified external trade as a key area for focus. News of Hong Kong's efforts to develop Hotline, a trade-oriented computer system (later renamed TradeLink) provided additional impetus. Funds and other government resources were now steered toward improving the trade process and infrastructure.

Early on, in contrast to Hong Kong, Singapore leaders recognized that no single organization could redesign the trade process independently, because it extended across many government agencies and private companies. Identifying relevant stakeholders and ensuring that redesign was based on a "common agreement" among them was another key success factor.

The previous relationship between Philip Yeo (chair of EDB and NCB) and Yeo Seng Teck (chair of TDB) helped them to identify the *need for a partnership* between their independent agencies and then to establish the partnership itself. Their relationship was fostered by the rotation of people through different organizations throughout their careers instead of "insulation" within a single organization. Frequent movement of key individuals among agencies and statutory boards allowed the transfer of knowledge throughout Singapore. Singapore's small size made personnel movements easier than in larger countries (or multinationals), where relocation involves geographic and/or culture changes. Yeo Seng Teck was CEO of EDB before moving to TDB. The CEO of NCB became CEO of EDB after Philip Yeo left that role, and Pearleen Chan moved from NCB to become CEO of SNS.

Together, the "two Yeo's" gained commitment from the necessary parties and provided project leadership. That high-level officials within Singapore had previously worked together closely and effectively was clearly an important factor contributing to the success of TradeNet. The statutory boards themselves are a good example. These quasi-governmental entities, comprising individuals from private business and government, were convened to perform important functions for society. The TradeNet Steering Committee was a special board created specifically to represent the interests of stakeholders and to manage it through the design phase. During implementation a formal organization, Singapore Network Services (SNS) was formed.

These organizations, constituting a social infrastructure for change, helped establish solidarity around the TradeNet vision, and brought together a community of interests that had as many reasons to resist working together as there were to cooperate. An important success factor in this stage of implementation was the actions taken to gain commitment by all interested parties. A process of *cascading levels of commitment* was used in both the *nature of agreements* and the *scope of involvement*.

The *nature of agreement* among stakeholders, early on, is an important point to emphasize. The case states that the initial agreement was to "streamline trade." The project was viewed not as an IT application development project, but as a *business process redesign* project, in which IT was seen as an important tool.

A second important point in understanding the level of commitment is captured by the phrase "agreement to agree." The group was not asked to reach consensus on the design details at this stage. Instead, they were asked to commit to the need for change, the focus, and the need to work together to accomplish the change. Later, as the design took shape, the group was asked to commit to specific design criteria that would change the way they did business. These changes were easier to accept because of the earlier agreements. This process of *cascading commitment* on the *nature of the agreement*, from general agreement on goals and process, to specific design details, was another important factor in the project's success.

Each representative on the committee was an influential leader of a larger group of stakeholders, with a duty to represent their interests and to ensure their commitment. This duty represented a second level of cascading commitment, based on the *scope of involvement* of interested parties (from few to many).

Redesign of the trade process

An important success factor during the design phase was the focus on the larger (interorganizational) process redesign, as opposed to each organization's piece of the process. First the *information content and flow* of the trade process were redesigned by consolidating information on a single form. This single, integrated form served as a visual symbol of integration of the process itself. It helped those involved in the design to clarify the impact on their organizations, which would have to redesign their own internal processes to meet TradeNet's new requirements. The ability to gain collaboration and commitment was fostered through a willingness to communicate a clear message of the change that would be needed. In addition, the single form symbolized the transfer of ownership of information from individual autonomous agencies to the TradeNet process itself.

The next design step was to prototype the redesigned trade process using an existing computer system, Trade Dial-Up. This system provided limited technical functionality, but enabled *proof of the concept* from an "operational" perspective, serving as a prototype of a new set of interorganizational processes. It is useful to ask students to discuss the choice of Merchants Air Cargo, Pte. Ltd. (MAC). Students readily identify the following characteristics:

> MAC was computer literate, had an in-house IT staff, and was considered an innovator in the use of computers to streamline its own operations.

> MAC was an example of "best practice" during development of the TradeNet requirements.

> MAC was a strong supporter of TradeNet and a respected representative for other air cargo freight forwarders.

Traditionally, the key characteristic sought in a prototype site is its "representativeness." MAC was *not* representative; it was "best of breed." *Prototyping during a business process redesign requires a different approach* than when an existing process is being automated. With the latter, the objective is to learn how a system will function in today's world; hence the choice of a "representative" site. If the process is to be transformed, the prototype helps identify the state of the possible, and a "*best of breed*" site is more suitable.

The decision to proceed with TradeNet was not made until after the prototype was assessed. At that point, a firm time frame for completion was set and detailed design begun.

TradeNet technical design and implementation

Most will agree that the technical design and implementation were well managed and successfully executed. Students can evaluate the level of risk inherent in the TradeNet application development project. Most would agree that it is a *high-risk project*. If time permits, the instructor can use the risk framework first presented in Cash, et al[7] to assess the *size, structure,* and *technology* risks of the TradeNet project, as summarized in **Exhibit TN-4**.

The project "went live" on January 1, 1989, meeting their deadline. IBM had only signed the contract 9 months previously - an impressive accomplishment. In addition to actions noted above and in **Exhibit TN-4**, other contributors to the success of the project included:

Strong, cohesive *leadership* at the highest levels of government and industry.

Presence of the necessary technical and human *infrastructure*.

Commitment to *industry standards* and widely available technology (e.g., MS-DOS), and early communication of these to all who would need to interface with the system.

Focus on basic information exchange and transaction-processing systems for initial implementation, while delaying work on database capabilities and user billing modules until after the system went live.

Providing small, medium, and large firms with *flexible usage options* (small firms could use TradeNet terminals in government offices)

To close this discussion, students can be asked to produce "hard" evidence of the benefits of TradeNet. Most point to *time savings,* from 1-4 days to 10-15 minutes to produce trade documents, and the *high user participation,* with approximately 45% of all trade documents processed through TradeNet by the end of its first year.

Beyond TradeNet

The *Singapore TradeNet (B)* case confirms the success of TradeNet, as illustrated in Exhibit 1 of that case. Furthermore, the TradeNet experience has led quickly to a broad SNS portfolio of numerous other EDI initiatives, suggesting that the unique government-business partnership supports significant organizational (and interorganizational) learning. Pearleen Chan is well on her way to the goal of having SNS be "the EDI provider for Singapore."

Students can also speculate on the impact of TradeNet and other Singapore EDI initiatives on countries outside the Pacific Rim. Robert Reich sees business in the future as a "global web" of relationships.[8]   Singapore appears to be positioning itself in the role of global facilitator for international finance and commerce. The instructor might share with students the text of a 1991 advertisement, which appeared in business magazines throughout the world, proclaiming Singapore as "the business architect with global connections... To see how your plans for Asia-Pacific can really take off, have a strategic planning meeting with the Singapore Economic Development Board, anywhere, any time."

In 1990, Lee Kuan Yew stepped down as Prime Minister of Singapore. A 1991 New York Times article summarized Singapore's current challenges[9] :

> *Twenty-six years after (Singapore) declared its independence, the fiber-optic cables are all laid, the skyscrapers are built, the computers are buzzing. But the days of hyperactive growth are over. The country's brilliant but autocratic Prime Minister of 31 years, Lee Kuan Yew, stepped aside a year ago, clearing the way for a new Singapore generation. The question now is whether the new generation can come up with a second act.*

Key Summary Lessons:

To achieve significant IT-enabled transformation, an organization - business, government entity - must first invest in the necessary educational, political, structural, and technical infrastructure that provides the necessary resources (skills, tools, money) to effect the change.

Stakeholder analysis can reveal issues concerning: *Who pays?* , *Who benefits?* , and *Who reconciles conflicting interests?* Interorganizational initiatives often require new ways of evaluating costs and benefits, especially when benefits are deferred until a large number of participants have bought in.

Large, complex, interdependent initiatives are more likely to proceed forward when a process of *cascading commitments*, from general agreement on goals and processes to detailed specifications, permit participants to gradually achieve consensus on the *nature of their agreements* and the *scope of their involvement*.

Project risk - size, structure, and *technology* - can be managed through astute selection of vendors and partners, use of outside consultants, development of various procedures, and attention to individual and organizational learning.

Suggested 80-Minute Teaching Plan

All four cases can be taught in a single 80-minute session, as described below. Alternatively, Hong Kong TradeLink can be taught on Day One, along with a lecture on EDI, interorganizational systems (IOS), business process redesign, and perhaps competitive analysis applied to nations and city-states. Students can be asked to assess how well Hong Kong is doing, and what business and government officials might do differently. Then, on Day 2, the Singapore cases can be discussed in comparison with the Hong Kong initiative.

The following lesson plan assumes a single 80-minute session for all four cases This rich material, however, is better suited to a two-class approach (or, for evening classes, a single 3-hour session).

1. How well is the Hong Kong TradeLink project going? (10 minutes)
   Review **Exhibit TN-1**

2. What is Lee Kuan Yew's vision for Singapore? What were the challenges and opportunities facing Singapore in the Eighties? (10 minutes)

3. TradeNet: Establishing Direction (15 minutes)
   Review Case Exhibit 1 (map): how important is trade to Singapore?

   What roles did Phillip Yeo and Yeo Seng Teck play ? Who else was involved early on? Note the small geographic size of Singapore, the frequent job rotation, and other mechanisms to facilitate the transfer of information and developing relationships.

   Note that news of Hong Kong's HotLine effort mobilized Singapore.
   Cascading Commitment: How important was the "agreement to agree"?

4. TradeNet: Early Design (10 minutes)
   What was the significance of the move from 20+ forms to a single form?
   Note: avoided "automating a mess;" emphasized business process redesign

5. TradeNet Implementation (10 minutes)
   Elements of Project Risk (see **Exhibit TN-4**)
   Review **Exhibit TN-2**

6. Singapore TradeNet Versus Hong Kong TradeLink (5 minutes)
   (Exhibits TN-1 and TN-2)

7. Beyond TradeNet: Singapore (B) (10 minutes)

8. Wrap-Up: Exhibits **TN-3**

Exhibit TN-1

Hong Kong TradeLink Implementation

1983   Hong Kong government creates Trade Facilitation Council, explores EDI

1984   Hotline proposed by the Council
Hong Kong government refuses to fund:
     "It's up to the private sector"
Private sector wants a neutral facilitator;
     Stalemate!

1987   Concern over TradeNet
Eight companies pull out of Trade Facilitation; form TradeLink
Coopers & Lybrand hired to study
Hong Kong government offers to contribute 10% of cost

Nov. 1988   TradeLink estimated completion date: 1990

Mar. 1990   Hong Kong government funds $9Million SPEDI project, to "speed up" TradeLink development

May 1991   SPECI project still studying the issue

Exhibit TN-2

Singapore TradeNet Implementation

1970s   IT targeted as a national initiative; CNC formed.

1980s   National education/literacy initiatives
Technology placed in government agencies/businesses

1986   Recession and news of Hotline spur development of TradeNet
TDB takes initiative to get all stakeholders to agree to participate
TradeNet Steering Committee formed

Dec. 1986   B.G. Lee formally announces TradeNet. Deadline: 1/1/89
Commits full authority/resources

Feb. 1987   Price Waterhouse Market Study
Pre-qualification solicitation (RFI):
       23 responses, 3 firms are finalists

Sept. 1987 RFPs from 3 firms

Dec. 1987 IBM wins bid, requests design review before signing contract

Mar. 1988 Singapore Network Services (SNS) created

May 1988   Contract with IBM signed

Jan. 1989   System Operational 1/1/89

June 1989 TradeNet completed

Exhibit TN-3

IT-Enabled Business Transformation

Establish Direction	Design/Redesign	Implementation
Define broad vision for change	Select partners	Develop roll-out schedule
Build Infrastructure: Human, Technical, Capital	Develop detailed design: process redesign structure, control, people, technology	Implement Change
Clarify vision, establish focus proof-of-concept prototype	Implement technology -- use project management tools, techniques	Manage individual and organiz'l learning
Gain commitment in cascading levels of agreement	Manage Risks	Keep on schedule and within budget
Assess risk/return	Detailed cost/benefit analysis	Develop education, communication materials
		Re-examine direction, design

Exhibit TN-4

TradeNet: Project Risks (Size, Structure, Technology)

Size: Large, complex project involving multiple interdependent users and vendors, high cost.
SNS, a new organization, lacks experience managing a project of this scale/scope.
Singapore statutory boards do have experience in successfully developing major,
capital-intensive projects.

Actions taken to manage project size:
Vendors selected based on track record for managing big, complex projects.
IBM's "Tampa Engine" would contribute 1.25 million lines of assembly code.
Custom coding on TradeNet's Information Exchange Engine: only 3000 lines.
Choice of Singapore's Computer Systems Advisors retained future expertise and
control over application code.
SNS personnel were on the application development team, ensuring transfer of
expertise to the organization responsible for the code in the future.

Project Structure:
Many, but not all, project requirements and outputs were specified.
Much uncertainty about translating requirements into technical specifications.
Much uncertainty about ability to interface with other government, industry systems.

Actions taken to manage project structure:
Price Waterhouse (PW) evaluated, defined requirements of 2200 agencies and firms.
PW studied basic information-processing needs of the trading industry.
PW specified applications that would enable TradeNet to function effectively.
IBM 3-month design review reassessed technical requirements and design.

Experience with the Technology:
SNS application development team lacked experience with necessary technologies.

Actions taken to manage technology risk:
Use of IBM's "Tampa Engine" substantially mitigated technical risk.
An experienced system integrator, IBM transferred knowledge to SNS and CSA
early in the project.

The Incident at Waco Manufacturing

Synopsis

This one-page, "armchair" case describes a fictitious incident involving controversial use of data collected through a company's "active badge" system. The issues raised in the case have been addressed in recent court battles concerning employees' privacy rights.

Employees at the fictitious "Waco Manufacturing" wear active badges which enables their whereabouts to be recorded throughout a large manufacturing plant. When a manager (Monk Barber) is criticized for falling behind on a critical project, he blames the lack of progress on three employees. Barber's supervisor, Monique Saltz, examines the active-badge tracking data, which reveals that the manager and his four team members have never been in the same room at the same time (or, more accurately, their badges have not been in the same room at the same time).

The implicit questions posed by this case are: has this manager overstepped her bounds in examining the data recorded in this system? Under what circumstances should firms invest in technologies that monitor employee behavior in this way? How might such technologies alter the explicit or implied contract between employer and employee, and what guidelines should govern their use?

Teaching Objectives

This case helps raise new issues concerning *employee privacy* which have come about as a result of technologies that enable organizations to more easily gather data, combine it with data in other databases, and analyze it more easily and inexpensively than ever before. The case can be positioned within a segment on IT and human resources issues, IT and employee privacy, IT and privacy in general (employee, customer, citizen), or IT and ethical dilemmas.

In *Building the Information-Age Organization* this case is placed in Chapter 5, *IT and the Individual*, which examines IT-driven changes in work tasks, working arrangements, and human resources issues. It is positioned after the Internal Revenue Services case, in which a new computer-based system includes employee monitoring and close tracking of individual productivity. In the IRS case, employee monitoring, combined with new working arrangements, leads to high dissatisfaction and turnover. In the Waco Manufacturing case, employees are apparently unaware that location-tracking data has been retained by management, and it is not clear whether the organization has developed any guidelines concerning who should have access to these data, and for what purposes.

Suggested Optional Reading:

Gogan, Janis L. and Jeanne W. Ross, "Managers and the Privacy Gap." Boston University School of Management Working Paper 91-71, 1991.

Kallman, Ernest A. "Private Matters". *Computerworld* 26(47): 85-87, November 23, 1992.

Johnson, Maryfran. "Wherever you go, They will Follow: Active Badges Allow Computer Network to Keep Silent Tabs on Employees' Whereabouts." *Computerworld,* July 15,1991.

Lacayo, Richard. "Nowhere to Hide." *Time,* November 11, 1991: 34ff.

Mason, Richard O. "Four Ethical Issues of the Information Age," *MIS Quarterly* 10(1): 5-12, March 1986.

Suggested Study Questions:

1. What are the benefits of a location-tracking system such as that described in the case?

2. What should Tomaso and Saltz do next?

3. What policies or guidelines would you suggest for governing the storage of and access to location data collected by the system?

Opportunities for Student Analysis

The case examines issues of privacy, management control, and ethical behavior. Despite its brevity (less than one page), it provokes a rich and controversial discussion.

Is the Data Accurate?

I start by asking what Monique Saltz and her boss, Shelley Tomaso should do next. While some students are immediately ready to discipline Monk Barber, who they believe has been "nailed" with incontrovertible evidence, other students - typically those with more experience - are usually more cautious. This initial discussion should reveal that the *accuracy* of the data which Saltz and Tomaso have just reviewed has not been established. The "active badge" technology has tremendous potential for capturing accurate information about employees' whereabouts, but one must immediately question whether conditions that would guarantee accurate tracking are really in place. For example, often an experienced student will observe that there is no guarantee in the case that employees wear their badges at all times. One of my students observed that "I don't want people able to reach me by phone at any moment of the day; I would only wear my badge if it was necessary to get through a security door." The instructor might at this point call to students' attention examples in the Mason article (listed above), in which inaccurate data about individuals caused them great harm. Or, mention the case of citizens of Norwich, Vermont, many of whom were incorrectly listed as having defaulted on their property taxes and subsequently were denied credit (see Gogan and Ross, above). It is not necessary to dwell on the issue of data accuracy for long at this point, but it is helpful to air it briefly so you can return to it in the wrap-up lecture.

Is this an Invasion of Privacy?

Next the instructor might ask students to assume that the data are accurate - Monk Barber has not met with the three engineers. Now what should Saltz and Tomaso do? Do they confront Barber with the data which they have just obtained from the system? At this point a student may comment that looking at such data may be illegal. "Employee privacy" has a rather ambiguous legal status. In general, certain specific employee information - such as medical data - is fairly well protected. Much job-related employee information - productivity rates, employee evaluations, travel expenses, etc. - is generally considered the "property" of the hiring organization, and not subject to privacy protection. Recent court cases concerning monitoring of employee electronic mail have been decided in favor of the employer, but publicity concerning these cases (such as Alana Shoars v. Epson) seems to be generating a lot of support for legislation limiting employer rights to access to some employee information.

This can lead into a discussion of IT and privacy issues. Students can be asked to define "privacy" and give examples of incidents which they feel would constitute an "invasion of privacy." This discussion can go on as long as the instructor will let it, since there is no one, widely-held definition of privacy invasion. A 1985 study[i] asked respondents to indicate the "perceived seriousness of various privacy invasions," some of which are listed below and can be mentioned if the discussion does not immediately take off:

> A person's previous medical health records are obtained by an insurance company without his or her consent after that person is involved in an automobile accident.

> A magazine company sells its subscriber list so that other companies can try to sell you goods and services.

---

[i] Neil Vidmar and David H. Flaherty. "Concern for Personal Privacy in an Electronic Age." *Journal of Communication* 35: 9-103, Spring 1985.

A closed-circuit TV monitor is installed in a work place so that worker behavior and productivity can be observed.

A government agency makes a list of the persons who attend a political meeting.

One store gives another store credit information about a customer who applies for a charge account.

Students can also be asked, in what ways can information technologies be used to invade one's privacy? The readings give numerous examples, a few of which are listed below:

An Ohio car dealership used video cameras to record license plate numbers of cars parked in their lot, which were easily matched with a Division of Motor Vehicles database to obtain the names of individuals browsing their lots after hours. The dealership followed up with sales calls, but some of these were met with complaints of privacy invasion.

Alana Shoars, an employee at Epson, is fired after her boss intercepts e-mail messages she sent someone else, in which she is critical of actions he has taken.

When news leaks of confidential plans appeared in the *Wall Street Journal*, Procter and Gamble managers authorized a computerized search of Cincinnati-area phone records, to identify who had called the *Wall Street Journal* reporter.

Management Goals versus Privacy Invasion

At this point it can be helpful to ask students to step back a moment and consider why Waco Manufacturing installed the system in the first place. What do you make of these active badges? The case describes them as part of a "security and information system." What sort of security risks do companies try to protect against? Students who have worked in defense-related industries may note that often there are areas where only individuals with a certain clearance level are authorized to enter. Students from electronics industries may note that theft is a big problem, and indeed, many computer chips and other expensive devices are easy to conceal on one's person. A discussion of the various tools and techniques used to secure a company's physical or intellectual property can help students see that companies have a range of choices in addition to active badges to prevent personnel from entering areas where they are not authorized, or keep track of who enters such areas. Many firms require employees to carry picture IDs. Some firms have high-tech entry systems that use voice recognition, finger-printing, even eye-tracking to establish an individual's identity. Other firms rely on security personnel or video monitoring to observe goings-on.

Why else is Waco using active badges? A student should note that this technology helps facilitate communication, since "a telephone call to an employee would ring at the phone nearest that person." A brief discussion can help students see that active badges are but one of several technologies that can help employees stay in touch. Public-address and paging systems, beepers, cellular phone, and other communication technologies could also be selected. Hence, students can see that firms have good reasons for investing in technologies like active badges, but they also have numerous alternatives.

Given that the system is in place, what policies should govern its use? Here the instructor has a choice: the students can be assigned to teams which will meet and report back at the next class (if a 2-class sequence is planned), or remain in the classroom to work on this question as a group. The assignment is to develop a policy governing a) access to the data generated by this system and/or b) access to other employee data (medical, lifestyle, job performance, electronic mail messages, paper mail, etc.). The policy should include:

> a definition of employee privacy
> brief statement of intent;
> definition of the types of data covered by the policy;
> specification of what data shall be retained, by whom, for how long, and for
>> what purposes;
> specification of the circumstances under which access to the data will be
>> granted;
> specification of a process for resolving employee privacy complaints.

Wrap-Up Lecture

The enclosed transparencies (**Exhibits TN-1, TN-2, TN-3 and TN-4**) reinforce the following themes:

> There is no single, universally-understood definition for "Privacy" or "Invasion of Privacy."

> Privacy law has not kept up with IT capabilities for data capture, storage, manipulation, and dissemination.

> Customer privacy has also become a big issue (preferably an entire class session would be devoted to this concern, using perhaps Lotus Marketplace: Households case - No. 9-392-026)

Management expectations for control may conflict with employee expectations for privacy, creating poor employee morale and even leading to lawsuits such as Shoars v. Epson.

Specific steps can be taken to "reduce the privacy gap."

Suggested 80-Minute Class Plan

1. What should Tomaso and Saltz do next?
   Do they have evidence that the team never met?
   Should Monk Barber be disciplined? Why/why not? (10 minutes)

2. Has Monk Barber's privacy been violated? Why/why not?
   How would you define "privacy"?
   How do you know when privacy has been violated? Is privacy an inalienable right?
   Do employees have privacy "rights"? Under what circumstances? (10 minutes)

3. Why did Waco Manufacturing invest in active badges?
   Why might other firms use them?
   Have you worked in an organization that used this technology?
   By what other means can organizations achieve the benefits they are trying to get
   with active badges? (e.g. security measures - passwords, fingerprints, voice
   recognition, eye tracking: communication measures - beepers, paging systems,
   cellular phones) (15 minutes)

4. Prepare a corporate policy concerning employee data and privacy. Specify the
   circumstances under which employee privacy will/will not be protected.
   Specify how access to employee data will be controlled. (20 minutes)
   In a 2-class sequence, this breakout assignment can be given at the end of this class. In the
   next class, students present their policy statements and the instructor wraps up with a lecture.
5. Lecture: IT and Privacy Concerns
   See **Exhibits TN-1, TN-2, TN-3, and TN-4** (15-20 minutes)

Key Summary Lessons

Choices concerning the use of information technologies to strengthen
management control may infringe upon employees' perceived privacy rights.
At a minimum, such choices should be made with an explicit understanding
of legal considerations and management and employee expectations.

Once information is revealed, it cannot easily be retracted. Hence,
management actions which may violate an individual's privacy should be
taken with full consideration of the possible ramifications for the individual
and the organization.

Organizations should develop and periodically review formal policies
governing the collection of and access to data concerning employees. Such
policies should conform to legal constraints and recognize employee and
employer expectations.

Private:

"intended for or affecting a particular person, group, or class"

"belonging to or concerning an individual person, company, or interest"

"not known or intended to be known publicly"

Privacy:

freedom from inappropriate surveillance

freedom from unwanted disclosure of private information

Privacy Issues:

What constitutes "inappropriate" surveillance?

What constitutes "private" information?

Legal Definitions of Privacy

Warren and Brandeis, 1890: "the right to be let alone"

Prosser, 1960: Invasion of Privacy:

1. intrusion upon one's seclusion or solitude

2. public disclosure of embarassing private facts

3. publicity that places one in a false light
   in the public eye

4. appropriation of plaintiff's name or likeness, by
   one who uses it for his or her benefit

Related Concepts: ownership

                             public

                             libel

                             free speech

Privacy and Information Technologies

Advanced information technologies facilitate:

data capture (scanners, voice recognition)

data storage (CD-ROM)

data manipulation (relational, object-oriented data)

data dissemination (networks, floppy diskettes)

"Privacy law

has failed to respond ... to technological changes that influence the degree of privacy to which we are accustomed... the computer alters the context in which privacy is defined."

- Graham, 1987

The Privacy Gap:

Marketers' expectations
            conflict with
                        customers' expectations.

Managers' expectations
            conflict with
                        employees' expectations

Consequences of ignoring the Privacy Gap:

    sunk costs/lost revenues
    lawsuits
    erosion of customer goodwill
    restrictive laws
    reduced employee morale

The Internal Revenue Service: ACS

Synopsis

This case shows how the IRS used information technology to greatly increase the productivity and effectiveness of a collections process that traditionally involved a complicated, labor-intensive and error-prone paper trail. The new system rationalized the work and brought more control through electronic monitoring. However, it also raised dissatisfaction among employees, who felt "chained to the computer" and were concerned about violation of their privacy rights because of the extensive use of electronic monitoring.

Teaching Objectives

The case examines how information technology:

> enables the redesign of a cumbersome business process,
>
> creates a new way of organizing work, and
>
> offers a wholly different level of control (a high degree of action or behavior control)
>> in a setting in which control was previously hard to achieve.

It also shows the unintended consequences which occur when the organizational and social ramifications are not considered. The electronic monitoring feature of the ACS system raises important ethical issues concerning IT and employee privacy.

Suggested Optional Reading:

Thomas Davenport and James Short, The New Industrial Engineering: Information Technology and Business Process Redesign," *Sloan Management Review*, Summer 1990.

Michele Galen, "Is Your Boss Spying on You?" *Business Week*, (January 15, 1990): 74-75.

Glen Rifkin, The Ethics Gap," *Computerworld* October 14, 1991, pp. 83-88.

Suggested Study Questions

> 1. Evaluate the change of the IRS's Collection function from the COF organization to the ACS system.

> 2. As Tim Brown, Assistant Commissioner for Collection, what would you do?

3. When, if ever, is computer monitoring appropriate? What safeguards can
   you envision that would protect an individual's right to privacy given
   the invasive potential of information technology?

Opportunities for Student Analysis and Discussion

Context of the IRS's collection operations

There are several background issues that must be borne in mind while teaching this case. The key points to note are:

> There are a lot of dollars at stake (a total of about $1 trillion in taxes collected by the IRS every year).

> As the primary revenue-generating arm of the Federal government, there are enormous pressures on the IRS to become more efficient, particularly in the light of a huge budget deficit, combined with a conservative atmosphere that makes raising taxes very difficult.

> It is difficult for the IRS to recruit new employees, since salaries in the private sector are more attractive. Those who do join the IRS view the Collection job as a first step from which they want to move on. Also, a large cohort of IRS managers will be retiring in the coming years.

> Overall, the IRS has a fairly old technology infrastructure and poor leadership of the I/T function.

> The IRS is a visible, highly scrutinized agency. Capital projects are audited internally and externally and auditors' reports are considered very seriously in approving new projects. Thus the IRS is under great pressure to make technology projects succeed and to learn from each initiative.

Assessing the change from the COF to the ACS system

A useful way to start the class is by asking: What are the key measures by which you would judge the performance of the Collection operations? This brings out the key metrics by which we can judge the performance of the new ACS system relative to the old COF system. It also gives students an opportunity to practice some of the concepts learned in the control chapter of the book (Chapter 3). The key metrics include operational indicators such as:

> number of cases processed and closed,
> percent of accounts receivable that are collected,
> employee productivity, accuracy and quality of cases processed;

measures of employee satisfaction such as grievances and turnover; and potentially, measures of customer service such as

      timeliness and quality of response, and

      quality of customer interaction.

Having established these performance criteria, one can then ask students to evaluate the change from COF to ACS.

In addition to assessing the performance of the new system, it is also useful to press students to analyze exactly how Collection operations have changed. During this discussion, one should try and cover as many of the issues summarized in **Exhibit TN-1** as possible.

After students have discussed how things have changed, I ask them to evaluate the new system again; in particular to explain why there was so much dissatisfaction with the new system. This often generates a heated debate, with about half the class feeling that the real problem was that employees felt the technology was controlling their work lives and invading their privacy. The other half of the class suggest that the most serious problem is not computer monitoring but the disruption of the friendly social system that existed earlier, and the sense that the new system produces feelings of isolation and anomie and drains employees' intrinsic motivation. A small number of students may feel that the technology itself -- as in all other cases -- is neutral. They argue that it is managers' choices which determine either the effective or ineffective use of the technology. This debate has enough energy to go for quite a long time and during the course of this discussion several ethical issues surrounding the impacts of information technology get raised. This heated debate is a great set-up for the action question: What should Tim Brown, the Commissioner of IRS Collections, do?

Changes that should be made to the ACS system

The discussion of what Tim Brown should do usually centers around the three alternatives presented at the end of the case:

    1) work teams;

    2) individuals working cases to completion; or

    3) an improved monitoring process.

    The advantage of a *team approach* is that it can enhance both identification with the task and the quality of social relationships. The immediate cost is that hardware will have to be retrofitted to assign inventory by teams. Training costs will also rise because each team member has to know all three functions. This will also affect wages. A move to teams can therefore be expected to take the longest time.

    The option of *individuals working their cases to completion* will also necessitate extra training. adaptation to the technology, and wage increases.

131

The last option, *leave things as they are*, but concentrate on the supervision process, is the least costly. However, it also has the least potential payoff, since individuals will still be working only on bits and pieces of the cases.

Even if the first two options are preferred by students they still have to deal with the supervision issue (i.e., option three will have to be addressed as part of the first two options). Irrespective of which option they prefer, it is important to ask students <u>how</u> they would go about implementing their proposal, specifically in terms of who they would involve in the design of the system. This gets at the topic of user involvement -- which in this case seems very desirable.

Another interesting question which can summarize the case would be to have students take the role of a Congressional auditor and do the equivalent of a project audit. They would assess what the Collection function should learn from this project and recommend how to proceed with future automation efforts. This exercise provides a natural way of summarizing the discussion and giving students an opportunity to produce the take-aways.

Post-Script: What has happened since the case was written

The Collection function has moved to a team based approach. Each team is given a batch of cases, and they are responsible for the whole case load. They make decisions about scheduling and assigning cases to different individuals and they are responsible for monitoring the performance of the group as a whole. The monitoring technology is still being employed, but with greater emphasis on feedback rather than evaluation. The team structure has not yet been implemented everywhere. Technology bugs delayed the project (as did the fact that this time there was much more active user input). Initial evidence from those sites that have adopted the new team approach is that there has not been much further improvement in operational efficiency to date. However, surveys report higher employee satisfaction and lower turnover. Turnover is still higher than under the old COF system (many people do not like the technology). There is considerable variance across offices, suggesting that how the technology is used and the office atmosphere are important determinants of the success of IT initiatives in work organizations.

Suggested 80-Minute Teaching Plan

1. Introductory remarks (5 minutes)

2. What key performance measures would you use to evaluate the performance of the IRS's Collection function? (5 minutes)

3. Describe and evaluate the change from COF to ACS. (20 minutes)

4. Why are employees dissatisfied with the ACS system? How legitimate are their complaints? Does ACS represent an ethically appropriate use of information technology? What steps should be taken to minimize potential abuses of the system and to protect individuals' privacy rights? (30 minutes)

5. What should Tim Brown do next? How should he implement the option he chooses? (15 minutes)

6. Wrap-up and concluding remarks (5 minutes)

Key Summary Lessons

Business Process Redesign. IT is a powerful tool to enhance organizational performance by facilitating the redesign of segmented work processes.

IT-Based Controls. IT enables unprecedented levels of "output control" (monitoring the results of work) and "behavioral control" (monitoring work as it takes place, such as employees' conversations with clients). Both work process and employee performance controls are available to management.

Organization of work matters. Employees under the new ACS system complained that they were unable to see their work through to completion. Moreover, they felt chained to their terminals eight hours a day. The loss of morale that can occur as a result of such poor choices in task design is important to avoid in designing an IT based work process.

No strong determinism to technology. Work organization is not totally determined by the technology. Indeed, managers can exercise quite a bit of discretion, which often determines how the technology is received by employees. For example, a system can be programmed to initiate work automatically, or this can be left to worker discretion. IRS managers decided to leave this up to the worker. With modifications to the system, an inventory of cases can be assigned to single individuals or teams. Also, monitoring can be used either as a positive coaching tool or a negative controlling tool.

133

	COF:	**ACS:**
Technology:	manual work using typewriter, pencils, calculators, computerized data base, step by step prescription for manual proceeding cases.	computer based, automated collection system; automated case retrieval, telephone dialing, letter generation, etc.
Work process:	diversified functions consisting of six groups of work procedures; frequent job rotation.	rationalization of job functions from six to three; quicker response time.
Control of work process:	control of accuracy of cases by supervisor reviewing employees' completed cases; substantial self-control by employees.	computer control of work generated, computer tracking of work in process.
Performance control:	control of work results and occasionally of work process by supervisor.	constant control of work results by computer; threat of constant control of work behaviors via telephone monitoring.
Supervisor's role:	full richness of supervisor's functions: planning, organizing, controlling.	almost singularly focused on the monitoring of performance.
Interactions with peers	frequent, concentrated around work and personal issues.	little interaction; lack of work interdependence shaping interactions.
Office climate:	busy, nonrestricted movement; a lot of interaction with peers.	individual cubicles, interactions with peers discouraged by supervisors.

Jacobs Suchard

Synopsis

In May 1989 Klaus Jacobs, CEO of Swiss-based Jacobs Suchard, a producer and marketer of coffee and confectionery products, considers what further steps to take after reorganizing the firm to better face the challenges of the coming unified European Common Market.

Teaching Objectives

The Jacobs Suchard case gives students an opportunity to examine a European company considering how to respond to what was expected to be a dramatic environmental change: the advent of the 12-nation European Economic Community. Klaus Jacobs wants his firm to be fully prepared to take advantage of lowered physical, technical, and fiscal barriers between European countries. Since this case the opening of Eastern Europe, war in Bosnia, and other events have made doing business in Europe even more complicated.

This case provides an opportunity to discuss issues that arise when the structure of an organization no longer complements the organization's strategy or competitive environment. In this example, the new Europe would dramatically reduce the need for local manufacturing, logistics, and marketing. Jacobs Suchard's structure, which was appropriate in a localized regulatory environment, would be burdened with excessive manufacturing and coordination costs in the expected unified regulatory environment. But a proposed new structure would dramatically change the roles of the business unit general managers who had played pivotal roles in the old Europe.

The case can be used either narrowly or broadly. When used narrowly, students can focus on questions of organizational structure, and engage in an in-depth discussion of the pros and cons of various structural alternatives, ending with a brief "bridge" discussion of management control issues to set up the next segment of the course. If used broadly, the case can serve as an integrative vehicle for discussing every element of the People, Information and Technology framework (although the case itself offers no information about IT management at Jacobs Suchard).

Suggested Optional Readings

Bartlett, Christopher A. and Sumantra Ghoshal. "Managing Across Borders: New Strategic Requirements." *Sloan Management Review*, Summer 1987: 7-17.

Bartlett, Christopher A. and Sumantra Ghoshal. "Managing Across Borders: New Organizational Responses." *Sloan Management Review*, Fall 1987: 45-53.

Bellack, Daniel W. "Exploiting EEC Marketing Potential." *Public Relations Journal* 46(1): 14-15, January 1990.

Francis-Laribee. "American Companies Exploring Networks in Europe: Alternatives. *Journal of Systems Management* 45(5): 6-11, April 1994.

Suggested Study Questions

1. How would you react to the changes that have already been announced at Jacobs Suchard if you were:
    a. a country manager?
    b. a manager of an international manufacturing center (IMC)?
    c. a global brand sponsor?

2. What would be your recommendations for the future if you were:
    a. a country manager?
    b. a manager of an international manufacturing center (IMC)?
    c. a global brand sponsor?

3. Looking ahead, what should Klaus Jacobs, chairman and CEO of Jacobs Suchard, do?

Opportunities for Student Analysis

Impact of the EEC

One or more students - preferably Europeans - can be asked to describe the changes in Europe that have come about with the European Economic Community (EEC). If you are teaching no other cases addressing this issue, it is an ideal opportunity to engage students in a brief discussion of the impacts so far of this change, as well as the unfulfilled expectations to date (for example, at this printing European nations are still far from consensus on a single European currency). One might begin by asking European students to describe how their lives as consumers, students, vacationers and employees have been changed by the EEC.

After a brief look at the EEC from a consumer perspective, the instructor can then ask students to discuss the implications of the EEC for companies doing business in Europe. What new opportunities arise? What are the strategic and organizational challenges? The goal of this discussion is to help students recognize that the reduced technical, fiscal, and physical barriers across European borders create both opportunities - to produce and sell more easily in multiple countries - and challenges - to achieve a strategy and a structure that capitalizes on these new opportunities and to be effectively positioned against competitors who are also changing to capitalize on these opportunities. Students should easily see that in many industries the switch-over to the EEC would necessitate a new look at marketing, manufacturing, finance and other activities. Under the old system of separate regulations and standards governing production, safety, transportation, data flows and other elements, many companies needed a local presence in each of the countries they served. Now those local offices and factories represent an unacceptable level of duplication and inefficiency. For US students, it is easy to drive this point home by asking if a US confectionery company would have separate chocolate factories in Massachusetts, Connecticut, Vermont, New Hampshire, Maine and New York - an area comparable in size to France, Germany, Switzerland, Austria and Belgium. A side board can be used to record students' comments on the EEC.

Jacobs Suchard in 1987

Students can then be asked to consider Jacobs Suchard's position at the end of 1987, when Klaus Jacobs asked Robert Carrott to implement the Vision 2000 recommendations. How healthy was the company in 1987? What specific opportunities and challenges did they face? A quick look at case Exhibit 1 reveals good progress in sales growth and income as a percentage of sales. Yet there are indications of inefficiency. For example, sales per employee had declined from more than sf480,000 in 1984 to about sf380,000 in 1987. The big jump in headcount (60% increase, from about 10,000 to about 16,000 employees) suggests that the 1987 acquisitions of E.J. Brach and Cote d'Or had not yet been accompanied by a correspondingly high sales increase. The confectionery division seems particularly inefficient, with 76% of the employees producing only 45% of the revenues.

Furthermore, the case description of the 19 confectionery manufacturing facilities, each producing only about 5000 tons of product, suggests there is ample opportunity to improve productivity by rationalizing manufacturing. Indeed, what Klaus Jacobs describes as an opportunity to improve the efficiency of operations is more likely a necessity, given the potential threat of new, leaner and more aggressive companies eager to grow market share in a unified Europe. The punch-line of this part of the discussion is the students' realization that Jacobs Suchard faces a compelling need to improve both their marketing and their operational efficiency. It is easy to see the potential benefits of consolidated manufacturing, especially for the basic ingredients like cocoa liquor and chocolate mass. The idea of global marketing is also highly appealing, although the margin of error also looks pretty large, due to varying consumer preferences on taste, texture, size, packaging, and languages used on the wrappers.

A side board can be used to record a few students' comments on Jacobs Suchard's performance and issues. Save some room for a few comments on the potential role of IT at Jacobs Suchard, as discussed next.

Potential Role of IT

The case unfortunately does not discuss the management of information technologies at Jacobs Suchard. However, it is helpful at this point to ask students to consider the implications of a unified Europe and potential changes in marketing and manufacturing strategies for information-resource management. Clearly there will be a need for closer attention to IT architecture issues, especially data management. Marketing will face the challenge of continuing to satisfy differentiated regional tastes while also introducing products with wide appeal. Test-marketing and promotional data will be far more refined, and there will be a far greater need to analyze these data to identify patterns in consumer tastes and buying behavior across regions. As for manufacturing, in order to consolidate production in a smaller number of sites, it will also be necessary to develop more sophisticated demand forecasts and order fulfillment systems.

It may be useful at this point to ask students to compare the potential role of IT at Jacobs Suchard with that at Mrs. Fields Cookies, another company producing a perishable consumer product. In that case discussion, students learned how IT can support central control of highly dispersed operations. However, there is a critically important difference between Mrs. Fields and Jacobs Suchard that should be drawn out in the discussion. At Mrs. Fields, there is very little need for demand forecasting. The basic ingredients of production are not highly perishable, and production occurs virtually on demand. That is, if a Mrs. Fields store manager realizes that they have run out of chocolate macadamia-nut cookies, s/he has literally about 12 minutes (the time it takes to mix and bake a fresh batch of cookies) to rectify the situation. If the shop owner realizes that there are too many chocolate macadamia-nut cookies on the rack, s/he can send an employee out on the street or in the shopping mall with samples to increase demand for that product. Production and sales are thus tightly linked at Mrs. Fields, with or without their sophisticated information systems. In contrast, at Jacobs Suchard there is a much longer link between sales and production. The lost opportunity if too few of a particular brand or size are produced can be substantial, and there can be similarly high costs if too much is produced (chocolates are perishable, although we are not given information in the case about their shelf-life). Complicating the demand-forecasting task are the fluctuating prices of the basic confectionery ingredients, a point which is made in the case. Under the old organizational scheme, Jacobs Suchard country general managers were responsible for striking this important balance between local supply/production and local demand/sales. Well managed, information technologies can help the company continue to effectively balance supply and demand while also supporting global marketing and achieving economies of scale which were unattainable in the geographically divisionalized organization.

Comparison of Alternative Structures

Now students can be asked to discuss the various approaches taken to restructure formal reporting relationships and decision rights at Jacobs Suchard. Because the case chronology is quite confusing as written, it may be useful to provide students with a handout such as is provided in **Exhibit TN-1**, in order to avoid unnecessary class time being given over to clarifying the case facts. To summarize:

Before the strategic shift to "global" brands and consolidated manufacturing, country general managers had jobs which they themselves considered represented the pinnacle of their careers. In each country the general manager had full profit and loss responsibility for trade marketing (sales), consumer marketing, and manufacturing, usually (but not always) for a single core category (coffee or confectionery). Unless they set unrealistically high goals, they participated in a bonus system that compensated them very well, for activities over which they had a high degree of control. There was a good fit between performance measurement and evaluation of general managers and their compensation. Most were apparently quite content with this arrangement, and the company generally showed an acceptable rate of growth in sales and profits. Were it not for the activity of the EEC, this arrangement might have continued for quite some time, for competition in the confectionery industry was generally on a regional basis, and Jacobs Suchard was able to hold its own in most markets (although it was not always the market leader). With reduced trade barriers, however, came a far more compelling rationale for economies of scale in marketing and manufacturing, and management concluded that the old structure was inadequate.

Vision 2000 and the Issenmann task force took manufacturing away from the purview of the country general managers, in order to reduce the inefficiencies inherent in local production of short, varied runs. This greatly reduced the general managers' control over the cost side of their profit equation, as well as over some of the factors that had traditionally gone into their bonus scheme. In addition, the first step was taken to provide for a structure - global brand sponsors - that would give increased attention to more broadly based consumer marketing, which further reduced the authority of the general managers. These two steps helped focus attention on global issues, but opened up a Pandora's box of conflict over resource allocation and decision rights.

The Harvard Business School team attempted to clarify matters and alter this structure in order to better align the new strategy with a new set of formal reporting relationships. By separating the role of global brand sponsor from that of general manager, this team was attempting to remove conflicting local and global interests away from individuals below the level of the Confectionery EVP (Zinser). The team also clarified that the general managers would no longer have consumer marketing responsibilities- further reducing their power and giving them fewer levers to influence the direction of their business activity or the size of their bonuses. On the other hand, the country managers are left with an easily measured activity to maximize (sales), so possibly some of them will be content to have a less complex (but also less prestigious and probably less well-compensated) job. By adding an organizational layer consisting of five global brand sponsors, a sales manager and a manufacturing manager, this team was attempting to provide a stronger mechanism for global coordination.

As of May 1990, the Harvard team's recommendations have not been accepted, and Klaus Jacobs has chosen to have Hermann Pohl, the manufacturing manager, report directly to him instead of to Zinser. Students can be asked what further changes they would recommend, if any. This can be done either from the CEO office perspective, or students can role-play the country manager, IMC manager or global brand sponsors. Some options that students might consider:

1. Restore the previous regional structure, giving general managers their former responsibilities. Clearly many general managers would like to see this, although few at this point expect Jacobs to turn back the clock. The argument in favor of this option is that significant regional differences in consumer tastes, language, and customs still persist, despite reduced trade barriers. Students may argue that in Europe, successful marketing will always have a strong local basis, an argument made in one of the suggested readings (Bellack, 1990).

2. Eliminate the position of general manager, replacing it with a lower-level sales manager position held by different individuals; and implement the other Harvard team recommendations. This argument views Europe as a single market, and heavily emphasizes high-volume global brands over locally-targeted niche products. A key assumption here is that mass marketing can be successfully implemented in Europe as it has in the US for confectionery products.

3. Various hybrid approaches: many students will argue that neither a heavily local nor a heavily global approach will work. They might argue that Europeans strongly value locally-sensitive advertising and packaging, even if they may accept common products inside those different wrappers. The optimal approach might be for a large percentage of production to be based on common formulas, yet with regional advertising, packaging and/or distribution mechanisms. This argument views the country general manager as continuing to play a pivotal role in identifying unique features of their regional markets, yet also acknowledges that substantial economies of scale are possible. One option would be to give every country general manager some global brand sponsorship responsibilities (perhaps two general managers could each share sponsorship of one brand). Currently it must be quite difficult for global brand sponsors to convince those who are still traditional general managers to make any changes, since there are no explicit terms in those general managers' compensation structure to reward contributing to global objectives. Another option is to eliminate the global brand sponsor

role, but incorporate specific global objective into each country manager's compensation terms.

4. A student may even propose that "structure doesn't matter," quoting Klaus Jacobs: "I don't believe in structure; I believe in people... personal relationships are what make this organization work." This is an opportunity to review why *both* formal structure (reporting relationships, business processes, decision rights) and informal networks are important mechanisms for achieving managerial goals. Jacobs is appropriately acknowledging the importance of informal networks, but may be overlooking the importance of formal structure.

The object of this discussion is for students to come to the realization that there are strong forces in favor of both local/decentralized and global/centralized structures. The optimal structure will be some form of hybrid, but homing in on a structure that will work is a difficult task, given the strong entrepreneurial culture of the firm (which favors continuing to be decentralized), uncertainties concerning consumer preferences (which will sometimes favor centralization, sometimes decentralization), and uncertainties concerning how soon various European trade barriers will really come down (despite the rhetoric, not all EEC recommendations would be implemented on January 1, 1992).

In addition, any choice which is made about formal reporting relationships and decision rights must be accompanied by choices about performance measurement and evaluation, incentives and rewards, values, and informal networks - that is, with important aspects of the company's *culture*. Traditionally, the Jacobs Suchard culture has favored extensive decentralization; shifting to a culture that accommodates a global perspective will not happen automatically.

Furthermore, it is not possible to make a well-informed choice regarding organizational structure without also taking into consideration issues of management *control*. The conflicts over resource allocation mentioned in the case revolve around how strategic objectives and tactics are set (planning) who has access to the relevant data to inform these decisions, who has the authority to make a decision (decision rights), and how each party's contribution will be measured (performance measurement and evaluation). A brief discussion of the relationship among the Control side, the Culture side and the Organization side of the People, Information and Technology framework will provide a conceptual bridge to the next segment of the course, which addresses Control issues.

Yet another key concern is conspicuously absent in the case: the role of *information technology*. Having set up the discussion concerning the potential role of IT early in the class, the instructor can ask students to consider this important element in their recommendations to Klaus Jacobs. Case Exhibit 2 reveals no function labeled "MIS" or "IT;" we can assume that probably this function falls under the box labeled "Controlling." If no student brings up the issue of data management in their recommendations above, the instructor might ask one, "If you were a consultant being asked to advise Klaus Jacobs, what would you want to know about the company's use of computers and data?" At this point in the course, students will not yet have read Chapter 4 (IT Architecture), but they will have discussed the Mrs. Fields case, so this brief discussion should probably focus at a high level on the ability to share data across the organization. Students should understand that, in the regional structure, general managers would have had little reason to worry about sharing marketing or manufacturing data with other country managers, so they may have each made choices that led to inconsistent data definitions and data base management tools from one country to another. Secondly, and very importantly, students can be led to understand that a well managed IT architecture can provide data-sharing and analysis capabilities that would help the firm to be responsive to local needs while simultaneously capturing economies of scale. In other words, careful consideration of IT issues can help management resolve much of the conflicting forces of decentralization versus centralization.

Post-script and Wrap-Up

If you wish to bring students up to date on Jacobs-Suchard, there are several items to note. First, Philip Morris acquired Jacobs Suchard AG in 1990 for $3.8B. At the time, Philip Morris declined to purchase the US-based E.J. Brach subsidiary, which was "in serious trouble," according to *Forbes**. The article reported that Klaus Jacobs had misunderstood the US candy market and made a number of personnel, product and distribution decisions that had not worked out. Abroad, Jacobs-Suchard continued to expand via acquisition, buying an Argentine ice cream company and a Lithuanian chocolate maker in 1993. In August 1993 Kraft General Foods (the Philip Morris division in which Jacobs-Suchard reported) announced that it had consolidated Callard & Bowser with J-S to form a wholly new candy company called Callard & Bowser-Suchard, Inc. A Bulgarian confectioner was also acquired in 1994.

The wrap-up will depend on whether the instructor has used this case for a focused discussion of organizational structure or as an integrative vehicle. The case emphasizes the interplay between formal structure, informal networks, resource allocation, performance measurement, incentives and rewards, and values. Decisions affecting any one of these elements will affect the other elements; decisions which take into account the dynamic interplay among them are more likely to effectively support organizational objectives.

---

* Feldman, Amy. "Arrogance Goeth Before a Fall." *Forbes* 148(7): 82, 87, September 30, 1991.

Suggested 80-Minute Class Plan

1. What is the impact of the EEC moves to a unified Europe on you as consumers, students, employees? (10 minutes)

2. What new opportunities and challenges arise for companies doing business in EEC countries? (10 minutes)

3. How well positioned was Jacobs Suchard in 1987 to compete in a unified European market? What specific opportunities and challenges did they face? (10-15 minutes)

4. What might all these changes brought about by the EEC mean for information management? How would you compare the potential role of IT at Jacobs Suchard with the role you saw at Mrs. Fields Cookies? (10 minutes)

5. Jacobs Suchard's structure is changing (hand out **Exhibit TN-1**), and management
is considering whether to make further changes. What do you recommend?
   (if desired, ask students to role-play general managers, global brand sponsors, IMC managers). (25-30 minutes)

6. Post-Script and Wrap-Up (5 minutes)

Key Summary Lessons

Importance of structure as a general management tool.

Aligning an organization's structure with a changing environment.

Difficulty in adopting a structure that adequately supports both global and local initiatives (and need for an effective IT architecture to meet this challenge).

Relationship among formal structure, informal networks, values, performance measurement and evaluation, incentives and rewards.

Exhibit TN-1 Comparison of Alternative Structures Proposed at Jacobs Suchard

	Structure in 1986	Issemann Task Force Proposal	HBS Team Proposal
Headquarters	"servants, not masters of business units"	ambiguous	separate executives for marketing, sales, manufacturing
General Managers	"GM's should make the most decisions" report to Confectionery EVP (Zinser) Responsibilities: local consumer marketing local trade marketing local manufacturing local resource allocation Compensation: based on responsibilities above; items over which GM has direct control. Very generous bonus terms. "my results, my people, my company"	report to Confectionery EVP (Zinser) Responsibilities: still do trade and consumer marketing, but under coordination of global brand sponsors. no longer manage manufacturing; do provide demand forecasts. Compensation: much less control over activities affecting bonus; less generous bonus terms	"sales unit general manager," report to European sales exec, who will report to Confectionery EVP Responsibilities: trade marketing (sales) only Compensation: based on sales volume
Global Brand Sponsors	N/A	5 out of 13 GM's get this added responsibility, specifically: international advertising, packaging, work with GM's on new product development, (unclear how) work with global manufacturing sponsor on capacity utilization (unclear how)	each global brand a "clear-cut profit center," 5 global brand managers to report to Confectionery EVP (Zinser). Responsible for consumer marketing and coordination with sales and manufacturing. Different people than sales unit general managers
Global Manufacturing Sponsors	N/A	all factories report to this manager, who reports to Confectionery EVP. ensure economies of scale, standards via "global product" production in some factories, traditional small-scale production at others	all factories report to this manager, who report to Confectionery EVP. Emphasize "global product" production as much as possible.

KPMG Peat Marwick: The Shadow Partner*

Synopsis

A large professional services firm faced over-capacity in their traditional audit business, and a need to grow its value-added advisory services. This case shows how an ambitious vision for capitalizing on emerging networked IT capabilities was articulated and communicated to members of senior management. While previous investments in IT had been aimed at automating various tasks, the so-called "Shadow Partner" initiative would informate knowledge workers. In this vision, the Shadow Partner - an online "reservoir of practice and knowledge" would provide partners of the firm with universal and immediate access to both the expertise of the firm contained in internal client reports, and external expertise contained in third-party data bases. The Shadow Partner concept was proven feasible in a series of technical prototypes. However, the cost - estimated between $30 and $100 million - and an inability to quantify or guarantee the benefits were large obstacles which needed to be overcome if implementation was to be approved by the firm's partners.

Teaching Objectives

The case examines:

> IT capabilities for developing the next generation of networked executive
> support systems.
>
> the role of IT in informating knowledge workers,
>
> the early stages of developing a strategic or transformational IT application
>
> issues associated with "critical mass" technologies, whose primary benefits are
> obtained only once a critical mass of users is achieved.
>
> the problem of garnering support for a costly IT project, when benefits depend on
> a critical mass of knowledge workers carrying out work in new ways.

The case also demonstrates the challenge of transformational change in professional work settings, in which sub-groups of diverse workers (in this case, auditors, tax accountants, and consultants) have considerable power to block change initiatives. Blocking can be due either to an unwillingness to commit funds to the project, or unwillingness to change established work patterns, which is necessary to realize the benefits.

Suggested Optional Readings:

Thomas H. Davenport, *Process Innovation: Reengineering Work through Information Technology* (Boston: Harvard Business School Press, 1993):
> Chapter 9, "Process Innovation and the Management of Organizational Change"
> Chapter 10, "Implementing Process Innovation with Information Technology"

Note: ***Exhibit TN-1*** *summarizes five articles describing Big Six accounting firms, the accounting industry, the rapid assimilation of microcomputers into the Big Eight/Big Six in the eighties, and specific KPMG Peat Marwick initiatives. In order to add context to the case, students can be asked to read the articles themselves or the summaries. The articles are:*

Anonymous. "Accountancy: All Change." *Economist* 325(7781): 19-23, October 17, 1992.

Foust, Dean. "The Big Six are in Big Trouble." *Business Week* 32(60): 78-79, April 6, 1992.

Gallun, Rebecca A., Thomas C. Waller and Dianne B. Love. "Microcomputers in the Big Eight." *CPA Journal*, October 1, 1987, pp. 1124-1127.

Stodghill, Ron, II. "Who Says Accountants Can't Jump?" *Business Week* Industrial/ Technology Edition 32(90): 98-100, October 26, 1992.

Strozier, Robert M. "Teaming Up." *World* 25(1): 6-11, 1991.

Suggested Study Questions

1. What are the challenges that KPMG Peat Marwick faces over the next 5-10 years?
   What are the organizational implications of these challenges?

2. What contributions can the "Shadow Partner" project make towards meeting these challenges? Attempt to map the potential impacts using the Benefits/Beneficiaries Matrix.

3. What other technologies could make a contribution?
   Have KPMG Peat Marwick managers converged too quickly on this set of technologies?

4. If you were a member of the US Operating Committee in February 1991 (when the project is being presented for a decision on funding) how would you vote? Describe the rationale you would use to explain your position to the partnership as a whole.

5. Critically evaluate the approach that was taken to develop the Shadow Partner initiative. Would you have proceeded differently? If so, be prepared to describe why your approach might be preferred to the one taken.

Opportunities for Student Analysis and Discussion

Strategic Challenges

The case discussion can be started by asking a student to describe the strategic challenges facing KPMG and how well are they positioned to address these challenges? Students with Big Six experience can be especially useful in kicking off this discussion.

The case provides a brief overview of the accounting industry. Previously a slow-paced, conservative, and collegial industry, the accounting industry was undergoing significant change in the Eighties. The case discusses the dramatic consolidation through mergers which occurred (resulting in a change from the Big Eight to the Big Six), suggesting that firms were struggling with over-capacity. The case mentions that growth of domestic accounting services was slowing, due to simplification of the tax laws and a softening economy. It notes that accounting services were increasingly viewed as a commodity product, and it mentions an increasing international focus. However, it does not fully discuss several important developments that took place during the eighties, and which experienced students may be able to address:

> As clients began to view audit as an *undifferentiated commodity*, loyalty declined (although the case states that KPMG Peat Marwick had successfully retained most of its client base), and price competition increased. To counter this trend, accounting firms explored two avenues: a) reducing costs through partner lay-offs, investments in audit automation technologies (allowing firms to compete more effectively on price), and identifying ways for client personnel to participate more extensively in non-critical audit tasks, and b) adding value to audit services by, for example, analyzing trends in a client's financial performance (allowing firms to compete more effectively on service differentiation).

> Risks of audit *litigation* were increasing, creating further pressure. For example, several Big Six firms were severely criticized in the press for failing to provide earlier warning of the extensive Savings and Loan crisis of the late eighties. To reduce litigation exposure, Big Six firms invested in statistical and expert systems software that allowed auditors to reduce the amount of financial data they directly examined, without increasing their risk exposure.

> All of the Big Six invested heavily in *microcomputers* during the eighties. The case does not mention that Peat Marwick was the first firm to provide all of its audit staff with microcomputers, a development which was heavily publicized in the mid-eighties. Most firms experienced some discontinuity, as junior members either entered with computing skills or quickly acquired them, while those who earned their college degrees before the eighties were generally not computer-literate (as of 1991, the case reports that fewer than 25% of KPMG

147

audit partners used computers). Most accounting firms initially emphasized the use of microcomputers to reduce audit hours (improvement in efficiency). Subsequently, emphasis shifted to improving audit quality by reducing risk exposure and by providing value-added services (improvement in effectiveness).

As audit became less central, and as consulting services grew, the differences in the skills and culture of *auditors versus consultants* became more evident. In one highly-publicized move, Arthur Andersen's consulting arm was spun off as a separate organizational entity. The partners mentioned in the KPMG case do not seem to be considering the issue of organizationally separating a mature business from a growth business. It can be worthwhile to ask students how the KPMG partners seem to be approaching this strategic challenge and whether they should be giving it greater attention.

The suggested readings address these issues, and it is not difficult to identify other articles describing the increased pressures on the Big Six to improve efficiency, reduce litigation risks, provide value-added services, reconcile conflicting cultures and business strategies, and compete internationally.

At KPMG, as elsewhere, partners were working harder for lower rewards. This must have had an impact on the firm's culture, which Bob Elliott described as a "high burnout" one.

While client loyalty reportedly was high, the 1989 client survey found that 80% of clients wanted the firm to offer more value-added services and a wider range of expertise. Consulting advisory services was targeted for growth, while traditionally it had been seen as a service to the audit business. One can infer that, as at other Big Six firms, a shift in power was taking place among the audit, tax and consulting groups.

From the case facts, it seems that KPMG thinks that they are ahead in utilizing information technologies (perhaps because of the leadership in acquiring microcomputers). However, it is unclear whether this perception is correct.

Role of the Shadow Partner in Addressing the Strategic Challenge

The vision of the Shadow Partner is to efficiently leverage the knowledge and expertise in the firm, as codified in the various reports and documents. In addition, the Shadow Partner would make available to all partners external data bases and an ability to communicate with each other any place at any time using e-mail and voice mail.

The Shadow Partner vision includes a data and communications infrastructure to "informate" professionals and hence enhance their ability to serve clients. The relationship with the client is assumed to be the critical comparative advantage that the firm has in competing with other sources of professional services. The traditional audit would provide a basis for determining additional client needs, such as better inventory control, opportunities for strategic alliances to share business risks, or evaluation of an investment proposal. The KPMG partner then can draw upon the Shadow Partner database to identify relevant information and sources of expertise.

The strength of the client relationship and the ability of the partner to access expertise should not go unchallenged in the discussion. Is the proposed technology solution sufficient to enable KPMG to compete against alternative sources of advisory services available to the client (as examples: for strategy consulting clients can go to McKinsey or Bain; for logistics consulting they can go to Federal Express or Rockwell; for mergers and acquisitions they can turn to Goldman Sachs or Morgan Stanley)?

Additional features of the Shadow Partner can come out in discussion.

> Enable client-centered versus product/service centered client service.

> Includes interactive training to assist partners in gaining expertise.

> Increases productivity through integrated management support tools
> (e.g., calendar and time management; telephone directory with auto-dial;
> project management tools, statistical packages; graphics; word processors)

At this point the Benefits/Beneficiaries Matrix (discussed in Chapters 8 and 9 of the book) can be put on the board to organize the discussion. One avenue is to note that personal computers were originally sold as individual productivity tools (Individual beneficiary, Efficiency and Effectiveness benefits). Accounting firms purchased them in order, first, to improve functional unit and organizational Efficiency. Later, as employees became more skilled workers, they were able to use sophisticated statistical, modeling, and expert-systems software to improve the quality of their work (Functional Unit/Organizational Effectiveness). The Shadow Partner concept, with its emphasis on networked access to information of many kinds originating throughout a widely-dispersed organization, is really oriented to Transforming the Organization by helping partners to work together in new ways, by reducing personal and organizational boundaries around information, and by providing new value-added services to clients. The instructor can also briefly discuss the use of the Benefits/Beneficiaries matrix for assessing emerging technology investments in general.

Investment Decision

In addressing the question of whether to go forward with the Shadow Partner implementation, the class is often split. The student that argues KPMG is facing strategic jeopardy if they don't go forward with the implementation can make a convincing case. And, she can carry the class for a time. Alternatively, the student that argues that the cost is too high and the benefits too speculative, can also make a strong case, and can carry the class for a time. One can generally go with the flow here until some student intervenes with the opposite conclusion.

Then, work with that line of reasoning until both sides have had a hearing. At this point, it is often constructive to ask the students to vote.

This juncture is a good time to explore issues at the next level of depth, such as cost analysis, benefits analysis and risk analysis.

Cost - The project to the prototype stage has cost $5 million. The sunk cost has proved the technology, but has not given a very good indication of benefits and the risk of acceptance and use by the partners.

The implementation cost estimate of $30-100 million represents a cost/partner of $5,000 - $16,000, and with partner salaries ranging from $120,000 to $1 million, this would be 2% to 6% of one year's compensation. This argument was used with some success in discussing the cost of implementation. However, the continued pressure on audit prices made already conservative partners even more conservative. Further downsizing in the industry exacerbated these concerns.

Changes in Power - Much of a partner's power in the firm depends on relationships with clients. Sharing information about clients with others in the firm changes that power base, and such a possibility was met with both overt and covert resistance.

Sponsorship - Elliott, a staff assistant to the Chairman, sponsored the project before the new chairman, Jon Madonna, was appointed. Students will express some concern for Elliott as project sponsor, and with the project being inherited by the new chairman.

Comparison with Phillips 66 Case

If the *Phillips 66 Company: Executive Information System* case (189-006) was assigned earlier in the course, it can be useful to compare the Shadow Partner concept in the early Nineties with the approach taken at Phillips 66 in the mid-Eighties. Most of the Phillips EIS internal corporate data were numeric information already on mainframe production systems. Because of severe cost pressures, the design team used purchased software - such as FOCUS a PC-based graphics package, and PROFS - supplemented by a minimal amount of custom development. External data consisted largely of manually-filtered news reports (today, companies such as Individual, Inc. in Cambridge MA distribute electronically filtered custom news reports using artificial intelligence techniques). In terms of organizational issues, Phillips 66 was experiencing severe pressures. It had downsized dramatically and restructured financially in order to avoid a corporate takeover. Despite these pressures, President Bob Wallace had enthusiastically endorsed a significant investment in software, hardware and staff for the EIS project, believing that this investment would be repaid in improved organizational effectiveness. In contrast, at KPMG Peat Marwick CEO Jon Madonna seems to be quite lukewarm to the idea that IT can provide a solution to the challenges facing the firm.

Another important point of comparison between the two cases is that both deal with a "critical mass" technology. The telephone, for example, is a critical mass technology in that it had very limited utility until a large number of individuals were using it regularly. E-mail is another critical-mass technology, while voice-mail and facsimile have hybrid characteristics (since there are alternative forms of storing and forwarding messages, such as secretaries, answering machines, Federal Express). At Phillips 66, Bob Wallace seemed to intuitively understand the importance of quickly generating widespread e-mail use, and several steps were taken to encourage executives to communicate with him in that way. Once the critical mass of e-mail usage was achieved, other uses of the EIS quickly followed (although there was some question of whether this usage pattern would be sustained after Wallace retired). At KPMG Peat Marwick, the primary benefits of the Shadow Partner project - in sharing knowledge and expertise - are unlikely to be achieved unless a critical mass of partners adopt this technology within a short time frame.

Implementation Scenarios

Implementation could start with an office, an industry, a practice or a function. As the class discusses the pros and cons of each alternative, they should be summarized on the board. The case does not provide any indication of hard analysis of alternatives with different cost, benefits and risk patterns or any development of time-based milestones.

Closing and Post-Script

Towards the end of the class, it is constructive to ask a student to assume that the discussion we just had happened at the February 1991 Operating Committee meeting. As a partner on the Operating committee, how would you vote? How would you explain your vote to your fellow partners at the Annual Partners meeting?

The Shadow Partner prototype is still operational in Montvale, New Jersey. The previous CIO took early retirement. Another CIO was brought in who had 8 years of experience as CIO with another major professional services firm. Still no major implementation funding has been approved. It is curious to many that the Shadow Partner initiative has neither been officially killed, nor approved.

Suggested 80-Minute Class Plan

The following is a broad guideline for the discussion (NOTE: If *Phillips 66 Company: Executive Information System* case has not been previously assigned, allow an extra 5 minute for segments 1,2 and 3):

1. Strategic challenge facing KPMG (10 minutes)

2. The vision of the Shadow Partner, and its relationship to the strategic challenge facing KPMG (10-15 minutes)

3. Key issues: costs, benefits, and risks (10 minutes)

4. Benefits/Beneficiaries Matrix (5-10 minutes)

5. Comparison with Phillips 66 Case (10-15 minutes)

6. Alternative actions and pros and cons of each - 15 minutes

7. Action and close - 5-10 minutes

Alternative use of video tape: Not mentioned in the case, a tough problem initially was to get the partners to understand how IT could help KPMG partners address strategic challenges. Richard Nolan, a member of the Technology Committee became aware of a 7 minute video tape, *The Knowledge Navigator*, prepared by Apple, showing how a university professor might work in the year 2010. This tape was shown to the Technology Committee and other senior KPMG partners, in order to suggest how a partner might work in the future. This became the basis for the Shadow Partner vision, and a way to communicate the vision to others in the organization.

The Knowledge Navigator video tape can be shown at the beginning of class Before showing it, ask students to write down all the technologies that they see, and when they think that these technologies will be commercially available. The answer: virtually all are commercially available. This underscores the point that technology itself is rarely a significant constraint.

Key Summary Lessons

1. Emerging information technologies offer enormous possibilities for transforming knowledge work and supporting strategic initiatives. But assessing the potential benefits in relation to the potential costs is complex and imprecise.

2. Critical-mass technologies, whose primary benefits are attained only when most members of an organization or social system use them, represent an especially difficult challenge.

3. Technology itself is rarely the critical constraint. In order to garner support for an ambitious technology initiative, it is necessary to assess the socio-political ramifications.

Surveying the Big Six*

The following article abstracts were drawn from the ABI/Inform bibliographic database. They describe five articles concerning Big Six accounting firms, and specific KPMG Peat Marwick initiatives. These articles provides a supplement to the "KPMG Peat Marwick: The Shadow Partner" case, no. 492-002.

Anonymous. Accountancy: All Change. *Economist* **325(7781): 19-23, Oct 17, 1992.**
Six large firms dominate the accounting industry. Ranked by worldwide fee income, they are KPMG, Ernst & Young, Coopers & Lybrand, Arthur Andersen, Deloitte Touche Tohmatsu, and Price Waterhouse. The 1980s tested auditing to its limits. Non-audit work - especially management consultancy - mushroomed, and the suspicion grew, that at some firms, auditing had become a loss-leader intended to pull in non-audit business. Changes are needed to restore the general public's confidence in accountants. One reform favored by the UK's Cadbury committee on corporate governance is the compulsory appointment of audit committees, composed of non-executive directors. Clearer accounting standards are also needed. The profession is allowed to define the conventions for presenting the company accounts required by law. Changing the job that auditors do would require changes to the firms they work for as well. For most firms, the partnership model itself is no longer sensible. If firms were to incorporate, management structures would be more straightforward.

Foust, Dean. The Big Six Are in Big Trouble. *Business Week* **32(60): 78-79,, April 6, 1992.**
As the search for culprits in the financial debacles of the 1980s continues, accountants face claims of more than $2 billion in damages, and regulators are preparing lawsuits demanding millions more. Private litigants are also suing. Most of the Big Six accounting firms face or have settled cases involving major financial hits. Insurance premiums for the Big Six have soared tenfold since 1985, while maximum coverage has been reduced by 1/2. For some firms, premiums and legal costs consume up to 25% of what would otherwise go to partners. In response, firms are trying to guard against future shocks. Ernst & Young will audit only banks that receive regulators' highest ratings. Another major firm will not take on government-securities dealers. To fend off future litigation, accountants are lobbying state legislatures for laws limiting plaintiffs to suing partners only in the office where an audit was performed. In addition, the American Institute of Certified Public Accountants has voted to require auditors to state unambiguously whether they had substantial doubts about whether a client could continue as a going concern for the following 12 months.

Gallun, Rebecca A., Thomas C. Waller and Dianne B. Love. Microcomputers in the Big Eight. *CPA Journal*, **October 1, 1987, pp 1124-127.**
This abstract is not from ABI/Inform. Following are quotes directly from the article:
As recently as the fall of 1983, several of the big eight accounting firms were just initiating major efforts to utilize microcomputers. Since that time, microcomputer usage by big eight accounting firms has increased dramatically... This article updates information on microcomputer usage by accountants in the big eight accounting firms.

In 1986, information and microcomputer usage by accountants was obtained by mailing questionnaires to 79 randomly chosen domestic offices of the big eight CPA firms... Replies were received by 51 offices...

... Over 43% expect a trend toward hiring accountants with microcomputer training or experience. 31% expect a trend toward hiring accountants with greater analytical skills...

The results of the survey indicate that microcomputers ... are currently being used by all of the big eight offices surveyed. All of these offices are using microcomputers for spreadsheet analysis, and almost all of them are using them for data base management, word processing, and telecommunications with a broad range of applications in each category... The results of this survey attest to the significant impact microcomputers have had, and will continue to have, on the accounting environment...

Stodghill, Ron, II. Who Says Accountants Can't Jump?. *Business Week* **3290 (Industrial/ Technology Edition): 98-100, Oct 26, 1992,**
In the 1980s, the Big Six CPA firms expanded amid unprecedented business activity. Lately, they have been battered by a shrinking client base and lawsuits over allegedly improper audits. The savings-and-loan crisis and other business failures stemming from the 1980s have eroded the Big Six's reputations. While other Big Six CEOs have made changes in response to the profession's problems, none has moved as quickly or as loudly as KPMG Peat Marwick's Jon C. Madonna since he took over in 1990. Just 4 months after taking over, Madonna eliminated 15% of Peat Marwick's partner roster. Auditors who had been generalists are being forced to develop expertise in certain fields or they will lose their jobs. In 1992, profits per partner are expected to increase 12%, despite flat revenues of $1.8 billion. At $230,000 per partner, those projected earnings would make Peat Marwick the 5th-most-profitable firm.

Strozier, Robert M. Teaming Up. *World* **25(1): 6-11, 1991**
In October 1990, the partners of KPMG Peat Marwick elected a new chairman, Jon C. Madonna, and a deputy chairman, James G. Brocksmith, Jr. In separate interviews, the 2 discussed their management philosophies and aspirations for the firm. Both men want KPMG Peat Marwick to be acknowledged as the best professional services firm in the markets they serve and to be the most profitable. They want to build the partnership into teams that understand their clients' businesses and industries and that add value to technical excellence in the services they provide. Madonna believes that a key element in building that teamwork is to get everybody to believe in short- and long-term objectives and how to achieve them. Communication is extremely important to this process. Brocksmith notes that teamwork is really an attitude that pervades the entire organization. He sees his biggest challenge as striking the right balance between empowering practice leaders and providing centralized support and direction from a national   office.

Lithonia Lighting

Synopsis

This case describes an interorganizational system (IOS) that Lithonia has pioneered to facilitate the sale of lighting fixtures. Light*Link is based on an ingenious reconceptualization of Lithonia's business, in which independent selling agents are placed at the center of an interorganizational network that includes building developers, lighting architects and specifiers, lighting contractors, distributors, and manufacturers like Lithonia. For their innovative design of this system, Lithonia won the prestigious Society for Information Management Award in 1988.

The dilemma that CEO Jim McClung faces is whether he should continue with aggressive further development of Light*Link in the face of declining revenues brought about by a slump in the construction business. Faced with the prospect of cost-based competition, McClung must evaluate if the competitive advantages that Lithonia enjoys from Light*Link are worth the estimated 2% of sales that Lithonia's Information Services Department budgeted to support Light*Link for the coming year.

Teaching Objectives

This case can be used as part of a module on interorganizational systems or in a segment aimed at assessing the economic and competitive impact of information technology. Ideally, it should be taught after a case like Frontier Airlines, which describes an IOS (a computerized airline reservation system) that created an enormous competitive advantage for carriers like United and American Airlines. In that case, the economic and strategic advantages obtained by the airline reservations systems are clear. In contrast, the Lithonia case offers an opportunity to evaluate a complex information system in which the economic benefits to the firm are not easily quantifiable, and hence the investment in IT cannot be easily justified on a strict cost-benefit analysis. The investment must thus be justified on strategic grounds. In arriving at a decision, students also need to take into account the evolution of information technology and the sustainability of competitive advantage attainable with IT initiatives. The case thus supports three broad teaching objectives:

> To examine the design and information architecture of a complex and innovative interorganizational system.

> To evaluate the costs and strategic benefits of investments in IT.

> To evaluate the sustainability of competitive advantage gained through information technology investments.

Suggested Optional Readings:

John Byrne, "The Virtual Corporation," *Business Week*, February 8, 1993, pp. 98-103.

Michael Hammer and G. E. Mangurian. "The Changing Value of Communication Technology." *Sloan Management Review*, (Winter) 1987.

Michael E. Porter and Victor E. Millar. "How Information Gives You Competitive Advantage, *Harvard Business Review*, (July-August) 1985.

Suggested Study Questions

1. Evaluate the design and architecture of the Light*Link system. What impact has the system had on the process by which Lithonia sells lighting fixtures?

2. How would you value the strategic benefits of Light*Link? Does Light*Link provide Lithonia a sustainable competitive advantage?

3. If you were Jim McClung, what would you do? If you were Charles Darnell, what would you do?

Opportunities for Student Analysis and Discussion

Design of Light*Link and its impact on various players

A good way to discuss the design of the Light*Link system is to draw on the blackboard its basic structure (as shown in case Exhibit 4) and ask students to describe each of its elements and their impact on various players. Before one gets into the details, one can ask students whether they agreed with Darnell's view that the agent had to be at the center of the system. It is a simple exercise to see that there is no other clean way to represent this system. The agents are the only players in this business who have a direct interaction with all other participants. The main reason that agents occupy such a central role is that the lighting business (like construction and real estate) is highly decentralized and depends upon the active maintenance of local relationships. It is simply not economical for a lighting manufacturer to have local sales offices in each region. Also, agents help manufacturers offer a full-line of products by combining their complementary product offerings. The importance of these local relationships was also the reason why the lighting fixture business had historically been such a fragmented and regional industry. National players such as Lithonia and Cooper were only able to emerge because agents provided a way to maintain local relationships. Light*Link offers a way for Lithonia to appear even more like a "virtual" regional manufacturer, since by providing real-time information to agents on pricing, delivery dates, and the status of an order, it enables them to represent Lithonia to its eventual customers as if Lithonia were itself present locally.

Another noteworthy feature of the overall structure of Light*Link is that it creates direct communication links among all players that need to communicate with each other. This is important because of the high volume of information flows in this business. As described in the case, much information is passed back-and-forth among various players before an order is placed with Lithonia. Once an order is placed it is important that information on its fulfillment schedule be easily available, since construction schedules are often very tight. It is important that various materials arrive on the construction site at the appropriate time.

In addition to these overall features of Light*Link, it is important to discuss each of the different elements of the system and the impact it has on the operations of the various players:

> *ACE+* is the element of Light*Link that resides in the agent's organization. It is a PC-based application that has a direct communication link with Lithonia. ACE+ gives the agent several capabilities. It includes a package which allows an agent to propose a lighting design for several standard situations in which a lighting specifier or architect may not be involved. It allows the agent to quote prices and delivery schedules on most Lithonia products from an updated electronic pricing catalogue, place an order and check on the status of its fulfillment. It also allows agents to communicate with distributors, Lithonia's sales management team, manufacturing divisions, and warehouses. ACE+ makes it easier for gents to do business with Lithonia and to be responsive to Lithonia's eventual customers. ACE+ also allows agents to focus on selling. As the Atlanta agency example demonstrates, with Light*Link most agents were able to reduce their administrative-to-sales staff ratio from 1:1 to 1:3. In addition, agents were able to provide more responses in real time, which reduced the number of phone calls they had to make and increased the accuracy of the information they provided. Overall, Light*Link probably had the greatest impact on the operations of Lithonia's agencies.

> *SPEC-L* was designed to influence specifiers of lighting fixtures to select Lithonia fixtures. SPEC-L makes the specifier's job easier because it incorporates complex calculations that identify the most energy efficient lighting design. The design is then translated into a list of Lithonia products (Two air conditioning manufacturers, Trane and Carrier, have similar software. Those systems help the engineer design optimal HVAC - heating, ventilation and air conditioning - configurations, and, not coincidentally, specify the host manufacturer's products.). By making it easy for specifiers to offer a Lithonia lighting solution, SPEC-L influences the purchasing decision. It is important to note that since specifiers could not directly place

an order with Lithonia, Lithonia's power as a result of SPEC-L was limited. Lighting contractors could specify equivalent products and order from those vendors offering the best terms.

DIAL-L enabled Lithonia distributors to check on the inventory of items in Lithonia warehouses and the status of orders. Lithonia had partially succeeded in convincing its distributors to adopt and use this system. Those distributors who did use DIAL-L greatly increased the volume of Lithonia business they did. One main reason for distributors' reluctance to use DIAL-L was that it was not a part of their regular inventory management system. They were often just as happy to call Lithonia's warehouses or agents on the phone or send them a fax. Moreover, since Lithonia was not so strong in the flow or stocked item business, distributors did not depend on them as much as Lithonia's agents did.

SELL was used by Lithonia's marketing and sales organization to quote prices on complex orders. Since much of Lithonia's business was for the lighting for specific projects, every order was unique and required a different combination of various elements. SELL enabled Lithonia's marketing organization to break an order into its component parts and price the order according to which parts were in stock, which were standard items that could be manufactured under an existing production procedure and which were unique and required custom production. It also allowed the marketing organization to generate a bill of materials that could be communicated to Lithonia's different production divisions.

ACE EXPRESS was used by Lithonia's manufacturing divisions to translate orders into production schedules and to make these schedules available to Lithonia's agents so that they could keep track of the status of an order. This application had a direct impact on how Lithonia's manufacturing divisions scheduled their work processes and managed the flow of materials.

SOS: Lithonia's warehouses used this system to manage inventory and the shipment of orders to distributors or for direct delivery or pick-up by the lighting contractor. SOS also linked warehouses to agents so that agents could track order fulfillment.

This somewhat detailed discussion of the various elements of the Light*Link system enables a more thoughtful discussion of the strategic advantage that Lithonia obtains from this system.

Strategic advantages of Light*Link

As the above discussion shows, Light*Link clearly allows Lithonia to differentiate itself as "being easy to do business with." It allows Lithonia to influence all the players involved in the lighting business and to make it easy for them to communicate with Lithonia. In an information intensive business, this capability is of considerable strategic importance. Note, however, that the advantages of Light*Link are much greater for the project or job segments of the lighting fixture market as opposed to the stock or flow segments. In the latter, information flows are much less important and price becomes a more crucial competitive factor.

Using Porter's value chain framework (see Porter and Millar reading), one can also see how Light*Link impacts Lithonia's ability to enhance the value-added in *marketing* (by enhancing its capabilities to flexibly specify and quote prices for various orders), in *production* (by improving its ability to schedule production runs and manage inventory), and in *outbound logistics* (by making the status of an order transparent to the customer at all times).

It is important to recognize that Light*Link, unlike the early airline reservation systems, provides Lithonia with only a limited degree of control over information flows in this industry. Indeed, one can ask students to compare Light*Link to an airline reservation system. Two main differences between these systems are worth noting. First, lighting agents do not influence the customer's buying decision as much as travel agents do. In the lighting business there are many more points of influence in the purchase decision, and Lithonia has limited control over these other buying influences. Secondly, unlike the airlines, Lithonia cannot use its system to offer differentiated pricing. Unlike airline seats, lighting fixtures are not perishable products. Yield management, so key in the airline industry, is not relevant to the lighting fixture business. Hence, Lithonia does not have the same flexibility as airlines do in setting competitive prices.

In light of these important but limited advantages, one can ask if the strategic benefits of Light*Link are worth the $20 million in capital investment that Lithonia has incurred to date in creating it, and the 2% of sales allotted for ongoing development. Based on a back-of-the-envelope cost of capital calculation and a variable cost calculation, one can ask students if Light*Link is worth the approximately 2% addition it requires in the cost of goods sold. This question directly leads to a discussion of McClung's dilemma.

McClung's dilemma

The dilemma that McClung faces is that the downturn in the construction industry presents him with the prospect of declining revenues and price competition. Moreover, the decline in new construction is likely to have its greatest impact on the project business, the segment in which Lithonia is strongest and from which it derives the majority of its revenues. By slowing down investments in Light*Link, McClung can postpone capital outlays and potentially add 1% to operating margins, which gives him greater flexibility in the event of price competition.

McClung is not contemplating abandoning Light*Link. He is merely wondering if he can slow the pace of its continuing evolution without losing competitive ground. One therefore has to ask what are the risks are of slowing down the continuing development of Light*Link. One clear risk is that competing systems are available and competitors might catch up with Lithonia, causing it to lose its first-mover advantage. Another risk is that a clamp-down could cause a significant loss of morale in Darnell's department. This could lead to defections by some of the most talented IS employees, who might even be tempted to join a competitor.

McClung's decision also depends on how long he expects the downturn in construction to last. The data in the case suggest that the recession is likely to be a long one.

Darnell's response

Darnell has to be conscious of McClung's concerns and should attempt to focus his efforts. He needs to realize that he must curb the wild abandon with which he has pursued new projects in the past and focus on those development efforts that are likely to have the greatest impact on the short-run problems being confronted by Lithonia, while still maintaining the long-run advantage of Light*Link.

There is one major change that Darnell should immediately make. He should place greater emphasis on internal applications that will help to rationalize key business processes, such as translating orders into a bill of materials and production schedule. By helping Lithonia achieve more operating efficiencies, Darnell can more clearly justify investments in Light*Link. In the present environment, a cost-benefit analysis is more compelling than the more vague promise of competitive advantage.

While he should focus on internal applications, Darnell should also work towards making the ACE+ system capable of dealing with other manufacturers' products. because emerging systems that offer that feature could otherwise become more attractive to users. Indeed, Darnell could even be encouraged to start planning how Light*Link might eventually become the industry platform. This would neutralize some of Lithonia's current strategic advantages; however, these advantages are already eroding.

Darnell should enhance the capabilities of the SOS system. Though Lithonia has been wary in the past of positioning warehouses in competition with its distributors, this is an area of enormous opportunity. Distributors enjoy good margins and Lithonia could capture some of this value.

Whatever Darnell does, he must bear in mind that his rationale for further investments in information technology will come under much greater scrutiny. He can no longer ride on the glory of Light*Link.

Suggested 80-Minute Teaching Plan

1. Introductory remarks. (5 minutes)

2. Do you think the design of Light*Link deserves the accolades it has won, such as the Society for Information Management award?
   How has the system impacted the way Lithonia sells lighting fixtures?
   What impact has it had on each of the other players involved in this interorganizational system? (30 minutes)

3. What strategic advantages does Lithonia derive from Light*Link?
   To what extent are these advantages sustainable?
   How much are you willing to invest to obtain the strategic benefits afforded by the Light*Link system?
   In what direction should Light*Link evolve? (15 minutes)

4. If you were Jim McClung, what would you do? How would you go about implementing your decision? (10 minutes)

5. If you were Charlie Darnell, what would you do?
   If you knew McClung was concerned, how would you influence him?
   How would you respond to McClung's decision? (15 minutes)

6. Wrap-up and concluding remarks (5 minutes)

Key Summary Lessons

IT can provide a variety of strategic and organizational benefits. The key is to understand how sustainable benefits are, and when and how easily they can be replicated by other firms.

Lithonia Lighting provides a good example of the trend towards creating the "virtual corporation," which is a system of inter-organizational linkages along a value-added chain, enabled by information technology.

Mrs. Fields Cookies

Synopsis

Mrs. Fields Cookies, Inc. has used information technology to permit rapid geographic expansion of their cookie store business throughout the US and Europe, without resorting to franchising. Networked computer systems are used to automate routine procedures and management control systems which, according to the company, frees up store managers to be more creative in the business of selling cookies. The systems also free up store managers to spend more time "managing people" rather than managing numbers.

It is important to note that Mrs. Fields Cookies describes a young organization (and hence a "greenfield" site for information systems). Students can readily comprehend that this company produces a simple product, with relatively simple operational and marketing processes, and primarily low-skill employees. Comparisons with other cases included in the book should explicitly note the greater complexity of many of the other organizations versus Mrs. Fields.

The case can be used to explore the role of IT to *automate* processes, and the attendant human resources issues. Instructors can use this as an opportunity to set up discussions of operational support versus decision support and automating versus *informating*.

Hence, the case enables a rich discussion of the interplay among technology, organizational structure, management control systems, and human resources.

Teaching Objectives

The case explores the use of IT to enable rapid growth while maintaining tight control. It presents a rare opportunity to study the design of an IT architecture within a "greenfield" site that developed during the eighties, incorporating modern technology into the original organizational design. The strategy, structure, controls, human resource management, and technology were designed in concert. The case can also be supplemented with recent articles about Mrs. Fields, such as those listed below, which raise issues about problems that can occur as a tightly integrated design changes. Topics addressed in the case include:

IT Architecture
IT and Organization Structure
IT and Management Control

Suggested Optional Readings:

Brown, B. How the cookie crumbled at Mrs. Fields. *Wall Street Journal*, January 26, 1989.

Ellis-Simons, P. Is the cookie crumbling? *The Marketer*, June, 1990.

Hollinger, P. Mrs. Fields quits London USM. *Financial Times*, February 16, 1993.

Suggested Study Questions

1. Describe and evaluate the organizational structure of Mrs. Fields. What alternative structures might the Fields have pursued?

2. Describe and evaluate the approach to management control systems at Mrs. Fields, in terms of those systems' ability to help management monitor operations, evaluate performance and make strategic decisions.

3. Describe and evaluate the role of information technology (IT) at Mrs.Fields.

4. Given their goals and the competitive environment in which they compete, have Randy and Debbi Fields made coherent choices about organizational structure, management control systems, information resources, and people?

Opportunities for Student Analysis

General discussion: role of IT at Mrs. Fields

The discussion can begin with a general question: What is the role of IT in Mrs. Fields Cookies? The goal is to get as many ideas as possible on the board with minimal interference from the instructor. It is helpful to ask students to save detailed descriptions for later in class. Once a fairly representative list has emerged, students can be asked to clarify what we mean by IT at Mrs. Fields. This provides a transition to a discussion of IT architecture.

IT architecture

Students can be asked to turn to Exhibit 4 in the case. A student with technical background can walk through the diagram and explain the various components. Be sure students distinguish between applications running on store PCs and those on minicomputers (S/38s) in corporate headquarters. Students should understand that the stores communicate with headquarters through modems; they are not "on-line" at all times, a common misconception.

Daily sales information is collected and uploaded to corporate in the evening. There, store controllers, each tracking 35 to 75 stores, analyze and aggregate the data. A summary report is shipped to Debbi and Randy Fields and to the vice president of operations on a daily basis. Problems are communicated directly to the store manager or to his/her boss. It is helpful to ask a student to walk through a store manager's day, to ensure that the class understands how the software influences the work of a store manager.

The discussion of the IT architecture can be summarized using the IT architecture framework shown in **Exhibit TN-1**, which appears later in the book as Chapter 4, Exhibit 5. If time permits, it is helpful for students to clarify alternative decisions that could have been made by Debbi and Randy as they developed their blueprint for IT at the company. In addition, security concerns can be discussed and evaluated.

IT and organization structure

Once they understand the basic IT architecture, the discussion can return to the influence of IT within the company. IT enables this hierarchical organization to "feel flat." Have students clarify what this means. There are two distinctly different reporting structures within Mrs. Fields. The traditional hierarchy is comprised of 500+ store managers, who report to 105 district sales managers, who report to 17 regional directors, who report to 4 senior regional directors, who report to a vice president of operations, who reports to Debbi and Randy. This is anything but flat! This side of the organization looks very traditional, with a span of control of approximately 1:5. Students should recognize that this side of the hierarchy relied on verbal and in-person supervision and reporting.

A second, formal reporting relationship exists in which the 500+ store managers report to 6 store controllers, who report to the vice president of operations, who reports to Debbi and Randy. The case indicates that the span of control between the store managers and controllers is 35 to 75:1. IT plays a key role here in the daily collecting, analyzing, and reporting of information. *This distinct separation of routine information and control, based on the numbers, from the human side of management is a key take-away from the case.*

Finally, there is an informal organization in which every store manager is connected to Debbi (and, presumably, to everyone else) through electronic and voice mail systems. This makes the structure "feel flat." Students can discuss how Debbi manages to communicate personally with 500+ people. What mechanisms keep her from being overloaded with messages? While data in the case are scanty, students can identify mechanisms that might be used to manage communications complexity in a networked organization.

Here one can also compare the span of control at Mrs. Fields Cookies with other companies. In addition to hierarchical span of control, discussed above, students can also compare staff-to-line ratios at Mrs. Fields (115:8000) with other organizations.

At this point it is helpful to raise the issue: Why didn't the Fields adopt a franchising strategy? It may be necessary to briefly discuss the pro's and con's of franchising:

Pro:
faster expansion, since franchisees shoulder much of the financial burden; shared risks, reduced exit costs

Con:
less direct control over operations; however, McDonald's is evidence that tight control is achievable. lower financial return per store

Apparently the Fields' decision not to franchise in the early years was based largely on their expectation that they could retain more profits by not franchising. Having made that decision, they implemented information systems that aimed at tight day-to-day operational control. This leads to the discussion of IT and management control, below.

IT and management control

Many quotes in the case provide a backdrop for discussion of control issues. For example, Debbi states:

> Management theory claims that it is wrong not to delegate authority to those that work for you. Okay, I'm wrong, but in my own defense, I have to say that my error came from caring too much. If that's a sin, it's surely a small one. Eventually I was forced, kicking and screaming, to delegate authority, because that was the only way the business could grow.

Students can discuss: How did Debbi "delegate" authority? What decisions were made at different levels of the organization? Would they consider Mrs. Fields to be a decentralized or a centralized organization?

Other case quotes that can stimulate discussion:

> Even when she isn't there, she's there - in the standards build into scheduling programs and hourly goals ...

> The technology has leveraged Debbi's ability to project her influence into more stores than she could ever reach effectively without it.

Students can be asked to take a stand: Is this kind of control "good" or "bad"? This often sparks a heated debate, with students lining up on each side of the issue (One student called Mrs. Fields Cookies "Orwellian Cookie Hell"). This discussion can be a forum for defining control systems and evaluating the role of IT in their design. Richard Walton's book[ii] devotes a chapter to Mrs. Fields Cookies. He states that technology can **force compliance** or support **voluntary commitment** to organizational goals. **Exhibit TN-2** summarizes his discussion.

It is helpful to ask students to describe a "typical" Mrs. Fields Cookies store manager. Students quickly point out that the average age is between 20 to 25 years, with 1 to 2 years of college education. Many Mrs. Fields store managers are probably college students working their way through school, as indicated by the 100% per year turnover.

Managers receive a low base salary and incentives for making sales quotas (set by district sales managers), with additional incentives for exceeding quota. Debbi and Randy want store managers who will convey the "feel-good" feeling of the product. They want "people" people, not "numbers" people. They want store managers to spend their time selling, not hiring scheduling, ordering, etc. They view IT as a tool for expanding the capabilities of store managers *in the role that Debbi and Randy wish them to fill.* Debbi

---

[ii] Richard E. Walton, *Up and Running: Integrating Information Technology and the Organization.* Boston, MA: Harvard Business School Press, 1989.

and Randy view their key challenge as hiring the right people to fit the store manager job as they have designed it. Be sure to verify that students recognize these as conscious management choices.

The information systems enable a new store manager to function effectively in a very short time. Minimal time and money are invested in training new store managers. This is critical to aggressive growth goals, given the high turnover and the decision not to franchise.

Since they follow a "promote from within" policy, it is assumed that a similar type of manager - good at dealing with people, selling, and generating energy and enthusiasm - is sought for positions higher in the organization. These managers are expected to develop the people below them. They focus on the human side of management (mentoring, motivating, developing), while store controllers and information systems manage the numbers.

Astute students may note that the firm's control system seems to have failed in 1987 and 1988. While revenues rose, earnings fell in 1987, were negative in 1988. Two common explanations:

> 1. The company expanded outside the cookie business, without developing the managerial expertise to run this very different business. Initially, Debbi and Randy had successfully used a "cookie cutter" approach to manage the rapidly growing company. Debbi's expertise at selling cookies and managing a cookie store was replicated in the information systems and accompanying organizational standards. When the firm attempted to expand outside the US and bought a bakery instead of a cookie store, the old system didn't work.

> 2. The losses represented R&D for the company as they developed new businesses (this is the rationale given by Randy).

The truth probably incorporates both explanations.

Insights for general managers

Many students, especially those in executive programs, have difficulty translating the lessons from the Mrs. Fields case to larger organizational settings. It is helpful at some point in the discussion to briefly discuss Mrs. Fields strategy and operations in light of the checklist below, which can be used in subsequent case discussions:

Product: simple (cookies satisfy a simple impulse, are easy to understand)
Processes: simple ("manufacturing" and inventory control are not complex)
Marketing: simple (transaction marketing, low information-intensity)
People: many, unskilled (friendly, "people" people)

When students evaluate IT choices at Mrs. Fields and subsequent cases in light of these characteristics, they are better able to understand there is no one "recipe" for perfect IT management. The product, processes, marketing, and people at a given company are some of the contingencies that determine how IT should be utilized.

Some helpful avenues of discussion include:

> To what degree can or should a company separate duties within the formal reporting system, so that people have more time to perform the "human" side of management, while IT helps with reporting the "numbers"? The degree of human intervention in the analysis of data is an interesting discussion area in light of the growing interest in, and technical functionality of, expert systems.

> How can an organization feel "flat," despite a hierarchical structure? Can people in the field feel "connected" to the top and to each other, despite geographic dispersion? Can the perspective of top management be integrated with the knowledge and perspective of those in the field? (Note: the Frito Lay series (case numbers 187-065, 187-123, 190-071 and 193-004), not included in the book, provides an excellent example of a large company that has used IT to support these organizational capabilities).

> What level of IT understanding is required of general managers to ensure they take advantage of the IT as they design their strategy, organization design, and control systems? Many managers wish to offload technical decisions to a consultant. A response might be: Whose philosophy do you want embedded within the software; yours or the consultant's?

Suggested 80-Minute Class Plan

1. Describe the roles of information technologies at Mrs. Fields.
   Describe Mrs. Fields' product, processes, marketing, people.
   Describe Mrs. Fields' strategy, structure, and control systems.
   This discussion can include students' perceptions of what it is like to work at Mrs. Fields. (25 minutes)

2. IT Architecture: introduction to basic concepts.
   What is the relationship between IT architecture, strategy, structure, and controls?
   What advantages did Mrs. Fields managers have in designing their IT architecture "from scratch"? (pun intended) (10 minutes)

3. Evaluate the risks and limitations of Mrs. Fields' approach to IT architecture and controls. What are the critical dependencies?
   At what point does the system break down?
   This discussion can examine uses of IT for operational support vs. decision support. It sets up the two following segments (10 minutes).

4. Note the decline in performance in 1987 (*the instructor might also wish to pass out one or more articles from the popular press - of which there are many - describing the reversal of fortunes at Mrs. Fields*).
   Were there flaws in the control system?
   Are there differences between managing cookie shops versus other kinds of bakeries? Did the system support cultural differences as Mrs. Fields expanded abroad? Was there too much reliance on the system, insufficient focus on other factors? (15 minutes)

5. Closing Lecture: review the framework introduced in Chapter 1. (15 minutes)

Key Summary Lessons

IT fundamentally changes the art of the possible.

Organizations arising in the Nineties have a unique advantage in being able to design their structure, control systems, and human resources in concert with new, networked information technologies. In contrast, organizations which formed in the Sixties or Seventies must cope with and gradually modify their "legacy" IT architecture.

IT choices (and a coherent IT architecture) are inextricably linked with strategy, structure, controls, and human resources.

Exhibit TN-1 IT Architecture

BASELINE ASSESSMENT:
THE EXISTING IT ARCHITECTURE

IT STRUCTURES	IT PROCESSES	IT TOOLS
Who Pays? Chargeout/ allocation policies	**Data Storage** How/where stored? How maintained and updated?	**Hardware Inventory** What H/W vendors? Standards? Upgrade schedule?
Who Manages? Centralized/decentralized responsibilities	**Data Transport** What types of networks? What network services? How maintained?	**Software Inventory** What S/W vendors? Languages/packages? How many? Standards? Upgrade schedule?
How Much? IT capital investment IT operating costs	**Data Transformation** What applications? What development tools and processes? What maintenance tools and processes?	**Data Inventory** What data? From what sources? How much? How often?

Exhibit TN-2   Dual Potentialities of IT Systems for Mrs. Fields, Inc.
                     Store Managers

Types of IT	Primary Business Purposes	Potential Compliance Effects	Potential Commitment Effects
Phone Mail and Form Mail	provide for fast and convenient two-way message flow	experienced as intrusive and controlling increase dependence of store managers on Debbi Fields and her office	experienced as opening up the organization, makes organization feel flat. increase amount of upward influence
Store Programs (Day Planner, etc.)	save time that is redeployed to selling; provide reliably satisfactory decisions; decrease period required for new store manager to function; leverage Debbi Field's knowledge and experience.	substitute for exercising judgment; local knowledge not utilized. remove incentive for expanding knowledge of the store business; undermine sense of responsibility for decisions covered by programs.	aid to exercising judgment; local knowledge well utilized. provide vehicle for learning about the business. increase store managers' sense of being on top of all aspects of store and feelings of responsibility.
Store Monitoring System	provides fast, detailed detection of problems along with prompt responses; relieves field management of minutiae.	experienced as impersonal, pervasive, and punishing surveillance.	experienced as legitimate monitoring, and as allowing field supervision to increase the focus on people aspects of store.

Source: Richard E. Walton, *Up and Running: Integrating Information Technology and the Organization.*
          Boston, MA: Harvard Business School Press, 1989.

172

Otis Elevator: Managing the Service Force

Synopsis

The service organization of a leading elevator manufacturer faces a decision regarding management of their large, decentralized field force. The primary job of the Otis Elevator field mechanic was to perform routine and emergency elevator maintenance and repairs. The traditional approach of using pagers to reach the field personnel disrupted the mechanics' work flow, and required that they spend valuable time locating a telephone in response to being paged. Two Otis Elevator field offices deploy alternative solutions to this problem. This case considers these alternatives and their potential for future impact on the business. The case provides an opportunity for students to examine the relationships among management control systems, organization structure, and information technology applications.

Teaching Objectives

This case examines:

> processes of selecting and assimilating an emerging IT;
>
> management of remote/mobile workers using information technologies;
>
> relationships among IT, organization structure, and management controls;
>
> importance of an appropriate and flexible IT infrastructure.

The case also demonstrates the challenge of introducing new technologies to unionized, geographically dispersed workers involved with complex manual tasks. These workers collectively have the ability to block successful implementation of the system, highlighting the importance of careful planning and a phased approach to insure acceptance.

This case study can be taught alone, or following the Otisline case (See Harvard Business School case series Otisline (A) and (B), #186-304 and 190-149).

Suggested Optional Readings:

Elmer-Dewitt, Philip. "A portable Office that Fits in your Palm," *Time*, February 15, 1993, pp. 56-57.

Forbes ASAP Supplement, September 13, 1993, pg. 48-92: Robert Cringely, "Who What and Why of Wireless," and James Daly, "Move over Dick Tracy."

Suggested Study Questions

1. Describe the information and communication needs of Otis Elevator's maintenance mechanics.

2. Evaluate the approaches taken by field offices to address the organization and communication problems faced by their field service organization. Which one would you recommend and why?

3. What difficulties should Bird anticipate with the roll-out of the KDT and OSM software? What actions can he take to mitigate these difficulties?

4. How might the KDT and OSM change the work done by the field mechanic? What impacts should be anticipated at the local field offices? At the headquarters in Hartford?

5. How should field service mechanics be measured? How might the deployment of a portable technology impact the performance measurement system?

Opportunities for Student Analysis

Description of the Business of Otis Elevators

The case discussion can be started by asking a student to describe the business of Otis Elevators. If this case follows the Otisline case, a student can summarize Otis Elevator's position in the elevator service business. If the case is taught alone, it is helpful to begin with a discussion of the elevator business in general. This case provides a brief overview of the elevator marketplace and the increasing competition for both sales and service customers. Otis is both a manufacturer and service provider of elevator and escalator systems. Although traditionally they are known for their manufacturing business, the case describes how an increasing portion of their revenues and subsequent profit are from the service and maintenance side of their business. Points to bring out of the discussion include:

Cyclical nature of construction business versus
steady nature of elevator service business;

Synergy between building and servicing an elevator system,
versus servicing it alone;

Manufacturers were large companies,
while service business included many small players.

The discussion can focus on the service business. A student can be asked "What characteristics are necessary to compete in the elevator service business?" or alternatively "What are the critical success factors for the elevator service business?" Students will usually respond with standard factors, such as:

responsiveness to the customer,
ability to handle both emergency and maintenance tasks,
knowledge of many different types of equipment,
reasonable price, and
quality service.

Astute students will realize that the service business is not as price sensitive as other service businesses. When an elevator is broken, or worse, when someone is stuck in it, the owner/manager wants it working as soon as possible. At that point, price is not the issue, but ability and responsiveness are. Further, the case describes the range of possible units installed around the country, from electromechanical systems almost 100 years old to state-of-the-art electronic equipment. Because full-service providers must be able to work on a wide range of systems, they need expertise on multiple technologies.

Otis's Response to Market Opportunity

Once students understand the business, they can be asked to describe how Otis is organized to respond to these opportunities. Otis's strategy was to provide premium service and to maintain a reputation for the best service in the business. In addition to Otisline, their centralized call-desk operation (described in Harvard Business School case series Otisline (A) and (B), #186-304 and 190-149), Otis had an extensive field service force of approximately 2500 field mechanics in 250 branch offices. Each branch office housed both a sales organization and a service organization, but reporting structures were separate.

Three-fourths of mechanics were responsible for routine maintenance and emergency repairs. The other one-fourth worked on larger, scheduled repairs which required more than one person or more than one day to complete. A third field force was responsible for construction of new systems in the region. Students should understand that the field force is very decentralized geographically, yet with the look and feel of a centralized organization.

Task, Background, and Information Needs of Maintenance Mechanics

The case focuses on the work of maintenance mechanics, whose jobs involve frequent exchange of information, and who are the key customer service providers representing the company. Although the case does not go into detail about a mechanic's typical career path, workers usually began as a construction mechanic, then moved into the job of repair mechanic, followed by promotion to maintenance mechanic. The highly desirable maintenance mechanic job was the most stable of the three. Construction mechanics were subject to the same cycle as the sales of elevators; they would be the first to be laid off during slow building periods. Repair mechanics did not have individual route responsibility; they were assigned tasks by repair superintendents. Each maintenance mechanic, on the other hand, was assigned a route consisting of between 40-70 units. The routes were relatively stable, giving mechanics an opportunity to get to know their customers as well as their systems. Seven percent of Otis maintenance mechanics were assigned to a single site and only serviced systems at that site.

The maintenance mechanic's job is important to understand. Students can be asked to describe the typical mechanic. The maintenance mechanic annually made between $50,000 and $80,000 (1989 dollars) including overtime. They typically had 2-4 years of college or technical school, followed by basic elevator classes taught by their union and specific equipment classes taught by Otis. In 1989 about 20 out of the 2000 maintenance mechanics were women. These workers are "blue-collar" (actually they wear green uniforms), unionized, and on their own most of the time. They manage their own routes, and are out in the field 90% of the time. Their route responsibilities include:

> emergency versus routine maintenance,
> talking with building engineers about the systems, and
> helping sales people identify sales opportunities.

These workers have to be mechanical engineers, electrical engineers, troubleshooters, mechanics, and customer service representatives. Since they are on customers' premises more often than any other Otis employees, maintenance mechanics serve as important Otis emissaries. They must be presentable, courteous, and competent. Successful mechanics are good time managers, good with customers, and good technicians.

It is helpful to go through a typical day for a maintenance mechanic, as the case describes for Boston mechanics. In the morning, mechanics put on their pagers, picked up their trucks (if they have a truck-based route) from the branch office and went to their first customer. Many mechanics did not have truck-based routes; for example a mechanic with a downtown route, or a cluster of buildings close together, would not need a truck. The mechanic picked which site to go to, and began working on a unit. With luck, the mechanic finished the job and moved on to the next unit. More likely, the pager went off during the middle of the job and the mechanic had to seek a pay telephone to call Otisline for instructions.

Finding a phone was not a simple matter. First, the mechanic cleaned up enough so s/he could proceed out of the machine room. Most pay phones are located in the public lobby of the building or, worst case, next door or across the street. Mechanics reported it generally took 20 minutes to locate a vacant phone. The mechanic called Otisline and found out why he was paged. If it was because someone was stuck in another elevator, the mechanic quickly returned to his previous job, cleaned up enough to leave the job for a while, and proceeded to the emergency. Many times the page was not an emergency, and the mechanic had to decide whether to return to the current job, or proceed to the new one.

Mechanics often cleaned up the current job immediately when they were paged and did not plan to return to it right away, since it was disruptive to the work to seek a pay phone and return the call. This meant that on many jobs only the basic work was done. Additional

176

maintenance, which might prevent another failure, was often left until the mechanic returned to the unit for an emergency repair or the next maintenance call. Workers were paged an average of 2-3 times per day; hence many maintenance jobs were incomplete or delayed.

Case Exhibit 4 summarizes this sequence of events. The key points to bring out are:

> mechanics had communication and coordination needs while out in the field
>> that were not currently being met;
> the current system was disruptive and kept mechanics from completing
>> routine jobs and doing additional maintenance, and
> mechanics had a lot of flexibility in scheduling maintenance jobs with the
>> current system.

If there is time, students can be asked to consider how a worker in Boston might get spare parts or technical assistance from a co-worker or talk with a supervisor. Workers had to call their branch office or Otisline and have the co-worker paged. The originating mechanic would then wait by the phone for a return call. Many pay phones did not take incoming calls, making it necessary to leave a message with Otisline or the branch office secretary and hope the co-worker received it. Likewise, supervisors had a difficult time locating workers because they, too, had to use the paging system. A supervisor who arrives at a job site would have to page a mechanic in order to find out where the worker was. Coordination was a nightmare.

Alternative approaches for managing field personnel

The discussion can then turn to management of field personnel. If supervisors must travel to the field to meet with workers, and coordination while out in the field was so difficult, the students can be asked, "How would you manage these workers if you were a supervisor?" During the discussion, it is important to bring out several points described below.

Supervisors were not able to frequently observe their workers doing elevator repairs and maintenance. Supervisors had an average of 6-8 mechanics working for them. To locate a worker in the field took significant coordination. A supervisor could not just arrive at a site and hope to find the worker. It was disruptive to the worker to respond to a page, and the supervisor typically had to have the worker paged in order to find him.

Mechanics were evaluated on "callbacks," the number of times a customer had to call in for service. The goal was to have 0 callbacks. Mechanics with a large number of callbacks, usually over 10 for one week, were asked to explain why. The number of callbacks per route were posted in the branch office for all to see. Students can be asked what a mechanic might do to reduce callbacks. Astute students will suggest giving the customer the direct number to the pager, bypassing Otisline, so the mechanic can respond to a problem without it being logged in.

Mechanics were compensated according to the union contract. Supervisors or branch managers could not give additional pay for high performance. Instead, they resorted to lunches, better routes, additional training classes and other non-cash rewards. Some students will suggest rewards such as paying more attention to high performance workers. In that case, the student can be asked if it is a reward to have your supervisor visit you while you are on the job. Most mechanics agreed they preferred to be left alone while out in the field.

Two offices were experimenting with alternative arrangements for their field workers. With a good understanding of the current operation, students can explore some of the alternatives, as presented by the Glendale and Dallas offices. **Exhibit TN-1** summarizes the three offices discussed in this case. In each office the task, management structure and skill sets were the same, but the choices made regarding IT, organization structure, and control system were very different.

Glendale developed a new organizational form called "pod maintenance". Teams included several maintenance mechanics and a repair mechanic. Scheduling and communications were facilitated with a Keyed Data Terminal (KDT) hand-held device connecting mechanics via a private radio network to each other and to Otisline. Students can be asked to discuss the pros and cons of this type of device. Mechanics called it "the brick." On the plus side, the KDT gave much more information to the worker than did the pager. In addition to receiving notification of a call, workers would receive a message of up to 128 characters on the KDT screen. They could scroll through the message to see what the problem was and decide whether to proceed to the new job or not. The KDT also gave the worker instant communications with co-workers, supervisors, and Otisline, relieving them of the search for pay phones. Workers could use the KDT to coordinate meetings, locate spare parts at co-workers' sites or trucks, ask/answer brief questions, and read Otisline-based customer records.

On the negative side, the KDT was another item to carry in an already overloaded 10-15 lb. tool-kit. Although intended to be worn on the belt in place of the pager, it was too bulky and too heavy (1 lb.) to be safely worn. Further, the KDT network was not yet ubiquitous, so pagers were still needed to reach workers who ventured outside the KDT network. It was data-based, not voice-based communications which required workers to type their messages. Similar to short e-mail messages, these communications were less rich than verbal communication, containing fewer indications of urgency, humor, and emotions.

In contrast, the Dallas office took a different approach to both structure and technology. Super-routes were developed, in which mechanics took turns answering emergency calls for their co-workers. This gave them uninterrupted time to complete maintenance work. They also had an opportunity to work on many more systems while "on call". The drawback to this arrangement was that mechanics were protective of their routes, and having someone else work on one of their systems meant sharing their route. During an emergency, the route mechanic wanted to be notified and consulted as he knew the system in question. Dallas also used a different portable technology. Voice-based radio gave them mechanics an ability to talk with each other, but not to interact with Otisline. The radios also did not give them direct access to customer records or to individuals who were not equipped with the radios.

Students can compare the advantages and disadvantages of each alternative. The instructor can bring up the issue of Otis' plans to deliver Otis Scheduled Maintenance (OSM), a new maintenance planning system which will help maintenance mechanics schedule their work. The Dallas office was the pilot for a paper-based version of this control system, called Otis Maintenance Management System (OMMS). Currently Glendale and Boston use the check-chart, a paper-based chart residing at the location of the equipment, which reminded mechanics of maintenance to do, and recorded when each task was done. OMMS and the subsequent OSM systems were designed to add structure to the maintenance activity. OSM was designed to work with the KDT system, making it accessible outside the machine room to supervisors, engineers, marketing, and other Otis personnel.

Students can be asked to assess the relative value of these systems. Students can also be asked to comment on the effect of standardizing work methods and planning, scheduling and tracking the maintenance work of mechanics. Is that de-skilling and excessive monitoring, or is it enabling and performance evaluating? Some students will perceive that standardizing work methods for these workers is de-skilling. On the other hand, it will be easier to train new mechanics and insure that necessary maintenance tasks are not inadvertently missed.

Impact on the field/region/corporate relationship

If time permits, the discussion can be raised a level to look at the impact of these new technologies on the branch office, region, and Otis corporate. The deployment of the KDT enables new management control metrics. Managers would now have access to detailed information on the length of time it took to do a job, comparisons between mechanics for the same job, hours worked by the mechanic during the day, time spent at particular locations, etc. There is the real possibility of information overload while at the same time, mechanics feared that "big brother" would be watching and criticizing their every move.

The region would have contact with field personnel on a real-time basis. If a customer escalated a problem to regional management, real-time access to the mechanic would mean instant information from the field, resulting in quicker resolution.

The ability for field workers to communicate with each other and the branch office enabled new organization structures. In addition to the pod and super-route approaches, mechanics could form self-directed work teams, communicating as needed between themselves. New structures would required new measurements and reward systems to keep workers motivated.

Finally, KDTs gave Otis corporate management an infrastructure on which to redesign their customer service offerings. If Otis could guarantee certain response times, and prove these guarantees with the KDT, an opportunity existed for redefining the service standard in elevator maintenance. Further, with access to Otisline and the automated dispatching system, mechanics could interact directly with Otis computers, giving the company more accurate, complete information about the marketplace, the environment, and their customers. With the KDT, it becomes more feasible to track parts usage to enhance inventory management, and identify recurrent problems not funneled through Otisline which could impact future designs.

Actions to be taken

Students can be asked to identify what difficulties Norman Bird should anticipate as he proceeds with roll-out of the KDT and OSM. What actions can Bird take to mitigate these difficulties? Implementation of the KDT and OSM to the rest of the 2000 mechanics is not a simple task. Workers, and possibly their unions, might resist the deployment, fearing additional monitoring. Workers might not use the KDT, preferring to continue to call Otisline directly. Workers might use the KDTs to communicate with each other, arranging meetings throughout the day and not doing their maintenance or repair work at all.

Discussion can conclude with the question "As Otis management moves forward with plans to equip the service force with communications tools, what should they be concerned about?"

Close and Follow up

Otis did distribute KDTs to all maintenance mechanics. Although originally scheduled for a 2-year deployment, complete coverage of all mechanics in North America did not occur until 1994 due to slower than expected shipments from the manufacturer. Initially OSM was not installed on KDTs. They were used simply for dispatching and communications between supervisors, co-workers, and Otisline. Mechanics could receive calls for service at their job location, respond to the call, then close out the call when the work was completed. The information went directly into the Otisline system, and was available when the next call came in on that elevator. Workers did initially use the KDTs to call each other. Bird pointed out that this was a way to get mechanics familiar with the KDTs, and they had probably wasted more time trying to find each other without this tool.

Implementation was done nationwide. Each region was allocated a portion of the KDTs as they arrived from the factory. Train-the-trainer sessions were held with key managers in each city prior to deployment, and training sessions were held with mechanics on the day of deployment. Mechanics were initially taught how to use the KDT for receiving calls, closing calls, and communicating with other KDTs. Each region was encouraged to supply an entire branch office at a time, rather than a few in multiple branch offices, to create a critical mass of users. In this way, the communications benefits spread via word of mouth to other cities, building up positive anticipation for the KDT arrival.

After about 8-weeks of using KDTs for communications, coordination, and dispatching, nearly all mechanics found these devices indispensable. Mechanics were still required to wear their pagers after the 2-year deployment, as the network was not strong enough to penetrate basements of many buildings. The plan was to work with the network vendor, ARDIS, to identify weak areas.

OSM was scheduled to be rolled out in 1994. It was piloted in 5 locations in 1993, and met with resistance from the mechanics and the supervisors. **Exhibit TN-2** summarizes the key take-aways from this case.

Suggested 80-minute class plan

The following is offered as a guideline for discussion. If this case follows a discussion of the Otisline case, then time devoted to sections 1 and 2 below can be cut to 5 minutes total.

1.   Description of the business of Otis Elevators (10 minutes)

2.   How Otis responds to market opportunities (5-10 minutes)

3.   Task, background, and information needs of field personnel (10-15 minutes)

4.   Alternative approached for managing field personnel (15 minutes)

5.   Impact on the field/region/corporate relationship (15 minutes)

6.   Actions to be taken (10 minutes)

7.   Close (10 minutes)

Key Summary Lessons

1. This case illustrates an emerging technology based on wireless computing, which provides communications, processing and storage capabilities to mobile workers. By combining the capabilities of cellular or radio-frequency communication with microprocessors, a new generation of notebook computers, hand held terminals, and personal digital assistants is offering new capabilities for supporting the needs of mobile workers.

2. In choosing whether to invest in a new IT capability, managers choose how to achieve a fit among the IT, organization structure, and management control systems. This case illustrated three arrangements for the same set of tasks done by three different field offices.

3. Careful consideration of database management needs and the IT architecture are important pre-requisites to getting optimal benefit from a new IT capability. Otis first developed the SMS database, then began to transform service delivery using Otisline, before giving hand held terminals to the mechanics. Now the elements are in place to redesign field service.

4. Implementation must be carefully planned and executed. At Otis, a train-the-trainer approach was taken, and managers responsible for the KDTs personally visited many sites to ensure successful implementation of this phase. OSM will require an equally careful implementation plan.

Exhibit TN-1

Summary of Office Configuration

	Boston	Glendale	Dallas
Organization Structure	Traditional Format	Pod Maintenance	Super-Routes
Management Control	Paper-Based Check Chart		Paper-Based OMMS
Information System	Telephone and Pagers	KDT Handheld Terminals	Portable Radios

Otis Elevator: Managing the Service Force
Summary

Control systems are increasingly embedded in the information technology platform.

The design principles for information technology, management control systems, and organization structure should not be artificially separated.

Information technology designed to impact one level of the organization often impacts all levels.

Leading edge companies project their organization into their customers' locations. Personal portable technologies are an increasingly popular way to link field personnel with corporate offices while at the same time achieving this projection.

Portable technologies can cause dual impacts. They can increase a field worker's task capacity, while at the same time de-skill the workers. KDTs at Otis increased the communications and decision-making capabilities of field workers, but were perceived as monitoring and control devices.

Phillips 66 Company: Executive Information Systems

Synopsis

The Phillips 66: Executive Information Systems case describes how President Bob Wallace managed Phillips 66 through the crisis of coping with debt incurred when the company fought takeover attempts by T. Boone Pickens and Carl Icahn in the mid-eighties. Parent company Philips Petroleum raised its debt ratio from 20% to 80%. Wallace responded to the financial crisis by downsizing and delayering, cutting management and staff by 40%. Before the takeover attempts, Phillips 66 had 14 divisions organized under two senior vice presidents. In June 1985 Wallace reorganized the company into nine divisions, consolidating marketing, accounting, and other staff functions. Nine division vice presidents, (six of whom were new to their positions), reported directly to Wallace.

Wallace recognized that a flatter organizational structure and higher spans of control, combined with an increasingly turbulent competitive environment created a greater need for timely access to information for management decision making. The case illustrates the redesign of management control systems to support decentralization of decision making and authority in time sensitive areas of the business (e.g., pricing, supply, inventory) and supports a discussion of the issues involved in identifying , presenting, and delivering "time-valued" information for decision making. A 15 minute videotape, *Phillips 66: Executive Information System—An Interview with Bob Wallace*, is available through Harvard Business School Publishing.

Teaching Objectives

The case can be used in support of several teaching objectives:

> 1. to introduce the technologies involved (database, 4GL, graphical user interface, e-mail, etc.) in an executive information system (EIS).
>
> 2. to explore the managerial information access and processing needs in a fast-moving business with significant cost constraints.
>
> 3. to introduce a unit on IT-enabled organizational transformation.

Every element of the *People, Information and Technology* framework (**Exhibit TN-4**) can be examined in this case.

Suggested Optional Readings

Hymovitz, C. "When Firms Cut Out Middle Managers Those at the Top and Bottom Often Suffer," *Wall Street Journal,* April 5, 1990.

Main, J. "At Last, Software CEOs can Use," *Fortune,* March 13, 1989.

Suggested Study Questions

1. What is the situation faced by Bob Wallace in early 1985? Evaluate the actions he took to manage the company through its crises.

2. Describe Phillips' EIS. What role did the EIS play in the organization's transformation? How has the system influenced organizational structure, management controls and decision making in the company? What other impacts has the system had on Phillips 66 and its employees?

Opportunities for Student Analysis and Discussion

The Situation in June 1985

The instructor might begin the discussion by asking a student to assume the role of Bob Wallace. What was the situation he faced in June 1985? How should he respond? The answers should evoke salient details and key operating factors of Phillips 66's business position and of Wallace's change agenda.

The company has been the target of two takeover attempts, one by T. Boone Pickens (November 1984 to January 1985), another by Carl Icahn (February 1985 to June 1985). The ensuing defense drastically altered the character of Phillips Petroleum and Phillips 66. The company sold more than $2 billion in assets, representing nearly a third of its net worth. Debt levels peaked at $8.8 billion, an increase from 20% to 80%. Profits dropped precipitously.

Wallace faces several significant challenges. Phillips 66's costs must come down, while the company's ability to compete must be strengthened. Managers must recognize and take advantage of new business opportunities. Wallace has little organizational or financial slack with which to maneuver. He has drastically reduced the number of people available to access, analyze, and deliver the information that is critical for making timely and effective management decisions.

Wallace has responded to these challenges by taking several steps. He has removed organizational layers, consolidated the number of divisions from 14 to 9 (six of his vice presidents are new to their positions), and cut the ranks of middle managers by 40%.

Role of Information Technology

The Management Information Systems/Operations Analysis and Control (MIS/OA&C) group reports to the controller. Several minutes can be spent discussing the development and structure of this group, which Gene Batchelder heads. MIS/OA&C includes the remnants of four previous groups: two MIS departments and two OA&C departments. When they were combined, the groups' overall staffing was cut in half. OA&C analysts, who previously prepared management reports were experienced as collectors, analyzers, and reporters of corporate-wide information. MIS analysts had provided access to information from internal data bases and developed analytical models and aggregated reports using FOCUS, a fourth generation information reporting package. MIS/OA&C provided a combined pool of skills and experience.

Students can be asked to describe the role of information technology in supporting the change agenda. Students should recognize that more timely and focused information was critical to Phillips 66's management. Wallace states,

> *I need rapid access to large quantities of information, condensed and reported in a manner that allows me to quickly identify problems and opportunities. Since the business is changing rapidly, the system must be flexible and adapt to the changes.*

The executive information system (EIS) was developed to enable timely delivery of information to managers at all levels of the company. Initially designed to support Wallace and the nine vice presidents who reported to him, it was quickly made available to other managers lower in the organization. It is helpful to have a student describe how the EIS supported pricing and inventory management, two critical, *time-valued* business processes.

Pricing: Prior to implementation of the EIS, pricing was executed and controlled centrally. Field sales representatives would drive through their sales districts, looking at the competition's pump prices, and call these figures in to a central pricing group which set prices for the three major regions of the country. All local stations within a region used the same price. It often took three to four days to change a price. Often the new price was based on incorrect or missing information from the field.

The EIS automatically drew local pricing information on Phillips 66 prices from each individual service station on a daily basis. This was integrated with daily pricing information on competitor's prices *in each local area*, and the daily spot price on the commodity market. Spot price data was purchased from an information vendor. The data were analyzed and displayed in graphs that provided information on Phillips 66 and local

187

competition's price. Students can be asked to explain what they would learn by having information available in this form.

Students may not be familiar with the dynamics of pricing in the oil industry, but they should identify the main points.

> The graph combines pricing and volume data, which helps managers learn about the "dynamics" of these related factors.

> The graph combines Phillips 66's local pricing data with pricing data for major local competitors over a 30-day period. This helps managers learn how competitors have recently responded to Phillips' pricing moves. The graph also shows the influence of changes in the spot market price and provides calculated margins that help managers understand how far a competitor can undercut the price without losing money.

> Through the information displays, senior management can communicate a pricing policy and standards, against which local managers can immediately compare their decisions.

> Timely updates enable managers to respond to prices on a daily basis rather than every three to four days. The information is accurate, detailed, and complete, giving managers a much better understanding of pricing.

What is this information worth to Phillips 66? The marketing vice president estimates at least $20 million per year. Given the availability of this information, students can be asked who should have responsibility and authority for pricing? Students are quick to respond that they would delegate responsibility and authority for pricing to local managers. When asked to describe the rationale behind their decision, they may cite availability to the local managers of the information they need to make effective decisions. Also, providing this information to local managers helps improve their understanding of the business, and should increase their commitment to the organization. (Bob Wallace discusses this important point in the videotape that accompanies the case.)

On the other hand, the EIS does not provide *all* of the information needed to make pricing decisions. Many subjective, nonquantifiable factors are involved. The major risk is that local managers may make poor pricing decisions, which could quickly cause significant problems. Students can be asked to discuss how they would manage that risk. Most will recognize that senior management also has access to daily pricing information and can track the influence of local pricing decisions on the "bottom line," quickly identifying problems. Some may suggest that the expert pricers based at corporate headquarters could be used to help local managers learn to make effective pricing decisions.

Inventory Management Process: A student can be asked to describe how the EIS influenced the way the company managed inventory. Prior to implementation of the EIS, understanding 12-month trends in inventory required a manager to review 24 different spreadsheets, each containing data that needed to be aggregated and analyzed to give a picture of inventory levels *two months* before, which was well past the time the manager could do anything to remedy the situation. Large inventory buffers were needed to deal with the uncertainty, and even then costly shortages occurred.

The EIS provided aggregated weekly information to local managers on inventory levels, which enabled a reduction of one million barrels. At approximately $18 per barrel (as the time of the case), this represented a significant infusion of cash. Equally important, even with significantly small inventory buffers, there were fewer shortages.

The instructor can also refer to the decision to postpone maintenance of the Heavy Oil Cracker at the Borger Refinery. Students may question the actions of Dick Robinson, VP of refining, in meddling in the decision of local management to close down the refinery. This situation presents an opportunity for students to clarify how they as managers would use operating information to manage and control the business.

These examples show how the EIS supported critical, time-sensitive, and information intensive business processes. The system enabled the top and bottom of the organization to become more tightly connected. The senior management team used the technology to focus managers' attention on critical areas of the business, the local managers to take a more active and effective role in managing the business.

Redesign of Management Control System

Prior to the reorganization, Phillips 66's 14 divisions were managed as profit centers, with extensive use of transfer pricing . Wallace asked the new set of nine vice presidents to reassess each division and determine the most appropriate management control structure. Though some (e.g., chemicals and petroleum products) remained profit centers, others (e.g., planning and transportation) were changed to cost centers. Managers were also asked to define criteria that would be most appropriate for managing and controlling their respective divisions.

The new management control system became an important part of the EIS. Managers were encouraged to identify criteria that focused on critical aspects of the business and to identify opportunities for increasing effectiveness. The system design was flexible enough to change as the business changed or as managers learned more about the dynamics of the business.

Design and Implementation of Executive Information Systems

An executive information system is defined as:

> *A computer-based system that enables senior managers to access a shared source of internal and external information that has been summarized in easy-*

to-access graphical displays. These displays can be developed and customized to meet the changing information needs of individual executives. Since the displays are created using data from a common store, the system helps promote a shared view of the organization. Most EIS are developed as one component of an integrated management support system that extends the use of the system beyond the senior management team to functional, divisional, and operational managers and their staff and extends the functionality of the system to include other management support applications (e.g., electronic mail, spreadsheet packages, program management systems, electronic calendars, and word-processing). The degree of integration among these various management support applications determines how easy it is for a manager to communicate information throughout the organization and to move from one component of the system to another.

Students can then be asked to evaluate the design and implementation of the EIS, starting with a description of its key features. Data were drawn from a variety of internal and external sources. FOCUS, a fourth generation information management and reporting system, was used to build links to internal and external data, analyze information, and store it in a separate EIS database . (Having a separate database kept executives from accessing operational databases directly, which would have slowed down the system.) A graphics package, ESS-VIEW, obtained from IBM's Hursley Laboratory was used to create and store the graphics displays. IBM's electronic mail package, PROFS, supported communication among managers.

Design of the EIS: The MIS/OA&C analysts were experienced in developing corporate information systems. They had already developed contacts with the major information providers and knew where and how to access information for decision making. They were experienced at using FOCUS (the heart of the EIS) to provide information for decision making to managers throughout the company.

Bobby Culpepper was brought from Corporate Information Systems to head the technical system design, when implementation reached the stage where corporate data would need to be accessed and linked into the EIS database. Frank Slaughter, the previous head of technical system design, was transferred from the EIS project to Corporate Information Systems. By exchanging key personnel Batchelder ensured a linkage between these two separate parts of the organization. This same approach is later used to "seed" business units with people who had previously worked on the EIS system project.

Finally, the implementation team used an interactive prototyping approach that allowed it to rapidly create working versions of the system that helped managers identify the information they would want and in an understandable form . A management support system must be capable of adapting to changing information needs.

This discussion can be summarized using the IT Architecture Framework (**Exhibit TN-1**) from Chapter 4 (pp. 172-173).

Implementation: Gene Batchelder played an important role as operating sponsor and project manager. Batchelder was not a technical expert. As a former controller, his expertise lay in understanding management control systems. Batchelder related well to the executives and understood their information needs. On the videotape, Wallace stresses the important role that Batchelder played in helping managers identify the critical information they needed to run the business and how to present that information to convey the maximum level of understanding.

Wallace served as executive sponsor and champion of the system. He asked that the first workstation be designed to meet his information needs. Once he was satisfied that the EIS could provide timely and focused information in a flexible and responsive manner, he made EIS available to his nine vice presidents. Wallace provided support for system implementation in four major ways.

> He set an active and positive example for other managers. It was clear to all that use of the EIS as part of his work routine was helping him to be better informed.

> He actively encouraged use of the system by putting meeting announcements and calendars on PROFS. He also used electronic mail rather than interoffice mail to send messages to the vice presidents.

> He encouraged mangers to customize the system to meet their personal information needs and the management style. They were able to design custom information displays and build customized cabinets for their workstations. He instructed the system developers not to bother the vice presidents, but instead to give them time to become familiar with the system.

In summary, Wallace encouraged the vice presidents to take ownership of the EIS on their own terms and for their own purposes. The flexibility and responsiveness of the system enabled each vice president to develop a personalized workstation drawing on the common information source. The examples of Ben Jones' and John VanBuskirk's adoption of the system enable a discussion of how Wallace overcame resistance to the system.

The only specific application Wallace strongly encouraged was the use of PROFS. It is helpful to spend a few minutes helping students see the benefit of strongly supporting a *critical mass* technology like e-mail, as compared with the more hands-off approach with their individual use and analytical applications. Critical mass communications technologies, like telephones or electronic mail are not useful until sufficient numbers of people (a critical mass) are using them. By reinforcing PROFS use, Wallace ensured that e-mail usage benefits would be achieved. This approach also ensured that members of his executive team "got their hands on" their keyboards, which increased their receptiveness to using other features of the EIS. PROFS was a gentle introduction to personal computing technologies, to a target population of users who were not yet computer-literate.

The videotape can be shown at this point to summarize the discussion.

Future Options

Students can be asked how they would manage the migration of the system to other levels of the organization. Most recognize that as the system moves down in the organization, the level of support from the corporate MIS/OA&C group will naturally decline. The instructor can inform students that the system has now been implemented in Phillips Petroleum corporate administration and in Exploration and Production. Each sales person now has access to a customized sales support system through a laptop computer. Recently, the company also developed an EIS workstation for independent service station owners, expanding the system from a strictly internal system to an interorganizational system.

The EIS has clearly expanded from a system to support executives to a system that supports managers and knowledge workers at all levels of the company. It has become an integral part of the management and control systems and has even become a key link in the establishment of interorganizational management and control systems. The system is now being managed by a team composed of managers from both the upstream and downstream portions of the business and corporate administration.

If there is time, students often enjoy debating whether the company should begin a new line of business and sell the system as a product. As the discussion becomes heated, the instructor can ask students to describe the product the company would market and sell. It soon becomes clear to the students that the physical product includes several off the shelf packages, such as FOCUS and ESS-VIEW (which is owned by IBM), and the information contained in the system. The information itself, the only part that is unique to Phillips, is highly confidential. Another valuable part of the product would be consulting services related to designing and implementing management support systems. By the end of this discussion, students are usually not surprised to learn that Phillips 66 managers were adamantly opposed to turning the executive information system into a product. They believed that they would be giving away a critical strategic advantage that was responsible for much of their success over the past few years. They also believed that they did not have the expertise to enter this new line of business, and that it would detract from their core business, which still demanded their utmost attention. Finally, IBM was not interested in a partnership venture with Phillips.

Wrap-Up

The instructor can wrap-up by summarizing the case in terms of Exhibits 6-5 ("Fast Cycle Capabilities") and 6-6 ("The Information Challenge") on pages 265 and 266 of the book (reproduced as **Exhibits TN-2 and TN-3)** and the People, Information and Technology Framework (**Exhibits TN-4 and TN-5).**

Suggested 80-Minute Teaching Plan

1. What was the situation faced by Bob Wallace in mid-1985? How did Phillips Petroleum respond to the takeover attempts of 1984-85? What steps did Wallace take over the next three years to strengthen Phillips 66's position? (5 minutes)

2. What has been the role of information technology in supporting Wallace's change agenda?
   How does the EIS support pricing?
   How does the EIS support inventory management?
   What other tasks/activities does the EIS support?
   What about Dick Robinson's Heavy Oil Cracker shutdown decision?
   (15 minutes)

3. What are the components of the EIS, in terms of the IT architecture framework:
   IT Tools (hardware, software, data)
   IT Processes (data storage, data transport, data transformation)
   IT Structures (who pays? who manages what? how much?)
   (15 minutes)

4. Evaluate the EIS implementation. What did each party bring to the table?
   What was Gene Batchelder's role?
   How about Bobby Culpepper?
   The MIS/OA&C analysts?
   Bob Wallace? (15 minutes)

5. OPTIONAL: show Wallace videotape (15 minutes)

6. In January 1989, what should Gene Batchelder do next? (10-15 minutes)
   (*note: if videotape is shown, probably will not have time for this discussion; good one-page paper assignment*).

7. Wrap-up (10-15 minutes)

Key Summary Lessons

A flatter organizational structure and higher spans of control, combined with an increasingly turbulent competitive environment creates a greater need for timely access to information for management decision making.

Information technology can play a key role in supporting organizational transformation, even in an environment of severe cost controls.

Information Choices (fit with business needs):

> EIS supported downsizing and broader span of control.
> Data available included events, trends, forecasts; numeric and text
> > ("hard" and "soft" data).

Technology Choices:

> Well-designed data base.
> Off-the-shelf software (Focus, PROFS, ESS-View); low technical risk.
> Interactive prototyping: rapid, customized designs, flexibility for future
> > changes.
> Friendly, graphical front end.
> Good test of perceived value: spending on IS increased in 1986-87,
> > contrary to industry trend.

People Choices:

> Gene Batchelder: former Controller in Chemicals;
> > focused on actionable information.
> MIS/OA&C analysts: experienced with Focus, decision support needs.
> Bobby Culpepper: linkage with Corporate Information Systems.
> Bob Wallace: knew what he needed; anti-aircraft gunner analogy.
> > Intuitively understood the "critical mass" concept:
> > "Talk to me via PROFS."
> > > Gave users choices (decor, reports desired, design of control systems)

FIGURE 4–4 Overview: Developing an IT Architecture

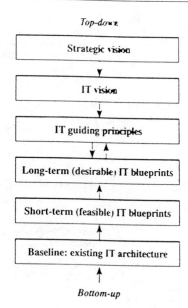

Top-down

- Strategic vision
- IT vision
- IT guiding principles
- Long-term (desirable) IT blueprints
- Short-term (feasible) IT blueprints
- Baseline: existing IT architecture

Bottom-up

FIGURE 4–5 Baseline Assessment: The Existing IT Architecture

IT Structures	IT Processes	IT Tools
Who pays? Chargeout/allocation policies	**Data storage** How/where stored? How maintained and updated?	**Hardware inventory** What H/W vendors? Standards? Upgrade schedule?
Who manages? Centralized/ decentralized responsibilities	**Data transport** What types of networks? What network services? How maintained?	**Software inventory** What S/W vendors? Languages/packages? How many? Standards? Upgrade schedule?
How much? IT capital investment; IT operating costs	**Data transformation** What applications? What development tools and processes? What maintenance tools and processes?	**Data inventory** What data? From what sources? How much? How often?

FIGURE 6-6   The Information Challenge

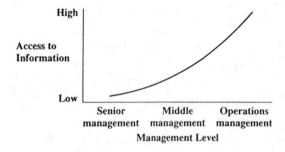

Operations managers often have the best understanding of local business dynamics.

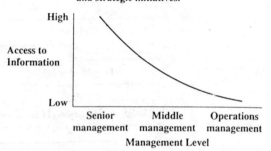

Senior managers often have the best understanding of overall business direction and strategic initiatives.

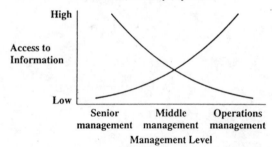

Traditionally, middle managers were thought to have had the best, though far from ideal, overall perspective.

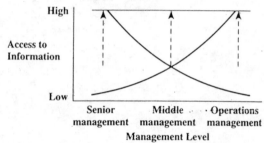

The challenge is to flatten and elevate the information curve.

Source: Lynda M. Applegate, "Information Technology and Organizations," Harvard Business School Note 9-191-136 (February 1991).

FIGURE 6–5   Fast Cycle Capabilities

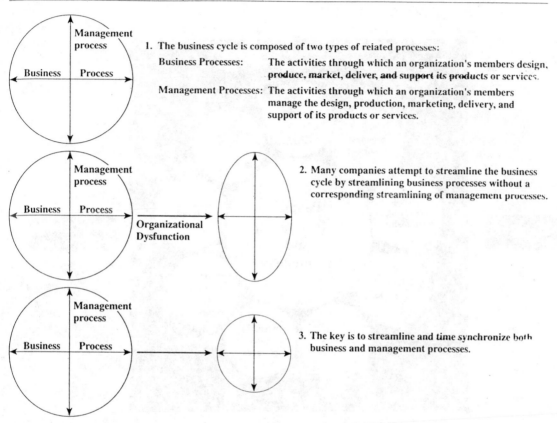

1. The business cycle is composed of two types of related processes:

   Business Processes: The activities through which an organization's members design, produce, market, deliver, and support its products or services.

   Management Processes: The activities through which an organization's members manage the design, production, marketing, delivery, and support of its products or services.

2. Many companies attempt to streamline the business cycle by streamlining business processes without a corresponding streamlining of management processes.

3. The key is to streamline and time synchronize both business and management processes.

Source: Lynda M. Applegate, "Information Technology and Organizations," Harvard Business School Note 9-191-136 (February 1991).

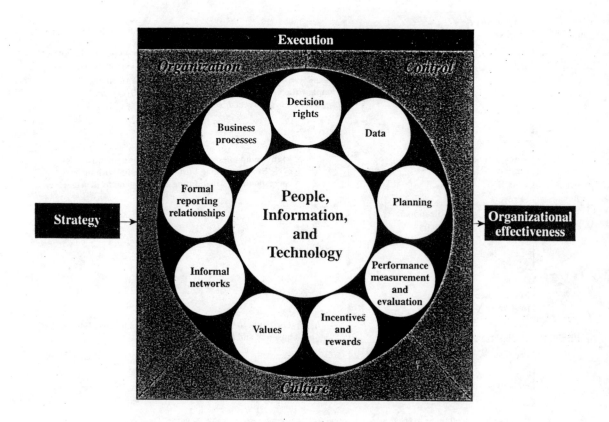

Exhibit TN-5   Applying the People, Information and Technology Framework to
                     Phillips 66

Technology: Well-designed data base. Off-the-shelf software (Focus, PROFS, ESS-View); low technical risk. Interactive prototyping: rapid, customized designs, flexibility for future changes. Friendly, graphical front end. Good test of perceived value: spending on IS increased in 1986-87, contrary to industry trend.

Data: EIS offered timely, customized access to relevant internal and external data. External news and competitor information more readily accessible and assimilated.

Planning: Ability to do more accurate analysis converts data to useful information, faster. Speedier decision-making, since participants share needed information. More effective meetings; fewer arguments about "the numbers."

Performance Measurement and Evaluation: EIS design consistent with managers' own performance monitoring criteria; no longer "one size fits all."

Incentives and Rewards: Customized performance criteria became basis for managers' personal responsibility statements and measurement criteria.

Values: PROFS fostered stronger cross-functional communication, improved understanding. Use of EIS displays in meetings reinforced grounded discussions - less "shooting from the hip."

Informal Networks: PROFS enabled tighter communication links (e.g., Ben Jones, laid up with bad back; managers on the road with laptops, Jerry Wilson communicating abroad).

Formal Reporting Relationships: Major restructuring in wake of takeover attempts: fewer divisions (14 to 9), fewer people (cut 40%) fewer layers --> broader spans of control. EIS helped make sense of data; middle managers used to do that.

Business Processes: EIS supported new ways of doing pricing, inventory management, equipment maintenance. Access to information from different sources leads to new decisions (e.g., cracker shutdown).

Decision Rights: With rapid access to competitor information, pricing decisions can be local, yet senior management can identify local managers who need guidance. However, potential local/central conflict when unfiltered data is widely available (e.g., Dick Robinson and the cracker shut-down).

Safeway Manufacturing Division:
the Manufacturing Control System (MCS)

Synopsis

This case describes an initiative to install an MRPII package in Safeway Manufacturing Division's (SMD) 38 plants. As stated in case Exhibit 1, the project was expected to cost $37 million and to take 5.5 years to accomplish. As of 1993, it was the largest project ever undertaken within SMD.

The case is positioned in 1991, just after Len Chapman was hired as project manager of MCS implementation. The case opens with Walt Schoendorf, senior vice president of SMD, wondering how he should advise Chapman and the MCS project team as they developed an implementation approach. Issues which needed to be addressed included:

> What additional resources would Chapman need to successfully implement MCS?

> How should the MCS project team be organized? Who should be on the team?

> In light of similarities and differences among plants, how many plants would the team need to visit?

> The MCS system would be based on a software package, PRMS, from Pansophic. Where there were mismatches between how work was performed in the plant today and procedures assumed by the software, what should the MCS team do: change the software or change procedures in the plant?

> How should a pilot be managed?

> How should education and training be carried out?

> What IT architecture needs to be adopted to support MCS?

Teaching Objectives

The main teaching objectives of the case are to:

discuss how to manage a large cross-functional software project;

give students an opportunity to propose and defend an implementation
plan for a large IT/organizational change project; and

introduce the opportunities and challenges of business process
reengineering.

The case can be taught alone or as part of a series on reengineering, in which this case,
illustrating the early stages of what could become a re-engineering project, would precede
Capital Holding Corporation -- Reengineering the Direct Response Group (192-001),
illustrating an organization farther along in a re-engineering effort.

Suggested Optional Readings

A Note on Manufacturing Resource Planning (MRPII) Harvard Business School Note
No. 687-097, 1987.

Davenport, Thomas, *Process Innovation*, Boston, MA: Harvard Business School
Press, 1993.

Hammer, Michael, "Reengineering Work: Don't Automate, Obliterate," *Harvard
Business Review*, July-August 1990, 104-112.

Hammer, Michael and James Champy, *Reengineering the Corporation*, NY: Harper
Collins Books, 1993.

Stewart, T., "Reengineering," *Fortune*, August, 1993.

Related Case Material

A follow-on (B) case, through the summer of 1993, is available: *Safeway Manufacturing
Division: The Manufacturing Control System (MCS) (B)*, No. 194-014. It is included here
as an appendix to this teaching note. If the instructor wants to hand it out at the end of
class, it can be ordered from Harvard Business School Publishing.

Suggested Study Questions

1. Assume you are Len Chapman. What should be your priorities as you move forward with MCS? Where do you think problems will arise?

2. How would you assess the risks of this project? What actions can be taken to mitigate project risks?

3. Assume you are Tim Leschinsky. Prepare a detailed implementation plan for presentation to Len Chapman and Walt Schoendorf, outlining how MCS implementation should unfold. Your recommendation should address both human and technical issues.

Opportunities for Student Analysis

Situation Analysis

In 1990, Safeway ranked third in the grocery industry, with sales of $14.8 billion. In 1986, KKR acquired Safeway's predecessor for $4.2 billion in what is often touted as one of the most successful leveraged buy-outs. In 1990, the company was still laden with a negative net worth and a significant amount of debt.

After the LBO, Safeway retail stores were only on the east coast and in the western US. As a consequence of the LBO, Safeway sold a number of stores but retained all but one of the manufacturing plants, which were geographically dispersed throughout the continental US. The 38 plants were grouped into 5 categories: grocery, meat/cheese, ice cream, milk and bakery.

Students may question why Safeway is in the manufacturing business. While this can lead to an interesting discussion, it is not relevant to the main issue of the case, so the instructor should not let it go on for too long. At the time of the case, Safeway management had made a strategic decision to stay in the manufacturing business. According to Chapman in 1993, most food manufacturers acknowledged that private label production was an area with high growth potential.[iii]

Students should be challenged to consider what it would be like to work in such a debt-laden organization. SMD managers were constantly challenged to do more with less.

[iii] See also Stern, Gabriella, "Big Companies Add Private-Label Lines that Vie With Their Premium Brands," *Wall Street Journal*, May 21, 1993, p. B1.

IS Use within SMD

Students should be asked to describe SMD's organization to support IS. The organization chart (case Exhibit 5) shows that the MIS organization, headed by Lon Metzger, was buried 3-4 levels down from Schoendorf and was completely separate from the group charged with implementing MCS. Yet Chapman cannot succeed unless he forges a close partnership with Metzger.

There appears to be a fairly low level of IS activity at the plants. Most systems were home-grown and computer literacy among plant personnel was low. The Benefits/Beneficiaries Matrix, described in Chapters 8 and 9 of the book, can be used to characterize how SMD had historically used IS. Traditionally, SMD used IS to support the efficiency and effectiveness of plant managers and employees in separate functional areas. The milk and cheese plants, for example, depended on computer-based numerical control devices to monitor the processing of their various products.

The IS organization's skills reflected the applications that were supported; employees had mainframe and personal computer knowledge. The MCS system, which ran on an IBM AS400 mini-computer, would necessitate development of new skills in the IS department.

It is generally productive to spend some time discussing the financial justification for MCS. An examination of case Exhibit 1 reveals that most expected benefits of the system will be due to material cost reductions, i.e., centralized purchasing. A student might question whether SMD could achieve these benefits without undertaking MCS. This can lead to a lively discussion regarding the kind of system that would really be necessary to enable centralized purchasing.

A student may criticize the financial justification for MCS, presented in case Exhibit 1. The instructor can ask, how do you justify a system such as MCS? Is it possible to quantify or even anticipate all the benefits that will accrue to the organization as a result of implementing such a system? This should prompt the class to enumerate the various benefits of MCS. For example, MCS will allow SMD to leverage and to standardize information flow between the plants and headquarters. MCS could also enable standardized processes across plants, and MCS could provide a base to more closely align retail sales to plant production.

Implementing MCS

MCS will result in significant changes in SMD's plants. In light of the size and scope of the project and the heterogeneity of SMD's plants, effective project management will be critical. Further, at the time of the case, the project team had not yet sorted out how many modifications would have to be made to PRMS (the MRPII software) to satisfy the plants' needs. Project management will be key to minimizing "scope creep," which could undermine the team's ability to stick with its project schedule.

At this point, it would be helpful to direct students' attention to the implementation questions which were posed in the case. For example, the software selection task force identified four stages for the MCS implementation: planning, conference room pilot, development, and rollout. Each stage can be discussed in turn, with a student stating how he or she would manage each phase.

Planning: The objective of the planning stage was to document the procedures in the plant and to match functionality provided by the PRMS software to that which plant managers felt they needed. Who should do this analysis? Students can be asked to describe the pros and cons of two or three alternative approaches. For example, a questionnaire could be developed and mailed to each plant manager to gather this kind of data. Alternatively, headquarters staff could visit each plant and interview managers and employees. Another option would be to pair a headquarters staffer with a plant person to complete the questionnaire.

Conference Room Pilot (CRP): The purpose of the CRP is to provide a "quick and dirty" walk- through of the PRMS software to determine what modifications need to be made to accommodate various plants' requirements . The CRP would serve as a mechanism to define MCS application requirements, and as a pilot plant where prototype applications could be tested.

Students can be asked to discuss the pros and cons of this approach. Questions the instructor can raise include:

> Why do organizations do prototyping?
> Who should get a chance to see the prototype applications?
> Why are they doing this CRP at headquarters and not within a plant?

Development and Rollout: During the development stage the software selection team proposed to scale up from prototypes to full blown systems. The case does not describe how they will choose the first plant to receive the system. The class should be challenged to think about this. Should this be rolled-out geographically? Should the rollout schedule be based on plant type?

Finally, students can be asked if Chapman has the necessary resources to be successful. What additional resources does Chapman need in order for the MCS project to succeed? For example, is Chapman's organizational level high enough to enable him to mandate or encourage the degree of change that will be necessary? Are there departments that MCS will rely upon that should be part of Chapman's organization but today report elsewhere?

Business process reengineering

Reengineering has been defined as a cross-functional initiative involving changes to structure, systems and culture, which is intended to produce dramatic performance improvements. As of September 1993, only Phases I and II of the MCS project had been completed. Those phases impacted how plants did purchasing, but had little impact on other plant processes.

Exhibit TN-1 summarizes the change tactics employed at Safeway Manufacturing Division. A similar exhibit is seen with the Capital Holdings teaching note, comparing Safeway and Capital Holding's approaches to their change efforts. It is useful to follow the Safeway case with the Capital Holding case, which represents a company further along in its reengineering efforts.

As the MCS team moves forward, what should be their goal? Students can be challenged to discuss the trade-offs associated with optimizing or reengineering processes based on "best practices" or merely ensuring that PRMS provides the needed functionality. Is it possible to accomplish reengineering when you are starting with a software package? What are the pros and cons of trying to accomplish reengineering with this project? If the team decides that its goal is reengineering, what obstacles should they expect?

The "B" Case

The "B" case describes an unfortunate turn of events in 1991, which made it even more imperative to be cautious with respect to spending. After four years of improved operating results following the LBO, Safeway experienced a downturn in operating profit as a percent of sales in 1991. In 1992, operating profit as a percent of sales remained low, while sales at existing stores fell 2.7% from 1991 levels. The major sources of difficulty included the recessionary environment of California, tougher competition from discount grocery chains and low inflation.[iv] In response to these environmental changes, Safeway senior management redirected the company's focus to include investing capital "wisely by ensuring that projects achieve targeted returns."[v] Generally, Safeway management only selected and approved new capital investments which forecast a pre-tax internal rate of return (IRR) in excess of 25%.[vi]

Safeway's increased focus on rates of return subjected the MCS project to additional scrutiny. The project was financially reviewed early in 1993. While MCS survived the review, it was scaled back. Some personnel assigned to the project were reassigned, and the project itself was stretched out. With fewer resources, the MCS team was forced to push the Phase II completion date out several months. Later phases were put on hold, awaiting further review and justification. Another project review was planned for

---

[iv] *Forbes*, March 15, 1992, p.166
[v] Safeway 1992 *Annual Report.*
[vi] Ibid

September, 1993. Further implementation depended on the team's ability to show the utility and cost savings achieved from Phases I and II.

The "B" case describes some organizational changes that took place between Spring 1991 and Spring 1993. In the Summer of 1991, Chapman was appointed Chief Information Officer -Supply. With this reorganization, the Supply Information Services Department, headed by Lon Metzger, and the Manufacturing Control Systems Group (MCS), headed by Tim Leschinsky, were brought together under Chapman. In February 1992, Chapman was promoted to Vice President, Finance and Information Services.

In Fall 1992, Walter Schoendorf, Senior Vice President of SMD, announced that he would retire at the end of 1992. Mike Bingham, who had been Vice President of Production, was named Senior Vice President of Manufacturing. Safeway management also announced the formation of a new division, the Supply Information Services/Finance Division (SIS/FD). Chapman was named head of this division. Both Bingham and Chapman reported to Executive Vice President E. Richard Jones. As Chapman assumed a wider range of responsibilities, Leschinsky assumed responsibility for day-to-day management of MCS.

In Spring 1993, after a corporate consolidation, Chapman's responsibilities were shifted from Information Services and Finance to Information Services and Supply Operations, including materials procurement, industrial engineering & logistics, and information services. Leschinsky became Supply Operation's Director of Information Services, heading both MCS and MIS. The summer 1993 SIS/FD organization is shown in "B" case Exhibit 4.

As for the MCS project, we find in the "B" case that an implementation team was formed, consisting of two management-level representatives from each type of plant. That team initially sought to identify "model" plants so they would not have to visit each plant. Finding that each plant was unique, they visited 32 of the 38 plants, and interviewed managers and employees at the other 6 plants by phone.

As of summer 1993, the project was succeeding. Phase 1 (centralized purchasing) was implemented without major problems. Phase 2 (some purchasing functions in the plants) was underway and also appeared to be going well. However, management's continued focus on short-term profitability threatened the future of the project. Phase 3 would be approved only after a benefits review was conducted for phases 1 and 2.

Suggested 80 Minute Lesson Plan

1. How would you characterize the business that Safeway Corporation is in? What role do SMD and MCS play in executing that strategy? (10 minutes)

2. Describe the Safeway IS organization.
   What is the relationship between corporate IS and SMD's IS group?
   Where would you place SMD on the benefits/beneficiaries matrix?
   What is your assessment of the MCS financial justification?
   (20 minutes)

3. As Len Chapman, what should be your priorities as you move forward with MCS? Where do you think problems will arise? Is SMD ready for change? (15 minutes)

4. What specific implementation recommendations would you make?
   How would you involve plant personnel?
   How do you get people excited about and willing to engage in change?
   (20 minutes)

5. Read and discuss the "B" case. (15 minutes)

Key Summary Lesson

To implement a complex, cross-functional IS project generally requires both senior management support and support of those who will use the system. Yet, it can be very difficult to get people to embrace change, especially in a highly dispersed, heterogeneous environment.

Change Tactics	Safeway Manufacturing Division
Management of the change process	* new manager brought in to manage BPR * outside consultants develop initial case for action * consultants also used for application development
Employee involvement	* high performing plant supervisors and manager selected, relocated to headquarters to design new approach to work
Communication	* reengineering team somewhat isolated during design phase * broadly communicate plans as design firms up
Communicated need for BPR	* self-improvement
Milestones	* firm initially; subsequently flexible
Changes to structure and culture	* changes deemed necessary, but not explicitly addressed at start of project

Safeway Manufacturing Division:
The Manufacturing Control System (MCS) (B)

In May of 1993, Tim Leschinsky, Director of Information Services for Safeway's manufacturing division, considered the progress of the MCS project. Overall, he felt that top management support and MCS team flexibility had led to a successful start. However, he expressed several concerns. First, he knew that successfully introducing PRMS to each plant was only a first step. Even though implementation-phase I was theoretically complete, he needed to insure that employees using the system would "take the next step." (See **Exhibit 1** for a description of the implementation phases.) Specifically, employees needed to move beyond using PRMS as an automation tool, and exploit its deeper capabilities. Only by using the system's deeper capabilities would employees begin to change the way they thought about and performed their tasks. Indeed, Leschinsky noted that it was only from this deeper level of use that the company would begin to experience the sought after financial returns.

Leschinsky also noted the importance of continuing the project, at least through phases III and IV, "Phase III is absolutely critical to getting the projected payback. We must set in motion the required discipline during phase II that will carry us successfully through phase III." He was confident that the lessons learned to date, along with top management commitment, would get the team through the coming critical phases.

Safeway's Changing Environment

After five consecutive years of improved operating results following the 1986 LBO, Safeway experienced a "down" year in 1992. According to CEO Peter Magowan, the operating environment had become more difficult.[1] The major sources of difficulty included the recessionary environment of California, tougher competition from discount grocery chains and low inflation.[2] In this increasingly hostile environment, Safeway's operating results suffered.

Doctoral Candidate Kevin Davis prepared this case under the supervision of Professor Donna Stoddard as the basis of class discussion rather than to illustrate either effective or ineffective handling of an administrative situation.

---

1. Safeway 1992 Annual Report
2. Forbes, March 15,1992, p.166

Operating profit as a percent of sales remained low, while sales at existing stores fell 2.7% from 1991 levels (**Exhibit 2**).

In response to these environmental changes, Magowan redirected company focus to include investing capital "wisely by ensuring that projects achieve targeted returns."[3] Steven Burd, hired in 1992 as President and Chief Operating Officer, echoed this concern, noting that management "must continuously evaluate every asset in the company to assess its contribution."[4] Magowan budgeted only $400 million in capital expenditures for 1993, down from the $525 million average of the previous three years. Generally, Safeway management only selected and approved new capital investments which forecast a pre-tax internal rate of return (IRR) in excess of 25%.[5]

MCS Implementation

In the Fall of 1991, an implementation team for MCS was formed at division headquarters in Walnut Creek. The team included management level representatives from each manufacturing plant type, as well as individuals representing each corporate process destined to feel the impact of MCS. The team was given responsibility for implementation phases I and II. Len Chapman, hired in 1991 as MCS Coordinator, was the team's early day-to-day leader.

The team began by conducting plant interviews to document current business processes. They had hoped to identify "baseline" plants, thereby avoiding the need to visit all 38 SMD plants. Unfortunately, it was difficult to generalize among plants. Therefore, team members were forced to visit 32 of the 38 plants, in addition to calling managers at the remaining 6. The team also documented relevant headquarters procedures that would be affected by MCS.

During the planning stage, the team decided that process optimization, or reengineering, was an important part of MCS. According to an internal memo, "The motivating force behind process optimization is CHANGE....to simply document today's business, and modify the MRPII package accordingly, would be to ignore the opportunities inherent to MCS."

After documenting business processes, the team simulated these processes using the PRMS software, and tested new ways of carrying out these processes. PRMS was tailored to meet specific business needs. Finally, modifications to the software were written and training procedures were developed.

Implementation of MCS was to take place in "phases." As the project progressed through each implementation phase, MCS would absorb a greater and greater number of SMD processes. Initially, the team expected a pilot plant to be operational by September 1993. The implementation team planned to roll out MCS in phases to the remaining plants beginning in January 1994. Two departments within a plant would be converted at a time. The team's initial schedule forecast MCS completion by December of 1995.

---

3. Safeway 1992 Annual Report
4. Ibid
5. Ibid

Early Results. In May of 1993, Chapman commented on the status of MCS. "We are very pleased with the implementation to-date. Phase I was completed on-time , and the pilot stage of phase II is underway." While some compromises were made to accommodate user requests, both the MCS team and the MCS users were quite happy with the many benefits of the PRMS system.

The biggest source of frustration seemed to stem from the resistance to reengineering. According to Jim Webb, MCS implementation manager, "We made modifications that we didn't need to make; the modifications forced us back to the old ways. There was resistance to reengineering."

Lisbeth Claus, Manager of Learning, expressed a similar sentiment.

There was resistance to change, particularly among supervisors and managers. They resisted what they felt was an invasion of their "turf." Instead they sought to have us replicate their old work patterns. Personnel on the MCS team lacked the power required to offset plant management's resistance to change. Finally, reengineering demanded cross functional agreements, which were difficult to obtain. Hence, the solutions were "negotiated."

Training Issues. Chapman and the implementation team recognized that the success of MCS would be predicated on the management of cultural change and education. Therefore, Chapman hired Lisbeth Claus, who possessed a unique combination of business and academic experience, to lead the education effort.

From the start, Claus realized that the education budget would be insufficient if MCS was implemented using traditional training methods. For example, the hiring of outside consultants to teach MCS and PRMS at each plant would easily exceed the $500,000 budget. She estimated that a "traditional" approach to training would require approximately $2 million. Hence, she opted to enlist the MCS representatives from the plants. She attempted to groom them as the "coaches," who would effect training from within the company. According to Claus, this approach ensured that those teaching MCS were knowledgeable about procedures and policies specific to Safeway. Therefore, the education was more likely to be immediately valuable.

Though she was generally satisfied with the training achieved in implementation phases I and II, she did have some concerns. First, there was resistance to conceptual learning; users and coaches constantly pressed to emphasize the "how" (e.g., specific keystrokes), rather than "why" (i.e., the conceptual big picture elucidating the need for MCS within SMD). In addition, many employees lacked basic PC skills. The company was forced to give future MCS users basic PC training before moving on to MCS training and education.

Organizational Changes and MCS

Several reorganizations took place between Spring 1991 and Spring 1993. In the Summer of 1991, Chapman was appointed Chief Information Officer - Supply. With this reorganization, the Supply Information Services Department, headed by Lon Metzger, and the Manufacturing Control Systems Group (MCS), headed by Tim Leschinsky, were brought together under Chapman.

In February 1992, Chapman was promoted to Vice President Finance and Information Services. In addition to his previous responsibilities, Chapman assumed responsibility for the finance group, comprised of accounting, planning, and credit for manufacturing, produce, seafood, and floral.

In the Fall of 1992, Walter Schoendorf, Senior Vice President of SMD, announced that he would retire at the end of 1992. Mike Bingham, who had been the Vice President of Production was named Senior Vice President of Manufacturing. Safeway management also announced the formation of a new division, the Supply Information Services/Finance Division (SIS/FD). Chapman was named head of this division. Both Bingham and Chapman reported to Executive Vice President E. Richard Jones. As Chapman assumed a wider range of responsibilities, Leschinsky assumed responsibility for the day-to-day management of MCS. In the Spring of 1993, after corporate consolidation, Chapman's responsibilities were shifted from Information Services and Finance to Information Services and Supply Operations, including materials procurement, industrial engineering & logistics, and information services. Leschinsky became Supply Operation's Director of Information Services, heading both MCS and MIS. **Exhibit 3** highlights the Summer 1993 organization.

The Future of MCS

While the MCS team had made great strides in the last two years, the future of the project was uncertain. Despite the project's apparent successes, Safeway's increased focus on rates of return subjected the MCS project to additional scrutiny. The project was financially reviewed early in 1993. While MCS survived the review, it was, at least temporarily, scaled back. Some of the personnel assigned to the project were reassigned, and the project itself was stretched out. With fewer resources, the MCS team was forced to push the phase two completion date out several months. In addition, personnel performing phase III preparations were assigned to phase II. Phases III through VI were put on hold, awaiting further review and justification. Another project review was planned for September of 1993. Further implementation depended on the team's ability to show the utility and cost savings achieved from the first two phases.

Jim Webb was confident that the team could continue to show the kind of success necessary to insure future funding. However, Webb noted that the problems faced by MCS were typical for any long term project. Specifically, long term projects lose momentum the longer they are around. There are always newer, "better" projects vying for scarce corporate dollars.

Finally, the MCS team felt that reengineering would enhance the returns from MCS; however, reengineering efforts had run into strong resistance. As Magowan noted in the 1992 Annual Report, "at all levels of the company, one of the best ways for us to reduce expenses without compromising service is by expanded use of technology." The MCS team had successfully reduced expenses through automation, but they knew that in order to maximize the expense reducing possibilities of information technology, they needed to reengineer company processes.

Exhibit 1   Safeway Manufacturing Division - Implementation Phases

Phase	Activity/Scope	Location	Original Schedule (Start date)	Revised Schedule
I	Accounts Payable; Purchasing Some Centralized MRP	Walnut Creek	14 Dec 92	Completed on time
II	Accounts Payable; Purchasing	Mfg/plants	14 May 93	Started on time, completion will slip several months, to Mar '94
III	MRP; Order Entry; Inventory; Shop floor control	Mfg/plants	16 Sep 93	On hold
IV	Forecasting; Master scheduling	Mfg/plants	16 Sep 93	On hold
V	S-Brands; Purchasing	Walnut Creek		On hold
VI	Order management system	Walnut Creek and plants		On hold

Exhibit 2   Safeway Manufacturing Division - Financial Highlights

	YEAR 1988	1989	1990	1991	1992	1993
SALES (millions)	13,612.4	14,324.6	14,873.6	15,119.2	15,151.9	
OPERATING PROFIT (millions)	398.9	462.4	535.3	433.3	441.6	400.0*
(AS A PERCENT OF SALES)	2.93%	3.23%	3.60%	2.90%	2.90%	2.6%**
CHANGE IN SAME STORE SALES			2.90%	0.10%	-2.70%	
CAPITAL EXPENDITURES (millions)			489.6	635.0	553.4	
(AS A PERCENT OF SALES)			3.3%	4.2%	3.7%	
STOCK PRICE						
March 31			***11.250	19.625	15.875	
June 30			14.375	18.375	12.125	
September 30			12.000	18.625	10.250	
December 31			12.250	17.750	13.000	

* Safeway 1992 annual report

** Estimate

*** Safeway went public at this price in April 1990

Exhibit 3   Safeway Manufacturing Division - Supply Operations Information Services Organization Chart

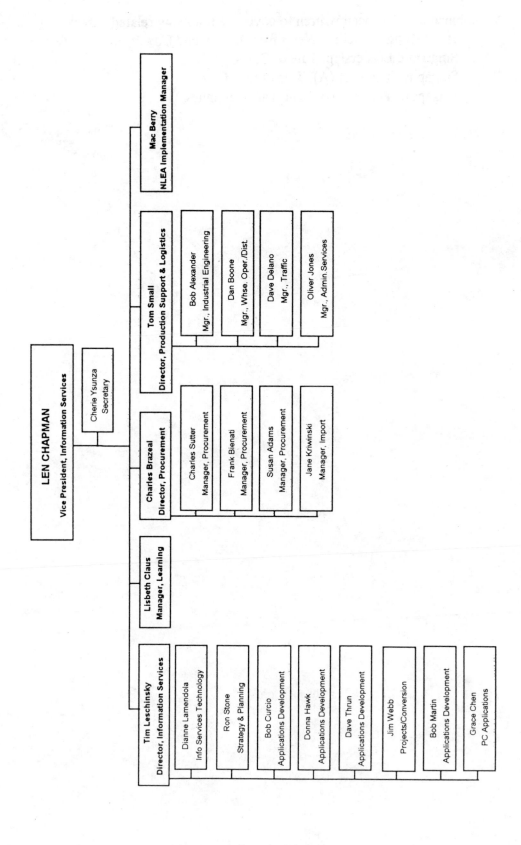

LEN CHAPMAN
Vice President, Information Services

Cherie Ysunza
Secretary

Mac Berry
NLEA Implementation Manager

Tim Leschinsky
Director, Information Services

Dianne Lamendola
Info Services Technology

Ron Stone
Strategy & Planning

Bob Curcio
Applications Development

Donna Hawk
Applications Development

Dave Thrun
Applications Development

Jim Webb
Projects/Conversion

Bob Martin
Applications Development

Grace Chen
PC Applications

Lisbeth Claus
Manager, Learning

Charles Brazeal
Director, Procurement

Charles Sutter
Manager, Procurement

Frank Bienati
Manager, Procurement

Susan Adams
Manager, Procurement

Jane Kriwinski
Manager, Import

Tom Small
Director, Production Support & Logistics

Bob Alexander
Mgr., Industrial Engineering

Dan Boone
Mgr., Whse. Oper./Dist.

Dave Delano
Mgr., Traffic

Oliver Jones
Mgr., Admin. Services

Singapore TradeNet

A combined note has been written to cover the following related cases:
    Hong Kong Tradelink: News from the Second City
    Singapore Leadership: Tale of One City
    Singapore Tradenet (A): Tale of One City
    Singapore Tradenet (B): The Tale Continues

See *Hong Kong Tradelink*

Symantec

Synopsis

Symantec, one of the fastest growing software firms, is one of the few that has successfully grown through a strategy of acquisitions. While the firm has been very successful in operational terms, there is a great deal of internal unrest — from the CEO down to lower level managers — regarding communication flows in the company. Concerns voiced include poor communication between the CEO and the rest of the firm, among different departments, and among top executives; and an E-Mail and a phone mail system that is constantly breaking down because of a presumably ineffective MIS department. The great puzzle in this case is what is really driving this unrest about internal communications? Is it the tone set by the CEO? The natural difficulties of very rapid growth? A mismatch between information processing needs and the communication media being employed? A flaw in the firm's structure? Poor leadership of the MIS function? The answer is probably "all of the above." It is important to be able to determine the relative weight of these underlying causal factors, because this assessment bears on the action question — who should do what and in which order to resolve these problems? As students wrestle with this question, lurking in the shadows is another: "how critical are these communication problems, anyway?"

Teaching Objectives

This case provides an opportunity to analyze a firm from an information-processing perspective. It helps students understand how information flows help a firm to effectively execute its strategy. It presents a range of communications media, including informal conversations, formal meetings, telephone and other electronic communication media, written documents, etc. Asking students to develop an infrastructure for information flows within a company is an important teaching objectives of this case. The case also provides an opportunity to examine the extent to which electronically-mediated-communication, such as E-mail and phone mail, can substitute for face-to-face communication . Electronic communications media allow organizational members to transcend the traditional boundaries of space and time, and to create the so-called "network organization."

Suggested Optional Readings

Albert M. Crawford. "Corporate Electronic Mail -- A Communication Intensive Application of Information Technology," *MIS Quarterly* 6:1-14, 1982.

Nitin Nohria and Robert Eccles. "Face-to-Face: Making Networks Work." In: Nitin Nohria and Robert G. Eccles (eds.), *Networks and Organizations*. Boston, MA: Harvard Business School Press, 1992.

Lee Sproull and Sara Kiesler. "Computers, Networks, and Work." *Scientific American* 265(3): 116-127, 1991.

Suggested Study Questions

1. Given the industry in which Symantec operates and its strategy, what information flows are important for the firm to be successful?

2. What are the communication problems that Symantec is facing? What are the reasons underlying these problems?

3. What should Symantec do to address its problems?

Opportunities for Student Analysis and Discussion

Symantec's strategy has been one of growth through acquisitions. The company has acquired firms with successful products in niche markets. A small number of others in the software industry, such as Computer Associates, have successfully pursued a similar strategy. However, many firms have not been successful at this strategy. After the case was written Symantec acquired Peter Norton — the maker of Norton Utilities. By all accounts this acquisition has also gone very well.

What benefits do acquired firms get by being part of Symantec? Why is the whole better than the sum of the parts? The answer may be that economies are gained by pooling the sales function and selling multiple products to a larger shared customer base. There may also be economies in sharing support functions like training and communications. There appear to be few other synergies across the different business/product groups that the firm is exploiting.

Evidence of Symantec's success is presented in the case. The firm is profitable, it has grown at a rapid rate, and it has successfully launched several new products and updates that have become market leaders. It boasts an enviable record of never having missed an announced shipping date, something which most other firms in this industry rarely accomplish. Though not reported in the case, the stock market has also been bullish on this firm, valuing it at $420 million on sales in 1990 of about $95 million. It was one of only three software firms on *Business Week's* 1991 list of small firms (revenues < $100M) to watch (the other two were Knowledgeware and Total System Services).

What explains the obvious success of the firm? One explanation is that they were good at picking the right firms and chose good niche markets in which they could establish leading products. While this has no doubt contributed to their success, another reason may be that they have not smothered the firms they have acquired. However, their hands-off post-acquisition approach may contribute to the communication problems that are discussed below.

With the firm doing so well, the concerns about communications are somewhat puzzling. I did not approach this firm with the explicit idea of writing a case on the information infrastructure of a firm. This was the issue that was uppermost on Gordon Eubanks's mind when he spoke to me, and it was also the burning issue when we interviewed other managers in the firm. Managers quoted in the case expressed concerns about:

> vertical communications (between Eubanks and the rest of the firm),

> horizontal communication (among the various business/product groups),

> cross-functional communication
>   (e.g., between sales and other support functions and product management),

> formal communications
>   (e.g., human resource policies and details of the new compensation plan),

informal communications
>(e.g. Eubanks has favorites and only talks to people in his inner circle;
>those who know people in MIS can get their projects quicker attention), and

the overall communication support framework
>(the lack of meetings of various kinds, the irregularity of performance
>feedback, and the frequent break-down of electronic communication media
>such as the E-Mail and phone mail system.

Such complaints are not uncommon and are likely to be heard in any firm; but at Symantec they had become a very big deal. If these problems became more severe, they could seriously hamper the performance of the firm, since in a fast moving industry communication failures can be costly.

The puzzle in this case is to figure out the reasons underlying the myriad communication problems. There are numerous potential contributors to the communication problem:

1. Some problems are merely the result of fast growth — when the company was small people could communicate without the need for formal communication systems. Now that the company has grown through acquisition and become dispersed in multiple locations, informal channels are no longer adequate and other channels have not yet been well developed. The company's rapid growth may also account for the infrequent performance reviews and lack of clarity regarding various company policies. Symantec managers are so task focused that they just don't have time to communicate about less immediate matters on a regular basis.

2. The strategy, supporting structure and control system may contribute to poor communications. All of the product groups have been newly acquired. Post-acquisition, they have not been integrated in any formal fashion. There are few meetings that bring people from different parts of the company together; a situation exacerbated by the fact that they are located in different places. The structure provides no integrating mechanisms. If anything, the control system encourages competition. Product groups are measured on a P&L basis and compete for resources such as sales and corporate communications. With neither incentives nor mechanisms to share information or resolve disputes, it is little wonder that there are poor horizontal and cross-functional communications.

3. It is possible to place considerable blame with Gordon Eubanks and the tone he sets. Eubanks is by all accounts a whimsical and eccentric character. In the case he makes weird comments about the difference between "opinions" and "policies." Couple that with his self-admittedly aggressive and intimidating style, and his habit of acting on the basis of information solicited from a small and select set of people (who may well be shunned by others in the firm as "spies"), and it is not surprising that this firm has communication problems. Eubanks does not fill out performance evaluation forms, and he allows people to go around him and talk to Hendrix (the company's technology "Guru" and "shrink"). As a role model at the top he does not set a very good example.

4. Another likely contributor to the communications problems at Symantec is the poor leadership of the MIS function. There has been poor planning, poor ongoing management and maintenance, and poor timing of technology upgrades. As Ed Paige, the MIS manager, rightly points out, there is no MIS strategy. Though Ed blames these problems on a "do-it-now, fix-it-later mentality," it is clear that he is overwhelmed and has lost the confidence of both his managers and users. System downtime is very frequent, and this is beginning to impact users' ability to get their work done (empirical research conducted by Infonetics Inc., an information systems consulting firm, indicates that the costs of LAN downtime can be very severe). Since Symantec's operational dependence on IT is very high, both for getting work done and for communicating on an ongoing basis, downtime is likely to be particularly aggravating. Perhaps the problem with the MIS department is the "bee in the bonnet" that has gotten everyone so riled up that other communication problems appear more magnified and salient. I am not convinced that this is the root cause. However, it certainly is a highly visible issue that can easily be dealt with, and should therefore be one of the first items on an action plan.

5. The company may rely too heavily on E-mail and voice mail. There is considerable research evidence that these communication media are ineffective when not augmented with face-to-face communication. Electronic media probably cannot substitute for face-to-face communication, though they can certainly enhance the overall flow of information within a firm. This also raises the related question: can the presumed benefits of long-distance, asynchronous communications be the basis on which to build an effective loosely coupled "federated" organization structure like the one that Symantec has chosen? Most successful senior executives spend an enormous amount of time in face-to-face interaction with all their managers, even if they possess a powerful electronic communication system (a wonderful example is Debbi Fields, the CEO of Mrs. Fields Cookies, who travels over 300,000 miles a year to meet face-to-face with her various store managers despite being connected with all of them via E-mail). One popular — and probably misguided — belief is that new "network" forms of organization will be made possible by linking people via electronic media such as E-Mail and video-conferencing. However, our position is controversial and can spark a lively debate (which is probably best to hold off until the final 15 minutes of the class).

Having discussed the reasons underlying the communication problems at Symantec, one can ask students what they would do to address these problems. One of the first items to be addressed is who should take the lead to solve these problems. Eubanks clearly recognizes the importance of these problems, but he would probably cause as many problems as he would fix. Hendrix, though more trusted by employees, has little real authority. Ed Paige enjoys little confidence from anyone in the organization. His days are probably numbered. Dave Sornson, the director of Human Resources has little leverage on most of these issues.

Bob Dykes is the only choice that emerges. Dykes can act quickly to address the MIS problem. He probably needs to replace Ed Paige, with a more experienced manager and provide the new manager with the necessary resources to solve the downtime problem.

Dykes also needs to work with Dave Sornson to communicate more clearly the new compensation and incentive scheme and to regularize performance evaluation. As CFO he probably has leverage with managers by threatening, for instance, to withhold all bonus payments to product groups that have not completed their evaluations. Since Dykes also appears to be convinced about the value of management training, he could work towards developing some programs to this effect. Such programs would also create closer ties and relations among managers from different parts of the firm, and may establish communication links across departments.

There is not much else that Dykes can personally do, although he can recommend that Eubanks create integrating mechanisms to ensure coordination and prevent communication failures. For example, cross-functional teams could meet regularly or at critical points in the product development and marketing roll-out process. Dykes could further encourage Eubanks to hold more company-wide meetings and informal meetings that create occasions for more face-to-face communication among the firm's employees.

After students have spent some time trying to figure out ways to address the communication problems, one might ask, how important is it to fix these problems, anyway? Could time and attention spent on this issue be more usefully spent doing other things? Is it possible that the tension and conflict in the system is actually keeping everyone on their toes and forcing them to find ways of addressing these issues so that the critical information flows are actually already taking place? The evidence in support of that conjecture is the incredible operational success of the firm. One could argue that what we see here is conflict and tension as a way of generating information and getting control. On the flip side, it could be that, if left unattended, these problems could potentially derail this firm. Its operational performance could be poised to take a nose dive.

Suggested 80 Minute Teaching Plan

It is important that this class <u>not</u> start with a discussion of the problems at Symantec. Students can often be very critical of Symantec and it is hard to get the discussion to be balanced after that. Once, when I started this way, students were ready to fire Bob Dykes, ask for Eubanks' resignation in the next Board meeting, and sell the company's stock short on the basis of this case. Having started this way, it was hard to get people to even look at the data on the company's stellar performance to date. To achieve a more balanced discussion it is important to first talk about Symantec's strategy and get students to internalize the great operational success of the firm. One can then raise the communication problems as an interesting puzzle in light of this stellar performance record. The following teaching plan works well.

1. Introduction (5 minutes)

2. What is Symantec's strategy? How difficult is it to execute this strategy? How successful has Symantec been at executing this strategy? How would you explain what has made them so successful? (10 minutes)

3. What is all this fuss about internal communications? What are some of the communication problems? How important are these communications for the continued success of this firm? (10 minutes)

4. What are the reasons underlying these communication problems? (15 minutes)

5. Who do you think should take the initiative to address these problems? What should that person do? Do we really need to do anything at all? (20 minutes)

6. Based on this case and the assigned readings, to what extent do you think electronic communication can substitute face-to-face communication? (15 minutes)

7. Wrap-up (5 minutes)

Key Summary Lessons

Since an organization is an information-processing system, building a robust communication infrastructure is a key management responsibility.

Different communication mechanisms are suited for different functions and contexts. Electronic media provide powerful asynchronous communication tools, but they cannot substitute for all face-to-face interaction.

Corporate/Individual Order Form

Harvard Business School
Publishing Division

MAIL to: Operations Department, Boston, MA 02163

FAX to: (617) 495-6985 or **PHONE: (617) 495-6117 or -6192**

(please mention telephone code **021A** when placing order)

[ ] [ ] [ ] [ ] [ ] [ ]

CUSTOMER NUMBER (FOR EFFICIENT SERVICE)

➡ _____
ORDERED BY   TELEPHONE

_____
ORDERED FOR

_____
ORGANIZATION

_____
TITLE/MAIL STOP

_____
STREET

_____
CITY   STATE

_____
COUNTRY   TELEPHONE

❑ Home address   ❑ Organization address

Telephone number of Personnel Department—*Verification of teaching status required for purchase of teaching material.*

BILLING ADDRESS
(if different from ordered for)

➡ _____
NAME

_____
COMPANY

_____
DEPARTMENT/MAIL STOP

_____
STREET

_____
CITY   STATE/ZIP

_____
COUNTRY

SHIPPING ADDRESS

➡ _____
NAME

_____
COMPANY

_____
DEPARTMENT/MAIL STOP

_____
STREET

_____
CITY   STATE/ZIP

_____
COUNTRY

❑ Home address   ❑ Organization address

ALL ORDERS MUST BE PREPAID

❑ Authorized purchase order **enclosed.**
   No international purchase orders accepted.

❑ American Express   ❑ VISA   ❑ MasterCard

❑ Check enclosed (payable to Harvard Business School Publishing Division in U.S. funds drawn on a U.S. bank).

➡ _____
CARD NUMBER   EXPIRATION DATE

_____
SIGNATURE

Item No.	Title	Quantity	x Price ea.	Total Price
	Minimum order $10.00 (except catalogs)		Subtotal	

Shipping and Handling:
Orders shipped within four business days. For overnight service, please contact us.
Continental U.S.: add 5%. (Minimum charge is $3.00) *All Other Destinations:* add 20%.

No postage and handling for videotapes or catalogs mailed within the continental U.S.	+	
Canadian customers add 7% Goods and Services Tax	+	
Prices and terms subject to change without notice.	TOTAL	